Two Paths to the New South

James Tice Moore

TWO PATHS
to the
NEW SOUTH

The Virginia

Debt Controversy,

1870–1883

The University Press

of Kentucky

ISBN: 0-8131-1302-4

Library of Congress Catalog Card Number: 73-86404

Copyright © 1974 by The University Press of Kentucky

A statewide cooperative scholarly publishing agency
serving Berea College, Centre College of Kentucky,
Eastern Kentucky University, Georgetown College,
Kentucky Historical Society, Kentucky State University,
Morehead State University, Murray State University,
Northern Kentucky State College, Transylvania University,
University of Kentucky, University of Louisville, and
Western Kentucky University.

Editorial and Sales Offices: Lexington, Kentucky 40506

*To My Mother and to
the Memory of My Father*

Contents

List of Maps

Preface

The 1870s and 1880s marked a transitional phase in Southern history. War and Reconstruction had shattered the antebellum regime, and a new order was gradually taking shape. The evidences of change were everywhere. In the field of race relations the main trend was toward Jim Crow, but a surprising degree of interracial contact persisted. Native whites occasionally attacked the caste system, while the plantation elite acted in its own cautious way to protect the Negroes. Politically, too, the situation was flexible. The "solid" South rocked with dissension between old Whigs and Democrats, mountaineers and planters, inflationists and hard-money men. Economic attitudes showed a similar fluidity. Slashing away at the old agrarian regime, a host of voices demanded industrial progress—a "New South" of factories and mines, power and prestige.[1] The whole region pulsed with new men and new ideas.

This progressive spirit proved fragile, of course. Poverty kept its grasp, blighting the face of the region. The South became, by the turn of the century, the land of lynch law and segregation, sharecropping and demagogues. Still, the earlier decades retain the curious fascination of the "might-have-been"—of a time of promise and hope. Perhaps the course of history could have been different. Perhaps, with better leaders and better luck, the South could have broken the grim cycle of despair.

Nowhere was this haunting possibility more evident than in Virginia. A struggle over the public debt shattered that state's ruling class in the 1870s, enabling a coalition of rebellious groups (popularly known as "Readjusters") to sweep into power. Negroes asserted their influence, while Grangers and Greenbackers used the Commonwealth as a testing ground for reforms. Debates raged over protective tariffs, civil rights, and railroad monopolies. The national Republicans extended their aid, moreover, and the insurgents spearheaded a drive against the entire Democratic hegemony in the South. This uprising collapsed after a few years, torn apart by racial antagonisms, but it left behind the most intriguing of the "might-have-beens." From 1879 to 1883 the rebels attempted to build a more progressive society in Virginia. Could they have succeeded, given more time? Could their example have invigorated the rest of the region? The possibilities are fascinating. In the following pages I have attempted to describe this upheaval. I hope that the story will have relevance for a South which is once again in turmoil, still troubled by poverty and race.

This study could not have been completed without aid from a variety of persons and organizations. Professor Edward Younger first introduced me to the Funders and Readjusters in January of 1967, and he has been an unfailing source of counsel, encouragement, and friendship ever since. Professor Paul M. Gaston, also of the University of Virginia, shaped many of my ideas on Southern history, particularly concerning the region's bid for industrial greatness after the Civil War. Professor Gaston further improved these pages with his criticisms, and Professor Willie Lee Rose of Johns Hopkins University offered perceptive comments as well. John S. Wise III of Charlottesville and Henry P. McGill of Petersburg graciously allowed me to examine vital collections of family papers. The research staffs of the various libraries cited in the bibliographical essay were uniformly helpful. The Woodrow Wilson and Danforth foundations provided indispensable financial aid, as did the History Department and the College of Arts and Sciences of Virginia

1. The term *New South* is sometimes ambiguous and deceptive. Writers have used it to describe several different phases of Southern history, ranging from the 1860s to the present. Others have employed it to describe a progressive, realistic state of mind; a change-oriented ideology; or (in recent years) a tendency to conceal the grim realities of Southern life with a myth of opulence and innocence. Recognizing this ambiguity, I have used the term in a limited and concise way. In this study the "New South" will refer to the utopian vision developed by the editors, businessmen, and politicians of the 1870s and early 1880s. These opinion-makers prophesied a future of industrial growth and racial harmony—a South that could share fully in American life. This book focuses on Virginia's Readjuster revolt, one of the earliest and boldest attempts to make this dream a reality. For a survey of shifting historical attitudes toward the term see Paul M. Gaston, "The 'New South,' " in *Writing Southern History: Essays in Historiography in Honor of Fletcher M. Green,* ed. Arthur S. Link and Rembert W. Patrick (Baton Rouge: Louisiana State University Press, 1967), pp. 316–36.

Commonwealth University. Mrs. Betty C. Leviner helped with a portion of the typing. I also owe a special debt to my wife, Louise, who contributed to this study in more ways than she probably cares to remember. She endured my clutter and absent-mindedness with admirable grace.

1

Doctor Bagby's Virginia

In the 1870s the celebrated Virginia humorist Doctor George William Bagby set out on a series of lecture tours which took him to every section of the state. He had established his antebellum reputation with the popular "Mozis Addums" stories, and the people still flocked to hear his witty, sentimental tales about the old plantation regime. Traveling by train or buckboard, he was a perceptive and sympathetic observer of the people and their troubles. Between lectures he filled column after column in the *Richmond State* with detailed and graphic accounts of his journeys through postwar Virginia. His health shattered by wartime deprivation, Bagby spent his last years composing these vivid word-pictures of a state in the throes of economic, social, and political turmoil.[1]

In some respects Bagby's Virginia of the 1870s was much like the Virginia of his youth. The economy was still geared to the production of agricultural commodities, and the overwhelming majority of the people continued to live on farms or in semi-isolated rural hamlets. By the 1870s, however, war and depression had stripped the veneer of antebellum prosperity from the land, revealing instead the grim realities of poverty and decay. Bagby's travels, particularly in the Piedmont and Tidewater, took him through miles of desolate countryside. His columns told of thousands of acres of gullied fields, a spreading broom-sedge wilderness, a butchered landscape of scrub oaks and stunted pines. Moving through the poverty-stricken central Piedmont, Bagby decried the ramshackled houses, the decayed fences, the "feeble attempts to cure galls and stop gullies with recently-cut pine tops," the "starved-looking cattle," the crumbling mansions, and the "dreary outland of scrub pines." [2] Much of the state's agricultural heartland presented the same dismal appearance.

These unpainted walls and emaciated livestock were symptomatic of deeper problems in the rural economy. The market value of farmland collapsed in the 1870s, and Bagby noted that in some localities cultivable plots went unsold even at ruinous prices which ranged as low as two dollars per acre. The national depression introduced a prolonged agony of deflated agricultural prices, high interest rates, and burdensome taxes. Competition from the rich prairies of the West, moreover, threatened to drive the products of Virginia's exhausted soils off the national markets. Even nature seemed hostile to the Old Dominion's beleaguered farmers, plagued throughout the decade by ruinous droughts, insects, and early frosts.[3]

No group suffered more during these hard times than the masses of agricultural laborers and tenants. White farmhands were paid somewhat more than Negroes, but workers of both races fared poorly in the depression years. Wages declined steadily during the 1870s, and at the end of the decade Bagby described a wage scale for rural laborers which ranged from only five to ten dollars a month during the crop season. During the winter many of these men had nothing to do, and their families subsisted on a meager diet of cornmeal, fat meat, and a few other staples. Emancipation had proved a cruel mockery for many of Virginia's blacks, transforming them into an unskilled and exploited peasantry. Some whites, observing the economic plight of the ex-slaves, speculated that the Negroes could not survive in a free economy and would gradually become extinct. In the meantime, however, the overseer's lash was being replaced by more subtle methods of control; the sharecrop and crop-lien systems were spreading over Virginia, shackling the agrarian masses into an endless cycle of poverty and debt.[4]

Bagby recorded these evidences of economic decay, but his attention was repeatedly drawn to an even more serious form of deprivation—a poverty of the spirit. A deadening and stupefying lethargy

1. For biographical information on Bagby see Joseph Leonard King, Jr., *Dr. George William Bagby: A Study of Virginian Literature, 1850–1880* (New York: Columbia University Press, 1927).

2. Letter to the *Richmond State,* August 3, 1881.

3. For information on agricultural problems see Richard L. Morton, *Virginia Since 1861* (New York: American Historical Society, 1924), p. 184; Charles C. Pearson, *The Readjuster Movement in Virginia* (New Haven: Yale University Press, 1917), pp. 93–94; and Nannie May Tilley, *The Bright-Tobacco Industry, 1860–1929* (Chapel Hill: University of North Carolina Press, 1948), p. 364.

4. Map 1 indicates the rise of the sharecrop system. See also Bagby's letters to the *Richmond State,* May 14, 1880; January 10, 11, May 20, 1881.

seemed to possess the rural mind, sapping all initiative and vigor. Illiteracy blighted the lives of nearly a fifth of the whites and almost three-fourths of the Negroes.[5] The ignorance and conservatism of the farmers made them reluctant to adopt improved methods of cultivation. This rural provincialism was intensified, moreover, by in-breeding and by the absence of new blood. The few immigrants who came to the state generally shunned the depressed countryside, and many of rural Virginia's most able and ambitious people fled to the West or to the towns. Other potential leaders were drained off by the migration of the old planter class to the cities. Abandoning their positions of authority in the rural power structure, a noticeable number of planters and their sons began new careers in urban commerce or the learned professions.[6] Deprived of their old leaders, the masses drifted into the ancient patterns of rural life, moving in tune with the phases of the moon and the changes of the seasons. Isolated by poor roads, many knew little of the great world beyond the pine barrens and the country store, and boredom spawned the grim diversions of alcoholism, violence, and an orgiastic religion. The very atmosphere, Bagby declared, "suggested poverty, monotony, a dreamy life always at ebb tide, hopelessness and almost despair." [7]

The rural scene was not, however, without signs of hope. Although the state's heartland was stagnant, several areas on the periphery were creating a more diversified and prosperous agricultural order. The Valley, the northern Piedmont, and some of the Tidewater counties showed impressive signs of enterprise, thrift, and good farm management. Even more significantly, almost all rural Virginia was swept by a trend toward yeoman agriculture. The number of farms increased by 60 percent in the first decades after the war, and by 1880 the average size of these farms had declined to 167 acres.[8] Bagby, who admired the old plantation system, noted with regret that many of the great estates were being carved up

5. U.S., Bureau of the Census, *Tenth Census of the United States: 1880. Population,* 1:919–25.
6. These population shifts are described in Marshall W. Fishwick, *Virginia: A New Look at the Old Dominion* (New York: Harper & Brothers, 1959), p. 151; Jean Gottman, *Virginia in Our Century* (Charlottesville: University Press of Virginia, 1969), pp. 122–23; and George M. McFarland, "The Extension of Democracy in Virginia, 1850–1895" (Ph.D. diss., Princeton University, 1934), p. 63.
7. Letter to the *Richmond State,* January 10, 1881.
8. Census Bureau, *Tenth Census: 1880. Agriculture,* 3:94; see also Gottman, *Virginia in Our Century,* p. 123.

and parceled out to aggressive and ambitious "new" men. The yeoman farmer, long dominant in the mountain regions, was extending his sway eastward, and such counties as Albemarle in the Piedmont and Nansemond in the Tidewater witnessed the rise of a considerable number of whites and a few Negroes into the property-owning class.[9]

This trend toward yeoman agriculture was only one of the progressive forces at work in the countryside. The towns and cities also exerted a pervasive influence on rural life, introducing the farmer to new ideas and new ways. The yeoman was tied to the urban market by economic necessity, and his hopes and fears focused on the mysterious fluctuations of its commodity prices and interest rates. Seeking to escape his drab surroundings, moreover, he looked increasingly to the towns for adventure and entertainment. The dusty main streets held a strange fascination for the rural mind, and on weekends and court days the country roads swarmed with excited families, drawn by the thousands to the more vibrant life of urban Virginia.

The towns provided the economic, social, and political nerve centers for the widely dispersed rural population. Linked by railroads and telegraph lines with the great cities of the North, they served to integrate Virginia's farmers into the national economy. Numerous merchants, hostlers, blacksmiths, and other small businessmen catered to the needs of rural customers. The county seats dominated local politics, moreover, and the lawyers and courthouse officials were generally able to control the votes of the disorganized farmers. Political harangues, barbecues, and picnics enlivened the court days, and enthusiastic crowds shouted approval as skilled debaters "chewed up" or "skinned" their unfortunate opponents. The towns also provided the focus for social and intellectual activities. Lodge halls, churches, and schools proliferated in the larger population centers, and even small villages could boast of their lyceums and agricultural societies. County fairs encouraged farmers to compare notes and to pit their livestock and produce in friendly competition. Weekly newspapers sprang up throughout the state, binding townsmen and farmers together with local gossip, market reports, and an apparently inexhaustible supply of maudlin short stories and

9. Bagby's letters to the *Richmond State,* April 14, 1879; May 27, July 16, 1881. See also William Edward Webb, "Charlottesville and Albemarle County, Virginia, 1865–1900" (Ph.D. diss., University of Virginia, 1955), p. 55.

doggerel poetry. These fledgling sheets were almost always printed with worn type and were saturated with partisan political invective, but they nevertheless exerted a powerful influence on public opinion. Together with the railroads, fairs, and court-day excursions, these newspapers helped to break down the barriers of rural provincialism and inertia.

Even the towns, however, could not completely escape the vitiating social and economic climate of the postwar decades. Most of the county seats which Bagby visited were only random collections of dilapidated houses and stores, huddled around grimy railroad depots or lonely crossroads. The dusty, unpaved streets turned into gashes of mud when it rained, and very few of the towns had sidewalks. The courthouses, more often than not, were shabby buildings with rusty tin roofs, and beggars infested the barren clay courtyards. Inadequate water and sewage systems plagued the municipalities, and the "niggertown" shanties teemed with disease and filth. Packs of stray dogs roamed about as scavengers. Drunken brawls punctuated the court days, and practically all of the towns harbored several gambling dens and the dismal saloons known as "blind tigers." More troubling than the bad water or even the lawlessness, however, was the stultifying lassitude which seeped in from the surrounding countryside. Bagby lamented the dispirited mediocrity of the small towns with their "ragged disarray of houses" and their "slip-shod men on sway-back horses." [10] In some of the villages cattle still wandered the streets, and the voracious broom-sedge wilderness gnawed at the outskirts, waiting to reclaim its own.

Only the larger towns and cities seemed immune to this virus of apathy and decay. Traveling through Lynchburg, Danville, and Staunton, Bagby applauded the energetic people and attractive buildings.[11] Spurred by increased tobacco manufacturing and railroad construction, such dynamic towns formed the spearhead of Virginia's economic recovery. Their bustling streets, lined with new businesses, opera houses, churches, and homes, evidenced a vibrant spirit of optimism and enterprise. The urban population surged upward during the 1870s, moreover, and several municipalities registered spectacular gains. Danville and Manchester, a Richmond

10. Letter to the *Richmond State,* January 10, 1881.
11. Letters to ibid., April 1, June 3, September 10, 1879; July 14, 15, 1880; April 13, May 20, 21, 1881.

suburb, more than doubled their populations, while Lynchburg led the state with an increase of 130 percent. Metropolitan Richmond claimed 70,000 residents, and the Norfolk-Portsmouth harbor complex mustered nearly 40,000.[12] Enthusiastic "boomers" trumpeted the advent of a new era of industrialism and prosperity. No goal seemed beyond reach, no ambition impossible. "The merchant and the manufacturer are now the princes of our society," a Richmond newspaper exulted, "and success in business is the test of merit." [13]

In spite of this bold rhetoric, however, Virginia's cities had numerous problems. Vexed by a potentially rebellious Negro proletariat in the tobacco factories, water shortages, sanitation problems, epidemics, high fuel bills, and incompetent municipal governments, the urban "swells" and "dandies" faced an uncertain future. All the flamboyant "New South" editorials, moreover, would not conceal the uncomfortable truth that the Old Dominion's cities still performed basically the same economic role as they had in the antebellum period. They continued to function primarily as agricultural marketplaces, mere adjuncts of the countryside, processing and transporting the produce of the farms. Heavy industry was virtually nonexistent in the urban areas, and even the production of consumer goods played a relatively minor role. In 1880 the tobacco factories, by far the largest of the manufacturing enterprises, stayed open for only eight or nine months a year and employed only 10,000 people in the entire state. Most of the townspeople worked as merchants, salesclerks, bookkeepers, domestics, teamsters, or skilled artisans, and only a small minority labored in the mills or industrial plants. The cities were undoubtedly bigger and wealthier than before the war, but the essential patterns of commerce were but little changed.[14] The industrialized "New South" remained only a tantalizing vision, ever receding into the dim reaches of the future.

The bold editorials, moreover, could not mask the basic conservatism of Virginia's dominant classes, urban as well as rural. The

12. Statistics derived from the *Warrock-Richardson Maryland, Virginia, and North Carolina Almanack for the Year of Our Lord 1884* (Richmond: James E. Goode, 1884), p. 31; and Ainsworth R. Spofford, ed., *American Almanac and Treasury of Facts, Statistical, Financial, and Political for the Year 1884* (New York: American News Co., 1884), pp. 294, 300.

13. *Richmond State*, August 2, 1881.

14. See the statistics on occupational groups in Richmond in Census Bureau, *Tenth Census: 1880. Population*, 1:898. See also Tilley, *Bright-Tobacco Industry*, pp. 517–18; and McFarland, "Democracy in Virginia," p. 63.

plantation heritage, hallowed by wartime heroism, continued to cast its spell over the state's cultural elite. Bankers, merchants, lawyers, and doctors, as well as the remnants of the old planter oligarchy, clung to the past for their standards and inspiration. These substantial citizens cherished the memory of the old aristocratic order, and they perpetuated such antebellum relics as the medieval tournament, the *code duello,* and the idealization of the "Southern belle." Bound together by the ties of personal kinship, they valued "good blood," the "Confederate cult," and the urbane sophistication of the gentleman. Insulated from the masses by exclusive social clubs, vacation resorts, churches, and professional societies, Virginia's elite lived in a rarified atmosphere of fashionable clothes and comfortable houses, good conversation and shared memories.[15] In spite of their successes in the hectic worlds of commerce and finance, moreover, they were careful to preserve an air of cool detachment. They spawned no tub-thumping Henry Gradys, and they murmured the vacuous "New South" platitudes with a genteel drawl.

Although the "New South" had made few inroads into Bagby's Virginia, there were unmistakable signs of a "newer" South in many areas of the state. The flourishing cities and ambitious yeomen invigorated social and economic life, and even the bombastic rhetoric of industrialism projected a new optimism and intellectual ferment. The geographical arrangement of the state, moreover, posed at least a latent threat to inertia and stagnation. Virginia's 40,000 square miles were divided into three great natural regions, each with its own distinctive terrain, products, and character. The railroads were binding these areas together, bringing mountaineers and planters, Negroes and whites, townsmen and farmers into closer contact than ever before. Although partially hidden by the mask of poverty, a "newer" Virginia was being forged by this collision of men and ideas, this kaleidoscopic interplay of Tidewater, Piedmont, and Appalachians.

The Tidewater, the easternmost of Virginia's regions, provided an interesting study in contrasts. Bounded on the east by the

15. For insight into Virginia's elitist social atmosphere see Perceval Reniers, *The Springs of Virginia: Life, Love, and Death at the Waters, 1775-1900* (Chapel Hill: University of North Carolina Press, 1941), pp. 250, 257; Beverley B. Munford, *Random Recollections* (n.p., 1905), pp. 83-84, 138-39; and Rosewell Page, *Thomas Nelson Page: A Memoir of a Virginia Gentleman* (New York: Charles Scribner's Sons, 1923), pp. 72-75.

Atlantic and on the west by the rocky shelf of the fall line, this coastal plain comprised some of the most progressive, as well as several of the most backward, counties in the state. The northern Tidewater, located between the James and Potomac rivers, had been devastated by the collapse of the plantation economy. Its impoverished and largely Negro population expanded very slowly during the 1870s, and many of its old estates reverted to woodland.[16] The southern Tidewater, however, presented a remarkably different picture. Its population grew rapidly during the decade, and most of its counties showed a fairly close balance in the number of Negroes and whites. Its landscape, a mosaic of small farms, abounded with truck crops, peanuts, corn, potatoes, and cotton—the products of a diversified agriculture. Scores of small boats plied the coastline for fish and oysters. The cities of Norfolk and Portsmouth bustled with activity, their streets teeming with hundreds of ambitious immigrants from Europe and the North. Steamships and railroads linked these ports with the markets of the world, and farsighted businessmen expanded harbor facilities to handle a mushrooming volume of trade. In 1874 alone Norfolk exported more than 400,000 bales of cotton, and steamers loaded with the Tidewater's fresh vegetables regularly embarked for the cities of the North. Optimistic and progressive, the coastal counties and cities below the James pulsed with new men, new money, and new ideas.[17]

The neighboring Piedmont, the gently rolling plateau between the mountains and the fall line, also exhibited a striking spectrum of progress and poverty. Its stable and predominantly white northern counties comprised one of the richest agricultural areas in the state. From Loudoun to Albemarle its large and diversified farms flourished with wheat, corn, fruit, and livestock. Settlers from the North, particularly from New Jersey, invigorated Fairfax County, and the region's beautiful and well-kept countryside reminded Bagby of New England.[18] The counties to the south, however, presented

16. Gottman, *Virginia in Our Century,* p. 123; Robert Somers, *The Southern States Since the War, 1870–71* (1871; reprint ed., University, Ala.: University of Alabama Press, 1965), p. 11.

17. The economic growth of the southern Tidewater is noted in Gottman, *Virginia in Our Century,* pp. 124–25; Thomas J. Wertenbaker, *Norfolk: Historic Southern Port* (Durham, N.C.: Duke University Press, 1931), pp. 300–315; and the articles on the region's counties in Virginia, Commissioner of Agricuture, *A Handbook of Virginia,* 1879, pp. 96–182.

18. Letter to the *Richmond State,* August 23, 1881. See also Howard R. Bayne and Peyton H. Hoge, *The Travels of Ego and Alter: An Epistolary Narrative of*

a much less hopeful appearance. The spreading pine wilderness had reclaimed large areas of the central Piedmont, and one traveler described Amherst and Nelson counties as a "desolate" and "forlorn" expanse of "rough craggy hills and bare fields." [19] The southern Piedmont, moreover, was an impoverished region of exhausted soils and apathetic Negro sharecroppers. Bagby sarcastically hailed this "Southside" area as the domain of the "sweet Virginia gulley, the rich Old Dominion gall, and the lovely scrubby blackjack." [20] The Southside's tobacco-based economy had been smashed by the war, and only a few localities showed signs of sustained recovery. Deprived of Virginia's dark tobacco during the conflict, the national market had turned increasingly to the superior white burley leaf of Kentucky and other states to the west. North Carolina growers quickly converted to the new variety after the war, but only a few of Virginia's counties had soils which were suitable for the production of bright tobacco.[21] This small, bright-leaf area, centered in Pittsylvania, enjoyed relative prosperity during the 1870s, but the rest of the state's tobacco belt suffered from poor land, inept labor, and the declining quality and popularity of its product. Bagby, traveling to Danville in 1879, provided a terse account of the economic status of the southern Piedmont. "In the bright tobacco belt of Pittsylvania," he noted, "there has been a great advance in lands, and an astonishing prosperity among individuals once very poor; elsewhere the county is in much the same condition as its sister counties—no sales of land, no new comers from England or the North." [22] The cities of the Southside made a more successful response to the bright-leaf challenge. Importing large quantities of the new tobacco from outside the state, the factories of Lynchburg, Danville, and Petersburg regained a considerable share of the national market during the 1870s. These thriving concerns drove many of their smaller and less efficient rural competitors out of business. Such trends only accentuated the chasm between the wealth of the towns and the poverty of the countryside, and the

a Tramp Through the Old Dominion (Richmond: West, Johnson & Co., 1879), pp. 13–16.

19. Orra Langhorne, *Southern Sketches from Virginia, 1881–1901,* ed. Charles E. Wynes (Charlottesville: University of Virginia Press, 1964), p. 4.

20. Letter to the *Richmond State,* May 21, 1879.

21. Tilley, *Bright-Tobacco Industry,* p. 150; B. W. Arnold, Jr., *History of the Tobacco Industry in Virginia from 1860 to 1894* (Baltimore: Johns Hopkins Press, 1897), pp. 34–35.

22. Letter to the *Richmond State,* June 23, 1879.

rural southern Piedmont staggered on the verge of economic paralysis.[23]

A radically different situation prevailed in the third of Virginia's great natural regions, the mountainous "West." The coves and valleys of the Blue Ridge, Appalachian, and Allegheny chains sheltered an energetic and rapidly increasing yeoman population, many of German or Scotch-Irish ancestry. The antebellum slave regime had made few inroads into the area, and the mountain counties had earned a reputation for independent politics and democratic proclivities. The region's Negroes were few in number, hard-working, and generally well liked. A diversified agricultural system predominated, ranging from the prosperous dairies and wheat fields of the Shenandoah Valley to the large livestock farms of the Southwest. Rich in coal and iron, the region clamored for new railroads, schools, immigrants, and investments. Towns and counties went deeply in debt to finance railroad construction, and small mines and foundries dotted the countryside. The underdeveloped counties of the Southwest, moreover, although isolated and poor, offered a genuine frontier for the adventurous farmer or investor. Relatively unhampered by racial problems, sharecropping, or exhausted soils, the western yeomen enjoyed burgeoning political and economic power during the postwar years. Bagby's description of Harrisonburg's bustling atmosphere provided an indication of the spirit of the entire mountain country. "Probably not ten men in the place," he insisted, "approved the war. Virginia traditions, the honor and glory of the past, are as nothing in the light of solid comfort and prosperity. Fame is a good thing, a great thing if you will, but as matters stand in this transitory vale a plenty to eat, a big crop, and a growing bank account are better. That is the kind of feeling that appeared to be in the air at Harrisonburg." [24]

Making his way through this mosaic of regions, Bagby observed an ever-changing panorama of economic, social, and geographical settings. In the most fundamental sense, however, his travels took him through two Virginias—the Virginia of despair and the Virginia of hope. The first of these, the destitute rural heartland, extended

23. Arnold, *Tobacco Industry,* pp. 35, 64; Tilley, *Bright-Tobacco Industry,* p. 489; McFarland, "Democracy in Virginia," p. 62.

24. Letter to the *Richmond State,* June 22, 1881. See also Bagby's letters to the *State,* April 30, 1879; July 23, 26, August 10, 1880; and May 10, 27, 1881. C. R. Boyd, *Resources of South-West Virginia* (New York: John Wiley & Sons, 1881), describes the economic potential of that area.

over most of the Tidewater and the Piedmont. The second encompassed the cities, the prosperous and diversified agricultural counties on the periphery, and the poor but ambitious Southwest. All the state's regions had their share of desolate countryside and ugly villages, but only the dynamic and vigorous areas of this second, "newer" Virginia showed real signs of escaping from the grim cycle of lethargy and decay.

2

The Collapse of
the Conservative Regime,
1869–1879

Conflicting social and economic currents swept across Doctor Bagby's Virginia. Races, sections, and classes maneuvered for position in the turbulent postwar decades, and a more modern society was emerging from the wreckage of the old. In spite of the turmoil, however, the state's venerable ruling oligarchy clung to power. Demonstrating a remarkable tenacity, it survived the trials of war and Reconstruction and gained a new lease on life by smashing the Radical Republicans in 1869. This potent agricultural-mercantile elite proved tragically unable to come to grips with the massive problems of the 1870s, however, and its blunders scarred the political history of the decade.

These durable patricians inherited patterns of aristocratic control which dated back to the first English settlements on the James. By 1700 the aggressive "cavaliers" had emerged as the major political force in the colony, and their great plantations dominated its economic life. Threatened by soil exhaustion and declining tobacco prices, these energetic planter-capitalists diversified their crops early in the antebellum period. As the years passed, moreover, they branched out into new activities. The planters had always acted as the merchants and bankers for their isolated rural society, and they quickly formed close ties with the emerging commercial classes of the towns. Some members of the tobacco oligarchy began prestigious careers in law or medicine; others sponsored railroad construction and a limited degree of industrial development. Flexible and realistic within the confines of their elitist heritage, the "best people" absorbed potential rivals instead of crushing them.[1]

The prewar ruling class demonstrated a similar tactical skill in controlling local politics. Its members monopolized economic power, and their educational and cultural superiority made them natural leaders. They bolstered these enormous advantages with restrictive suffrage requirements, *viva voce* voting, and disproportionate representation for planter areas. Self-perpetuating county courts dominated local affairs well into the nineteenth century, and the ignorant and generally apathetic masses had little influence. The democratic upsurge of the Jacksonian era weakened this system, of course, but failed to destroy it. New state constitutions expanded voting rights in 1830 and 1851, and the western yeomen won occasional concessions on taxes and legislative apportionment. Still, Virginia politics retained a distinctively elitist tone, surpassed only by John C. Calhoun's South Carolina.[2]

Disdaining any rigid political straitjacket, the prewar oligarchy allowed its members considerable freedom of action. On national questions they split into Federalists and Republicans, Democrats and Whigs, Secessionists and Unionists. When state issues arose, however, they united to maintain the rule of "gentlemen." Refusing to discuss state problems in their campaigns, they approached these issues through behind-the-scenes political deals and "log-rolling." Skilled in the fine art of compromise, they dominated antebellum politics with a deft touch.[3]

The Civil War shattered this delicate aristocratic framework.

1. Sources on the evolution and attitudes of Virginia's ruling class are, of course, legion. For a provocative modern study, however, see Morris Talpalar, *The Sociology of Colonial Virginia* (New York: Philosophical Library, 1968). The elite's willingness to adopt new agricultural methods is described in Avery Odelle Craven, *Soil Exhaustion as a Factor in the Agricultural History of Virginia and Maryland, 1606–1860* (Urbana: University of Illinois, 1925), pp. 25–121. Jack P. Maddex, Jr., *The Virginia Conservatives, 1867–1879: A Study in Reconstruction Politics* (Chapel Hill: University of North Carolina, 1970), pp. 9–11, provides a brief description of the state's antebellum industrial growth.

2. Two perceptive analyses of Virginia's antebellum political order are Charles S. Sydnor, *Gentlemen Freeholders: Political Practices in Washington's Virginia* (Chapel Hill: University of North Carolina Press, 1952); and Anthony F. Upton, "The Road to Power in Virginia in the Early Nineteenth Century," *Virginia Magazine of History and Biography* 62 (1954): 259–80.

3. For insight into the elite's political tactics see Upton, "Road to Power," pp. 260, 276; Maddex, *Virginia Conservatives,* pp. 11–16; and George M. McFarland, "The Extension of Democracy in Virginia, 1850–1895" (Ph.D. diss., Princeton University, 1934), p. 40.

The plantation system lay in ruins after Appomattox, and Virginia's electorate mushroomed to include nearly 100,000 ex-slaves. The new "Underwood" Constitution, patterned after Northern models, democratized local government and expanded educational opportunities for the masses. Vigorous Republican leaders sought to weld Negroes, carpetbaggers, and mountain Unionists into a powerful coalition. Backed by the congressional Radicals, these ambitious men worked to establish a new political order in the Commonwealth.[4]

The patricians soon responded to this challenge. Working to rebuild their fortunes, they sold outlying areas of their ruined estates and used the proceeds to modernize their farm operations. Many took advantage of the burgeoning sharecrop and crop-lien systems by renting their land to the impoverished blacks and skimming off the profits for themselves. Others began lucrative careers in the towns, and the elite became more urban-oriented than ever before. They formed close ties with the great railroad corporations, adopted the flamboyant "New South" rhetoric, and aligned themselves squarely with the dominant economic forces of the day.[5]

Recognizing the magnitude of the Radical challenge, moreover, the realistic patricians schemed to broaden their political base. The aristocratic "Old-line Whigs" tried unsuccessfully to infiltrate the Republican organization and to take control from within. Spurned by their ex-slaves, the elite fanned the flames of discord in the Radical ranks. They submerged their antebellum political differences, organized the powerful "white man's" Conservative party, and waged a gubernatorial campaign in 1869 that was a masterpiece of *Realpolitik*. Seeking to split the Radical vote, the Conservatives withdrew their nominees and backed a splinter ticket of moderate "True Republicans." This dissident slate, headed by New York native Gilbert C. Walker, swept to victory on a landslide of white votes, and the jubilant Conservatives packed the state and local offices with their henchmen. Buttressed by efficient political organization and railroad money, they completely crushed the Radical threat. An ex-Confederate, James Lawson Kemper, took over the Governor's Mansion in 1874, and native Virginians controlled every branch of the government.[6]

4. For an extensive examination of Virginia's Reconstruction experience see James Douglas Smith, "Virginia During Reconstruction, 1865–1870: A Political, Economic, and Social Study" (Ph.D. diss., University of Virginia, 1960).

5. Charles C. Pearson, *The Readjuster Movement in Virginia* (New Haven: Yale University Press, 1917), p. 92; McFarland, "Democracy in Virginia," pp. 63, 153–54.

Entrenched in power, the Conservatives increasingly lost touch with political reality. Their new urban orientation cut them off from the tragic problems of the rural masses, and the shocks of war and Reconstruction made them more fearful of popular democracy than ever before. Like their antebellum predecessors, they sought to defend property rights and to maintain the rule of "gentlemen." Unlike their predecessors, however, they seemed to forget the need for flexibility and compromise. Time and again they championed measures which flew in the face of the economic and social realities of the day. Rebellious farmers, mountaineers, and Negroes demanded concessions throughout the 1870s, but the government ignored them. Adopting a defiantly dogmatic stance, the Conservative elite grimly waited out the storm.

The state debt, a bitter legacy from the antebellum period, did more to poison the political atmosphere than any other issue. Before the war the dominant oligarchy had borrowed millions of dollars to construct an extensive network of railroads and canals.[7] These ambitious empire-builders had invested the money wisely, but they could scarcely have foreseen Virginia's bleak future. The Civil War turned the state into a battleground, shattered the slave regime, and killed or maimed a generation of potential leaders. By shearing off mountainous West Virginia, moreover, the conflict deprived the Old Dominion of even more of its wealth and population. The debt, however, heedless of wartime destruction, mounted higher and higher. By 1870 it stood at more than $45 million, and each Virginian shouldered a per capita debt burden more than twice the national average. The war-ravaged Commonwealth, its tax-paying ability cut by at least two-thirds, staggered on the verge of bankruptcy.[8]

Virginia's desperate plight was by no means unique. All the Southern states grappled with serious financial problems during the 1870s, and the decade's chaotic political climate only aggravated the situation. Faced by enormous Reconstruction debts, such "redeemed" states as Alabama, Georgia, and the Carolinas repudiated

6. The Republicans collapse is described in Richard Grady Lowe, "Republicans, Rebellion, and Reconstruction: The Republican Party in Virginia, 1856–1870" (Ph.D. diss., University of Virginia, 1968), pp. 336–61.

7. William Luster Grenoble, "A History of the Virginia State Debt" (M.A. thesis, University of Virginia, 1937), pp. 29–30.

8. Pearson, *Readjuster Movement*, p. 8; Charles E. Wynes, *Race Relations in Virginia, 1870–1902* (Charlottesville: University of Virginia Press, 1961), p. 16.

millions of dollars in purportedly fraudulent bonds.[9] Virginia's case was complicated, however, by the undeniable validity of its antebellum debt and by the legal intricacies of dividing it with West Virginia. The two governments attempted to reach a negotiated settlement in 1866 and again in 1870, but the talks broke down amid embittered accusations of bad faith.[10]

These setbacks failed to dampen the elite's enthusiasm for the property rights of the bondholders. Anxious to restore the state's "good name," the 1866 General Assembly declared that Virginia would honor its entire debt. Congressional Reconstruction nullified this bold pledge, but the defeat was only temporary. Led by Governor Walker, the resurgent patricians enacted the controversial Funding bill in 1871. This lenient measure permitted the creditors to fund two-thirds of the debt and unpaid interest in new, 6 percent bonds and offered them potentially valuable "certificates of indebtedness" for the remaining third. The fate of these interest-bearing certificates, which represented West Virginia's share of the debt, would be determined by future negotiations between the states. Seeking to encourage the creditors to turn in their old securities, moreover, the law stopped all interest payments on "unfunded" bonds and made the coupons on the new ones receivable for state taxes.[11]

This Funding bill proved to be the most disastrous piece of economic legislation in Virginia history. Instead of putting the government on a sound financial basis, as its proponents claimed, it shackled the state into a grinding cycle of deficit spending. Within a matter of months it became obvious that Governor Walker and his aides had grossly overestimated the state's financial resources. They had made their debt calculations on a predicted tax base of nearly $725 million, but a subsequent assessment discovered only half that amount. Government revenues slumped accordingly, even though outlays for state services skyrocketed to almost three times Walker's original estimate. The tax-receivable coupons, the "cut-worms of the Treasury," flooded in at a rate of $1 million a year, draining off badly needed cash. An anticipated budget surplus of $61,000 was swallowed up by a series of chronic annual deficits which ranged as high as $850,000. Frequently victimized by incompe-

9. Reginald C. McGrane, *Foreign Bondholders and American State Debts* (New York: Macmillan Co., 1935), pp. 282, 291, 311, 340; B. U. Ratchford, *American State Debts* (Durham, N.C.: Duke University Press, 1941), p. 192.

10. Grenoble, "Virginia State Debt," pp. 44–47.

11. Virginia, General Assembly, *Acts and Joint Resolutions,* 1870–71, pp. 378–81.

tent leaders, the state government could not afford to carry out its normal functions and meet the huge interest payments at the same time.[12]

Tremors of unrest rolled over the countryside, producing the first real cracks in the Conservative phalanx. The yeomen, driven to the wall by high interest rates and low commodity prices, rebelled against this coddling of the bondholders. Even the elite recognized the urgent need for change, and the 1872 General Assembly moved to scuttle the unpopular debt settlement. The legislators passed a bill suspending the funding process, but Governor Walker vetoed it. Adopting another approach, they overrode a Walker veto and repealed the section of the Funding Act which made the interest coupons receivable for taxes. This effort was blunted, however, when the state supreme court struck it down for violating Virginia's contract with those creditors who had already funded their bonds.[13] A loophole in this decision allowed the state to offer its remaining securities to the public without the tax-receivable coupons, and the government took advantage of the opportunity by splitting its bonds into the categories known as "consols" and "peelers." The $20 million worth of consols, issued before the decision, still had their tax-receivable coupons, but the $10 million in new peelers were useless for tax purposes. During the poverty-stricken 1870s the consol owners paid their taxes with coupons or sold them on the open market, but the defenseless owners of the peeler bonds received virtually no return on their investment.[14]

In spite of vetoes and a hostile judiciary, the legislators continued their crusade against the Funding Act. They taxed the coupons and imposed a heavy license fee on the stockbrokers who handled them. These measures did little, however, to stop the flood of worthless paper. The Conservatives tried to convince the bondholders to agree to a lower interest rate voluntarily in 1874, but their efforts proved almost as fruitless as Governor Walker's suggestion that the United States should assume Virginia's debt. Efforts to bludgeon the creditors into line by postponing or arbitrarily reducing interest payments only increased their hostility. Rebuffed on all sides, the elite was rapidly exhausting its options.[15]

12. Maddex, *Virginia Conservatives*, pp. 218–20.
13. Ibid., pp. 235–36; Pearson, *Readjuster Movement*, pp. 42–43.
14. McGrane, *Foreign Bondholders*, p. 370; Pearson, *Readjuster Movement*, p. 43.
15. Maddex, *Virginia Conservatives*, pp. 236–45.

The increasing polarization of public opinion added to the climate of urgency. Although Virginia's leaders had traditionally avoided political controversy on state issues, the financial debacle assumed such huge proportions that it could not be glossed over by secret deals or patronage manipulations. Abandoning their routine platitudes, alarmed government officials voiced dismay and concern over the situation. Embittered editorials and fiery court-day speeches appealed for mass support, and the Conservative organization began to splinter under the impact. Bitterly debating the debt question, the party's leadership split into quarreling factions known as "Funders" and "Readjusters." The economic crisis transcended everyday politics, and it threatened to shatter Virginia's traditional patterns of political behavior.

Quickly gaining control of the party machinery, the Conservatives' Funder element dominated the state during the 1870s. In spite of their faction's name, which implied an enthusiastic commitment to the Funding Act, the Funders generally condemned the disastrous debt settlement and endorsed the early efforts to repeal its most harmful features. Discouraged by adverse judicial decisions, however, they concluded that no substantive changes could be made without the consent of the bondholders. They assumed a conciliatory stance and unhesitatingly admitted the state's liability for the debt, including unpaid war and Reconstruction interest. The Funders pointed out that the state still benefited from the railroads and canals which the bonds had financed, and they insisted that any attempt at repudiation would violate the basic principles of Christian ethics and economic orthodoxy. They emphasized the importance of encouraging investments in Virginia, moreover, and argued that no capitalist would risk his money in a state which refused to pay its just debts. If the bondholders refused to compromise, the "debt-payers" maintained that the people would have to make the necessary financial sacrifices, shoulder the interest burden, and uphold the "honor" of the state.[16] Gearing their appeal to the substantial citizens, the men of influence and property, the Funders rallied Virginia's traditional ruling class to their banner.

16. For more extensive statements of Funder views see John W. Daniel, *The Public Debt: Letter of John W. Daniel to M. Clennan, Esq., July 27, 1877* (Lynchburg: n.p., 1877), broadside in the Virginiana Collection, Edwin A. Alderman Library, University of Virginia, Charlottesville, Va.; Charles Herndon, *Address of Hon. Chas. Herndon on the Public Debt and the Funding Bill* (Fredericksburg: Virginia Star Print, 1877), pamphlet, Virginiana Collection; and John W. Johnston, "Repudiation in Virginia," *North American Review* 134 (1882):149–60.

The rebellious Readjusters, on the other hand, represented the fringe elements of the Conservative organization and expressed the "common sense" opinions of the inarticulate masses. Sneering that Funder "honor" could not "buy a breakfast" or "set a leg," they demanded a downward "readjustment" of the debt to match the state's reduced ability to pay. They pointed to the countryside's wretched poverty and insisted that the creditors should be made to bear their share of Virginia's tragic losses. Noting that wealthy English and Northern investors owned most of the bonds, the Readjusters argued that these "outsiders" had no valid claims on the state because they had contributed to its military catastrophe; they lamented the disastrous results of the Northern invasion and insisted that the English had aided the enemy's war effort by tolerating Lincoln's "illegal" blockade. Ransacking the lore of international law, moreover, the political insurgents argued that the conflict had destroyed the antebellum state of Virginia and canceled its debt. Turning their attention to the Funding Act, they branded it as the immoral creation of a bribed legislature, and they defied the courts by claiming that it could be repealed or modified in accordance with the popular will. During the early 1870s the Readjusters lacked a unified plan of action, and their proposals ranged from drastic demands for total repudiation to less ambitious schemes for minor cuts in the interest rate. They agreed, however, that the debt burden was excessive and that the state had the sovereign right to force a new settlement on the bondholders if they refused to compromise. Stressing the harsh economic realities of the day, the insurgents made a powerful appeal for the votes of the depressed agrarian masses.[17]

Faced by this ominous democratic challenge, most of the Conservative patricians moved into the Funder camp. They filled the air with emphatic declarations that the state would keep faith with its creditors, but their optimistic speeches could not conceal the mounting deficits. Haranguing the court-day multitudes, the energetic Readjusters attracted numerous converts, and the kindred Granger movement organized more than 16,000 of the Old Domin-

17. Examples of Readjuster arguments are provided by Alexander B. Cochran, *Speech of Alexander B. Cochran, Senator from Augusta County, in Vindication of His Course on the Funding Bill* (Richmond: Enquirer Book and Job Printing, 1873), pamphlet, Virginiana Collection; Frank G. Ruffin, *Facts, Thoughts, and Conclusions in Regard to the Public Debt of Virginia* (Richmond: John & Goolsby Book and Job Printers, 1885), pamphlet, Virginiana Collection; and H. H. Riddleberger, "Bourbonism in Virginia," *North American Review* 134 (1882):416–28.

ion's rebellious farmers. In spite of the persuasiveness of the insurgents' speeches, it is doubtful that their debt arguments alone could have sparked such a massive revolt. The problems of high finance confused many voters, and the elite's rhetorical flourishes about the state's "sacred honor" and "unblemished name" appealed strongly to most mid-Victorian Virginians. Unfortunately for the debt-payers, however, the fiscal crisis soon infected almost every aspect of governmental affairs. High taxes, school closings, and other hardships brought the issue home to the masses in unmistakable fashion. The insurgents hammered away at a broad range of unpopular Conservative policies, and the massive upsurge of unrest reflected a deep-seated alienation from the traditional ruling class. Devastating the Old Dominion's political order, the debt issue served as a catalyst for generations of pent-up resentment and anger.

High taxes, in particular, caused widespread dissatisfaction. Crushed by the national government's deflationary fiscal policies, Virginians also suffered from federal protective tariffs and excises which siphoned nearly $13 million out of the state every year. State and local taxes took almost $5 million more, and the Funders' search for additional sources of debt-paying revenue stirred up a hornet's nest of opposition. Virginia's peak antebellum tax levy had been only forty cents on each $100 of assessed property value, but the postwar Conservative regime boosted the rate to fifty cents and maintained it at that record level throughout the depression-ridden 1870s. The elite also contrived a complex system of business license fees, and by 1880 the per capita tax burden mushroomed to more than twice its prewar size.[18] The regressive and inequitable distribution of the tax load, moreover, stoked the fires of mass hostility. The banks, insurance companies, and other corporate interests paid relatively little, and even these minuscule sums could easily be shifted to impoverished rural customers in the form of higher prices and interest rates. Avoiding county taxes by the use of old charter exemptions, the railroad corporations also evaded most of the state levy because the government foolishly allowed them to assess their own property for tax purposes. Their assessments were ridiculously low, of course, and as late as 1879 these multimillion dollar enterprises paid the state less than $46,000. The urban financial manipulators saved money by paying their

18. Maddex, *Virginia Conservatives*, p. 170; Robert Clinton Burton, "The History of Taxation in Virginia, 1870–1901" (Ph.D. diss., University of Virginia, 1962), pp. 56, 83.

taxes in depreciated interest coupons, while the farmers generally paid dollar for dollar. Local newspapers published long lists of delinquent taxpayers, and resentment flared against the ever-expanding tangle of property taxes, license taxes, poll taxes, road taxes, dog taxes, and liquor taxes. Disgusted by the government's apparent indifference to their economic plight, the lower classes increasingly identified the Funder elite with unjust and excessive taxation.[19]

Many Virginians also objected to the way that their tax dollars were being spent. Seeking to balance the budget and pay the debt, the Funders slashed expenditures for social services. The farmers complained about poor roads, exorbitant railroad rates, worthless fertilizers, and dishonest tobacco warehousemen, but the government took no effective action. Hampered by inadequate funds, the state commissioner of agriculture, Thomas Pollard, could not even afford an office of his own.[20] Other officials also felt the sharp blade of the retrenchment ax. The overcrowded mental institutions received insufficient appropriations, and many of the mentally ill were shunted into local jails and poorhouses. Weakened by budget cuts and declining enrollments, the state-supported colleges reduced teacher salaries and course offerings. Virginia's central penitentiary was small and dilapidated, moreover, and its female prisoners were confined in rickety out-buildings enclosed by plank fences. Large numbers of male convicts, too numerous to be housed in the congested prison, were leased to railroad and canal companies for hazardous construction work, and many died in the disease-infested swamps and pine barrens.[21]

The masses were even more disturbed by the plight of the new public school system. Assailing the limited educational progress of the antebellum years, the aggressive Radical Republicans had laid the constitutional groundwork for these tax-supported "free" schools in the Reconstruction period. Their actions had angered many of the wealthier whites, fearful that this "carpetbagger" innovation would foster socialism and break down class lines. This hostility persisted even after the elite's triumph in 1869, but the

19. Maddex, *Virginia Conservatives,* pp. 147–48, 170–71; Pearson, *Readjuster Movement,* pp. 56–57; Joseph A. Greene, Jr., "A Critical Investigation of Virginia's System of Taxing Railroads" (Ph.D. diss., University of Virginia, 1951), pp. 18–19.

20. Pollard to Henry H. Hurt, March 2, 1878, Hurt Papers, Edwin A. Alderman Library, University of Virginia, Charlottesville, Va.

21. Maddex, *Virginia Conservatives,* pp. 217, 224–29, describes conditions in Virginia's colleges, mental hospitals, and state penitentiary.

bulk of the Conservative leadership accepted the constitutional mandate and worked diligently to get the new schools into operation by the fall of 1870. Ably directed by William Henry Ruffner, state superintendent, the system recruited an energetic teacher corps and attracted more than 130,000 pupils during its first year. The schools won widespread popular approval, and in 1876 Governor Kemper declared that public education could no longer be considered a subject for debate.[22] In spite of its initial success, however, the system's position was extremely precarious. The flood of tax coupons crested at more than $1.2 million in 1878, and the state's financial stringency forced a drastic reduction of educational funds. Appropriations dropped from $443,000 in 1876 to only $241,000 in 1878. The number of schools and students plummeted. In some counties every school closed its doors, and the government owed the teachers more than $250,000 in back salaries. Ruffner protested angrily that the state's financial officers had diverted more than $1.1 million of the system's money into interest payments on the debt.[23] His aggressive statements aroused a storm of controversy, and the reactionary enemies of the free schools demanded a return to the less expensive antebellum educational order. Leading Funder spokesmen inflamed the situation with extremely impolitic statements. Frederick W. M. Holliday, who succeeded Kemper as governor in 1878, declared that the public schools were a nonessential "luxury," and prominent state Senator John W. Daniel insisted that it would be better to burn them than to default on the debt.[24] Such remarks angered the rebellious yeomen, and the educational crisis drove many into political revolt. Championing the schools, the Readjuster insurgents gained thousands of new supporters.

In spite of the Funders' inadequate appropriations for social services, it would be wrong to brand them as heartless reactionaries. Most of them supported the schools and the other charitable institutions, and they did not relish the politically disastrous policy of retrenchment. They were, instead, the victims of economic depression and the tax-receivable coupons. Misled by Governor Walker, they had believed that the state could support its colleges,

22. See ibid., pp. 204–14, for information on the establishment of the public school system. See also Cornelius J. Heatwole, *A History of Education in Virginia* (New York: Macmillan Co., 1916), pp. 220–21.

23. Virginia, Superintendent of Public Instruction, *School Report,* 1881, p. 126, provides a summary of Ruffner's protests from the 1870s.

24. C. Vann Woodward, *Origins of the New South, 1877–1913* (Baton Rouge: Louisiana State University Press, 1951), p. 61.

schools, and mental institutions and fulfill the terms of the Funding Act at the same time. When the depression of the 1870s hit Virginia, however, the government's tax base contracted, revenues declined, and the tide of interest coupons reached its peak. Confronted by this grim situation, the elite reluctantly adopted the unpopular course of raising taxes and reducing expenditures. Governors Kemper and Holliday attempted across-the-board cuts in official salaries and other outlays, but the savings were small. The treasury remained empty, and the masses rightly suspected that they were getting less and less for their tax dollars. The failure of retrenchment further depleted the Funders' rapidly dwindling political capital.[25]

The miscalculations and blunders which warped the state's fiscal policies were indicative of deeper problems. The government's administrative machinery was honeycombed with incompetence and, in some instances, corruption. Following in the footsteps of the antebellum elite, the Conservatives parceled out state jobs, including judgeships, according to the dictates of the spoils system. Nepotism and political influence dominated appointments, and even a conscientious man such as Governor Kemper could do little to upgrade the quality of the civil service. General Assembly committees made cursory annual investigations of the various administrative departments, but the legislators lacked the time, the motivation, and the expertise to keep a close watch on affairs. Deprived of adequate coordination and supervision, Virginia's officials carried on the government's business in an atmosphere of mistrust, jealousy, and intrigue.[26] The bitter clashes between the school superintendent and the state's financial officers set the pattern for similar, though less publicized, vendettas at the Medical College of Virginia, the Agricultural and Mechanical College, and the school for handicapped children in Staunton.[27] Lax administration frustrated legislative efforts to regulate the corporate interests, moreover, and effectively

25. Maddex, *Virginia Conservatives,* pp. 220–24; Robert R. Jones, "Conservative Virginian: The Post-war Career of Governor James Lawson Kemper" (Ph.D. diss., University of Virginia, 1964), pp. 317, 320, 322.

26. Maddex, *Virginia Conservatives,* p. 114; Charles C. Pearson, "William Henry Ruffner: Reconstruction Statesman of Virginia," *South Atlantic Quarterly* 20 (1921):148.

27. For details on the problems of these institutions see Wyndham B. Blanton, *Medicine in Virginia in the Nineteenth Century* (Richmond: Garrett & Massie, 1933), p. 61; James H. Skinner to Frederick W. M. Holliday, August 31, 1880, F.W.M. Holliday Papers. William R. Perkins Library, Duke University, Durham, N.C.; and John Perry Cochran, "The Virginia Agricultural and Mechanical College: The Formative Half Century, 1872–1919, of Virginia Polytechnic Institute" (Ph.D. diss., University of Alabama, 1961), pp. 111, 116–17, 120–26.

nullified ambitious tax levies on liquor consumption and oyster harvesting. Lawyer "cliques" and "rings" dominated the courthouse towns, and local school officials and tax assessors were frequently subservient to neighborhood pressure groups. Many of the county treasurers and clerks skimmed off state money for themselves, and by 1878 their accounts with the government were in arrears by more than $330,000.[28] Poorly organized and staffed with political hacks, Virginia's administrative machinery was threatened with complete paralysis.

A series of extremely damaging scandals repeatedly drew attention to these administrative failures and fanned the flames of political revolt. The unsettled conditions of the 1870s spawned corrupt officials throughout the United States and Europe, and the Old Dominion's Conservative regime did not escape the blight. The doorkeeper of the House of Delegates falsified records and embezzled state funds, and the register of the land office neglected his duties for the saloons and gambling halls of Richmond. Governor Kemper fired several penitentiary officials for conspiring to swindle the government on supply purchases, and in 1880 investigators discovered that the institution's general agent had stolen more than $31,000 during his four years in office. Although under indictment for bilking the Commonwealth out of $160,000, state Senator Bradley T. Johnson continued to enjoy the influence and friendship of Governor Holliday. The most unsavory scandals, however, involved the Old Dominion's financial officers. Joseph Mayo, treasurer, and William D. Coleman, Sinking Fund secretary, engaged in illegal bond manipulations and embezzled more than $15,000 before coming under fire in 1874; Coleman was subsequently jailed for forgery, and Mayo managed to escape imprisonment only by pleading insanity.[29] In spite of the removal of these corruptionists, suspicions continued to focus on the financial offices in the basement of the Capitol. In 1877 the second auditor's staff discovered that $35,000 in prewar bonds had been funded, stolen from the treasurer's office, and funded again. A subsequent House investigation revealed that more than $90,000 in interest coupons, already used for the payment of taxes, had mysteriously disappeared from the second auditor's office during the 1870s and might illegally be used again.[30]

28. Virginia, Senate, *Journal,* 1879–80, Document 17, p. 11; *Senate Journal,* 1883–84, Document 21, p. 5.

29. Maddex, *Virginia Conservatives,* pp. 113–17, 224, describes Virginia's governmental corruption in the 1870s.

Extending beyond these administrative functionaries, the taint of corruption also spread over the legislative chambers and into the Governor's Mansion. Strategic bribes played a key role in pushing the Funding bill through the General Assembly, and Governor Walker was deeply implicated in the wrongdoing. In 1870 the government began to sell its prewar railroad holdings to private investors at cut rates, moreover, and a host of well-heeled lobbyists converged on Richmond. Money, stock certificates, and free railroad passes were the "solvents of integrity" in fierce legislative battles over corporate charters and other governmental favors. Although the Old Dominion had experienced its share of political corruption during the colonial and antebellum years, the 1870s marked a new low in its public morality.[31] Accustomed to the petty graft and favoritism of the old aristocratic order, the elite did nothing to combat the institutional shortcomings which bred corruption. The Funders' perorations about the state's "sacred honor" had a hollow ring against this sordid background of debauched legislators, "fancy women," "wet groceries," and punch bowls full of greenbacks.

Faced with an increasingly rebellious electorate, the Virginia Conservatives employed repressive political methods which only increased the alienation of the masses. Fearing a recrudescence of the Radical threat, the Funders pitted the efficient and well-financed Conservative organization against the insurgents. They repeatedly raised the specter of "Negro rule" to frighten the whites into line, and they rigged elections through ballot box frauds and wholesale bribery. Local nominating conventions merely registered the dictates of the courthouse cliques. Further buttressing their position, the Conservatives used their control over the General Assembly to kill reform measures in committee. They struck at the political rights of the poor, moreover, by making the prepayment of the poll tax a prerequisite for voting. Governor Kemper even suggested that the secret ballot should be replaced by the old *viva voce* procedure. The elite's retrenchment policy also served to remove the government from popular control, forcing a substantial cut in the size of the House of Delegates and the substitution of biennial legislative sessions for the Underwood Constitution's

---

30. Virginia, House of Delegates, *Journal,* 1881–82, Document 2, p. 5; see also the *Richmond Daily Dispatch,* December 7, 1877.

31. Maddex, *Virginia Conservatives,* pp. 93–99; Allen W. Moger, "Railroad Practices and Policies in Virginia after the Civil War," *Virginia Magazine of History and Biography* 59 (1951):427.

annual ones. The Conservative leaders gerrymandered county boundaries to neutralize the Negro vote, abolished the democratic township system of local government, and gave every indication that they intended to restore the aristocratic prewar political structure in its entirety.[32] Alarmed by these developments, the lower classes responded eagerly to Readjuster promises of a "free ballot" and an end to "ring rule."

Identified in the public mind with high taxes, deficit spending, corruption, and repression, the patricians had alienated thousands of voters by the end of the 1870s. They had exhausted the patience of the masses, and many of the people no longer trusted them. Why did the Old Dominion's traditionally flexible ruling class allow this debacle to take place? Part of the answer lies in the group's increasing isolation from the problems of the rural poor. Second, the state's leaders were the tragic victims of the economic depression and the intransigence of the bondholders and the courts. In the broadest sense, however, they failed because they could not understand the economic and social realities of postwar Virginia. Their basic attitudes and values, including their devotion to the property rights of the bondholders, had been shaped by the antebellum culture and were very slow to change. They could easily have maintained their position by stealing the Readjusters' thunder, defying the courts, and forcibly reducing the interest burden until the return of prosperity. Refusing to do this, they ignored the wishes of the rising yeoman class and opposed the powerful trends toward political and social democracy unleashed by the war. Suspended between the aristocratic past and the harsh realities of Gilded Age America, the patricians were strangers in their own land. Their behavior during the 1870s constituted a blueprint for political suicide.

32. McFarland, "Democracy in Virginia," pp. 87–100; Maddex, *Virginia Conservatives,* pp. 194–203; Wynes, *Race Relations,* p. 13.

3

The Funders:

Men against Their Time

Battered by circumstances and crippled by their own mistakes, the Funder patricians were losing their grip on the Old Dominion by the end of the 1870s. In spite of their blunders, however, they retained several significant political advantages. They dominated the state's economy and had easy access to campaign donations from wealthy bondholders and railroad executives. Their control over the Conservative party machinery, moreover, gave them a powerful hold on a majority of the white vote. Most significant of all, the Funders were bound together by an intricate and durable web of shared values and beliefs. These ideological bonds gave their cause a coherence and solidarity which their Readjuster opponents lacked. Although temporarily discredited by administrative failures, the Funders were still a powerful force during the bitter campaigns of the 1870s and early 1880s.

The debt-paying faction benefited greatly from the high caliber of its leaders. Drawn from the ranks of the traditional elite, the party's spokesmen were the sort of men that Virginians had been electing to office for generations. An analysis of biographical data on sixty-seven prominent Funders reveals that they were a remarkably homogeneous group. Reflecting the social and economic trends of the day, the overwhelming majority had begun professional or mercantile careers in the towns and cities. Lawyers, editors, and other professional men dominated the party councils, and only eleven of the sixty-seven had engaged in farming to any significant extent. According to this sample the typical Funder politician was a middle-aged lawyer with a good family background, a University of Virginia education, and a distinguished war record as a Confederate officer. Although some had been soiled by the corruption of the 1870s, most were respectable gentlemen whose opinions carried much weight in their communities. United by ties of kinship, education, and experience, they provided a powerful nucleus for their party.[1]

These leaders could count on a solid core of support from the white voters, particularly from those who were thoroughly integrated into the traditional agricultural-mercantile economic order. They consistently won sizable majorities in such trade centers as Richmond, Lynchburg, Staunton, and Alexandria, and they generally outpolled the Readjusters in the crossroads towns and county seats. "The cities," declared one of the party's newspapers, "are said to be the strongholds of Funderism in Virginia. It is natural that they should be so. Men engaged in commercial pursuits are apt to be but little tolerant of repudiation and readjustment, and other such modes of getting rid of honest debts. . . . However this may be, it is certain that the mercantile classes, the bankers, the lawyers, and moneyed men generally, are supposed to be as a rule arrayed in solid phalanx in favor of maintaining the credit of Virginia."[2] The faction also garnered a high percentage of the white vote in the state's agricultural heartland, the Piedmont, where racial fears deterred potential rebels from breaking with the "white man's party." The prosperous farmers of northern Virginia were relatively immune to the Readjusters' appeals, moreover, and the Funders swept these counties handily in election after election. They were much less successful, by way of contrast, with the dynamic and restless yeomen of the Valley, the Southwest, and the southern Tidewater. Nevertheless, the combination of the mercantile classes of the towns with a large bloc of farm votes provided the debt-payers with a numerically strong and economically potent political base.[3]

1. At least 54 of the 67 had been lawyers or had studied law, and editors, teachers, doctors, and preachers constituted an overwhelming majority of the remainder. A minimum of 48 had attended college or law school. At least 41 had served the Confederacy during the war, and 27 of them had held high positions in its civilian or military hierarchies. In 1880 the median age of the group's members was 46 years; the average age was 46.3 years. See Appendixes A and B.

2. *Richmond Daily Dispatch,* November 5, 1881.

3. These generalizations are based on the election returns from 1879 to 1883. For the results of the 1879 legislative contest see the *Richmond Daily Dispatch,* November 19, 22, 1879. The *Warrock-Richardson Maryland, Virginia, and North Carolina Almanack* (Richmond: James E. Goode) provides a convenient source for other vote totals. Its 1882 issue, pp. 30–31, contains the results of the 1880 presidential election in Virginia, and its 1884 issue, pp. 30, 34, has the totals for

This coalition of townsmen and farmers, capitalists and aristocrats, was cemented by a common commitment to the traditional values of Virginia society—economic orthodoxy, a hierarchical social order, and elitist government. The Funders' conservatism had been intensified, moreover, by twenty nerve-shattering years of war, Reconstruction, and economic collapse. Troubled by the social upheavals of Gilded Age America, they adopted what amounted to a siege mentality and traced most of the nation's ills to the disproportionate power of the industrial Northeast and the destruction of "constitutional government" by the Civil War. In a typical editorial the *Richmond Dispatch* lamented that the conflict had laid the foundations for a "consolidated despotism . . . upon the ruins of the republic." [4] The Union victory had shackled Negro suffrage and carpetbag governments on the reconstructed South, but conservative Virginians insisted that the conquerors could not escape the suicidal consequences of their own acts. Governor Frederick W. M. Holliday warned that "Northern society is on a Volcano and the crust is not an inch thick." [5] The ex-Confederates expressed a perverse satisfaction, therefore, when the North was racked by governmental scandals and the great labor disorders of the 1870s. Beneath their surface cynicism, however, the Funders were deeply concerned about nationwide trends toward corporate monopoly, mob violence, atheism, and political radicalism. The editor of the party's newspaper in Harrisonburg wondered if the country could survive the endless wrangling of "Republicans, Democrats, Nationals, Greenbackers, Repudiationists, Communists, Women's Righters, Knights of Labor, Native Americans, Grand Armies of the Republic, Murphy Leagues, Kearneyites, Tramps, and all the ism ills that the world, the flesh and the devil are heir to." [6] The debt-payers regarded their Readjuster opponents as the local manifestations of these decadent trends and repeatedly compared them to the socialists, communists, anarchists, and nihilists of Europe and the North. Beset by fears of impending chaos and class war, some of the Funders succumbed

---

the 1881 gubernatorial race and the 1882 election for United States Congressman-at-Large. For the 1883 legislative races see the *Richmond Daily Dispatch*, January 16, 1884; and Ainsworth R. Spofford, ed., *American Almanac and Treasury of Facts, Statistical, Financial, and Political, for the Year 1884* (New York: American News Co., 1884), p. 262.

4. *Richmond Daily Dispatch*, March 4, 1880.

5. Holliday to Thomas F. Bayard, December 12, 1881, copy in the F.W.M. Holliday Papers, William R. Perkins Library, Duke University, Durham, N.C.

6. *Harrisonburg* (Va.) *Old Commonwealth*, August 8, 1878.

to despair. Several argued that a benevolent national dictatorship would provide the only real chance for social harmony, and Doctor George William Bagby abandoned his customary role as a humorist to predict another civil war and the creation of a brutal military regime headed by General Grant. Virtually abandoning hope for the South during his lifetime, educator and philanthropist Jabez L. M. Curry declared that only Christianity and education could possibly save the region. William H. Ruffner was also fearful about the future. "The era of the oak," he noted grimly, "is giving way to the era of the pine: God forbid that we should pass on to the era of broomsedge and prairie fires." [7]

Most of the Funders, although apprehensive, never completely despaired of the situation. Preeminently legalistic in their frame of mind, they believed that the universe, society, and man were governed by immutable natural laws, and they argued that the nation had courted disaster by violating or ignoring them. The overwhelming majority traced the origin of these laws to the Christian God, while a few of the more adventurous employed a Darwinian rhetoric to explain the nature of things. All agreed, however, that the descent into anarchy could be halted only by a return to these essential precepts, by obedience to the time-honored and proven teachings of experience and practice. They insisted that a sensible regard for this traditional wisdom would restore the nation's economy, social order, and governmental institutions to health and vigor. "In the language of our fathers," the *Southern Planter and Farmer* pontificated, "the time has come for a recurrence to 'fundamental principles,' and for the practice of those homely virtues, which alone make a people prosperous, great and happy." [8] Although deeply distressed by the turmoil and corruption of this "transition period in our political history," the Funder *Richmond State* also expressed a cautious optimism. "But in spite of the fact that things have gone very far wrong," the newspaper argued, ". . . we still have faith in the ultimate triumph of the right and the complete vindication of the system." [9]

7. Virginia, Superintendent of Public Instruction, *School Report,* 1881, p. 118. See also [G. W. Bagby], *1860–1880. John Brown and William Mahone: An Historical Parallel, Foreshadowing Civil Trouble* (Richmond: C. F. Johnson, 1880), pamphlet, Virginiana Collection, Edwin A. Alderman Library, University of Virginia, Charlottesville, Va.; and J.L.M. Curry to Robert C. Winthrop, February 7, 1882, J.L.M. Curry Papers, Manuscripts Division, Library of Congress, Washington, D.C.

8. [L. R. Dickinson], "Note by the Editor," *Southern Planter & Farmer, Devoted to Agriculture, Horticulture and Rural Affairs* 39 (1878):486.

9. *Richmond State,* August 23, 1879.

In the area of economic policy the embattled Funders called for a return to the sound financial practices of the prewar years. Capital and labor were at each other's throats, and the Virginia conservatives insisted that governmental paternalism was at the root of the problem. Devoted to the laissez-faire principles of Adam Smith and the other classical economists, the Funders maintained that the nation's prosperity was based upon the efforts of each individual to accumulate private property by his own independent exertions. "If all will stop hoping for impossibilities," the *Richmond Dispatch* intoned, "and if every man will go to work for himself, make what he can and save all he can, society will be lifted up from depression and made independent and contented." [10] Brought up in a pretechnological economy of scarcity, the Funders believed that the human race was condemned to a harsh and unending struggle to wrest its livelihood from a niggardly world. They called for a policy of "practical economy and rigid utility" and insisted that man was the prisoner of inexorable economic laws.[11] Beneath this dismal and apparently heartless rhetoric, however, a strongly Calvinistic moral tone pervaded the Funders' economic thought. The "good" man, the industrious laborer or the thrifty capitalist, could generally expect to prosper, but the wastrel or parasite would almost invariably suffer the evil consequences of his folly. By the same token, a government which observed the rules of economic probity and fair dealing could expect to elevate the moral tone and ensure the prosperity of its citizens; a state which lived by fraud and deceit, on the other hand, would amost inevitably lead its people to disaster.[12] The Funders' ethical bearing, moreover, tended to mitigate the most vicious theoretical aspects of the competitive system. According to their way of thinking there could be no valid cause for class war since the independent efforts of each individual contributed to the general good. They assumed the existence of a "harmony of interests" between the "productive" classes—capitalists and laborers alike. The *Richmond Commonwealth,* for example, firmly avowed that the interests of labor and management "are identical, and . . . there is no collision between them except what is stirred up by idle and trifling and selfish

10. *Richmond Daily Dispatch,* September 28, 1878.
11. Ibid., July 6, 28, 1879; *Richmond State,* October 16, 1878; George Frederick Holmes, *A Science of Society* (n.p., 1884), p. 41.
12. The Funders used this argument repeatedly in their fight to prevent the repudiation of Virginia's state bonds. See the *Richmond State,* June 25, 1878, August 23, 1879, for examples of these appeals.

agitators." [13] The ferocity of competition was also tempered, at least in theory, by a rigorous though informal code of personal honesty and fair dealing, by "the belief in and practice of principles of justice and integrity between man and man." [14]

The only legitimate economic functions for the state in this essentially self-regulating economic order were to defend property rights, enforce the obligation of contracts, and promote trade by maintaining the stable value of the nation's currency. Efforts to expand the role of the government beyond these traditional and rudimentary services were likely to prove either harmful or ineffectual. As one of the party's Tidewater newspapers declared, "The natural laws of trade and commerce are more important than the statutory enactments of governments." [15] The editor of the *Southern Planter and Farmer,* speaking for the wealthier agricultural classes, offered a concise statement of the Funders' laissez-faire views. "Let the people of Virginia never admit the idea," he intoned emphatically, "that they must look to government, State or Federal, for prosperity. If only government can be kept from doing harm, and the people be left, without let or help, to provide for their own interests in their own way, we have all that we have a right to expect or desire. The great duty of government consists not in doing, but in not doing. It should be negative, not active. The individual should be protected at all hazards, and at any cost; but when it proceeds to meddle with his business, to control his domestic arrangements, it becomes odious and tyrannical." [16]

Applying these theories to the great economic issues of the 1870s, the Funders sought to protect property rights and to curtail the government's meddling in the economy. They denounced the nation's system of protective tariffs as a corrupt scheme for stifling international trade, fostering corporate monopolies, and forcing the price of consumer goods to unnatural heights. Angered by this paternalistic coddling of the Northeastern "money kings," the Funders generally advocated either free trade or a low "tariff for revenue only." [17] On the other great issue of the day, the currency, they adopted a staunchly conservative hard-money stance. The

13. *Richmond Commonwealth,* April 15, May 18, 1880.
14. *Richmond State,* June 25, 1878.
15. *Warsaw* (Va.) *Northern Neck News,* May 30, 1879.
16. [L. R. Dickinson], "Note by the Editor," pp. 486–87.
17. *Richmond State,* July 8, 9, August 18, October 11, 1879; March 29, May 19, 1882; *Staunton* (Va.) *Vindicator,* February 3, 17, 1882; *Harrisonburg* (Va.) *Old Commonwealth,* June 15, 1882.

party's leaders flirted briefly with the Greenback craze during the 1878 congressional election, but their basic commitment was to a stable money supply backed by gold and silver. "All theories," the *Dispatch* noted, "that teach the people that the government can enrich them by printing paper and calling it money are hurtful and injurious to those to whom they are taught." [18] Insisting that the public credit was the fountainhead of prosperity, moreover, these conservative Virginians insisted that the United States government should pay its bonded indebtedness in specie and ignore Greenbacker demands for payment in depreciated paper money.[19] Viewed within the broader context of these "sound" financial policies, therefore, the faction's spirited defense of the Old Dominion's bondholders was not surprising. All in all, the Funders' economic stands reflected the needs of the traditional economic order in their state. Earning their living by producing and marketing agricultural staples, they believed that their tariff, currency, and debt policies would gain them easy access to the markets and credit facilities of the world.

These economic arguments were closely linked to the debt-payers' views on the nature of society. Shocked by the upheavals of the 1860s and 1870s, they became obsessed with the need for order and stability in a nation which seemed to be tearing itself apart. "The necessities of civilized society," the *State* maintained, "are subordination to law, belief in law and appreciation of law—order, confidence, and intelligence." [20] In spite of the divisive trends of the day, however, they took comfort from what they believed to be the long-term patterns of social development. They regarded their society's built-in safeguards for life and property as the end result of thousands of years of evolution and struggle. In the past men had been bound together by force and fear, but the progress of civilization had largely replaced the spear with the contract, the bludgeon with more enduring bonds of trust and mutual respect. "Faith between man and man," the *Southern Planter and Farmer* declared, "is the great ligament that holds society together." [21] The

18. *Richmond Daily Dispatch,* July 13, 1878.

19. *Richmond State,* July 7, August 25, 1881; R.M.T. Hunter to J. Randolph Tucker, August 29, 1878, Hunter-Garnett Papers, Edwin A. Alderman Library, University of Virginia, Charlottesville, Va.

20. *Richmond State,* June 25, 1878.

21. "Some Comments on the Address of the State Executive Committee of the Conservative Party to the Teachers and Friends of the Public Schools," *Southern Planter & Farmer* 40 (1879):508.

experience of generations, moreover, led the Funders to believe in the permanence of social classes and the unequal division of property. Theologian Robert L. Dabney, an arch-Funder, argued that class lines were of divine origin. "God has made a social sub-soil," he thundered, "a social foundation in the dust, for the superstructure—the utopian cannot unmake it, least of all by his patchwork." [22] These social inequalities, according to conservative Virginians, simply reflected the varying talents and abilities of the people, and they insisted that in a free market economy all the classes would voluntarily cooperate for the general good. Just as there were natural class divisions in society, moreover, the debt-payers argued that there were also irrevocable caste lines between the races. Confident in the superiority of the whites, they insisted that Negroes should accept a subordinate role in society and politics. They cherished the image of the cheerful and tractable "darkey" of slavery times and were sure that the blacks would voluntarily and naturally assume a position at the base of the social pyramid.[23]

Sustained by their faith in social classes, private property, and racial subordination, the debt-payers were convinced that American society was fundamentally sound. True, problems had arisen from the "too rapid increase and concentration of wealth," [24] but the impact of competition and other natural laws would eventually restore stability and order. During the transitional period, however, the Funders insisted that "utopians" and "demagogues" posed a great threat. Looking across America, they observed the bitter fruits of fanaticism in the nationwide Greenbacker movement, the North's labor strife, California's anti-Chinese agitation, and Virginia's Readjuster uproar. The *State* denounced these radicals for appealing to the "inherent instinct" of the idle and vicious "to break through all the restraints of civilized life, and to return to the primitive condition of society." [25] In spite of the extreme gravity of the situation, however, the Virginia conservatives argued that the remedy was simple. They insisted that all that was necessary to ensure the nation's safety was a firm union of the industrious,

22. Robert L. Dabney, "Dr. Dabney Again," *Discussions by Robert L. Dabney,* ed. C. R. Vaughn, 4 vols. (Mexico, Mo.: Crescent Book House, 1897), 4:202.

23. Holmes, *A Science of Society,* pp. 204–5; *Richmond Daily Dispatch,* November 23, 1877; *Richmond State,* May 21, 1879, January 20, 1881; *Richmond Commonwealth,* July 2, 1880; *Norfolk Landmark,* September 4, 1879; Dabney, "The Negro and the Common School," *Discussions* 4:177–85.

24. Holmes, *A Science of Society,* p. 143.

25. *Richmond State,* August 10, 1878.

productive, and law-abiding people of all classes against the demagogues and the rabble. "In other words," the *State* declaimed, "the two estates [laborers and capitalists] who compose the muscle, brain, and wealth of the country must combine against the third, or hoodlum estate, and put it down." [26] This accomplished, the country could survive the crisis and resume its accustomed paths of peace and prosperity.

Determined to maintain the power of the conservative classes, the Funders devoted considerable attention to the problems of politics and government. They argued that the state existed in order to protect life and property, and they accordingly emphasized its judicial and police functions. "The State is to its citizens," the *Southern Planter and Farmer* declared, "the standard of justice, the sacred embodiment of right, the mirror in which individual actions are to be viewed and judged, the source and the inspiration of morals." [27] Sharing this exalted opinion, Governor Holliday insisted that the state was an earthly "counterpart of that Divine Government under the shadow of whose wings we rest." [28] This moralistic orientation led the Funders, naturally enough, to maintain that only the elite was fit to rule, and they persistently demanded that every community should be controlled by its "intelligence" and "property." Arguing that an unrestrained democracy could be just as tyrannical as a one-man dictatorship, they denied the egalitarian assertion that each individual had to have a vote in order to be free. Conservative Virginians maintained, by way of contrast, that freedom involved different conditions for different people. For the intelligent and the able, freedom meant full participation in the rights of citizenship; for the less intelligent, the less able, it meant the right to live under a just government controlled by capable men. Reflecting the debt-payers' elitist bias, the *Dispatch* maintained that the conduct of all public officials should mirror "the culture, the civilization, and the right standard of comfortable life and usage" in their community.[29]

26. Ibid.

27. "Some Comments on the Address of the State Executive Committee," p. 508.

28. Frederick W. M. Holliday, *The Higher Education, the Hope of American Republicanism: Annual Address Delivered Before the Society of the Alumni of the University of Virginia, June 29, 1876* (Winchester, Va.: *Times* Office, 1876), pp. 48–49, Virginiana Collection.

29. *Richmond Daily Dispatch*, March 3, 1879. See also Holliday, *Higher Education*, pp. 6–8, 25–26, 32, 39–42.

Turning to the governmental problems of the day, the Funders were appalled by the excesses and the vulgarity of Gilded Age politics. In a typical editorial the *Harrisonburg Old Commonwealth* expressed dismay at the country's "surfeit of charlatans, epaulets and flash; of mediocrity, of fraud, of rings, of shoddy." [30] On the national level conservative Virginians demanded that the boss-ridden and corrupt Republican party should be driven from power and that the Democrats should restore a pure and simple government based on states' rights. The *Staunton Vindicator,* for example, warned that the trend toward the concentration of power in Washington had to be reversed. "Centralization," the Funder newspaper intoned grimly, "means the death of free action, free speech, and finally of free thought." [31] On the local and state levels the debt-payers placed themselves in opposition to the democratic forces unleashed by the war. Particularly disturbed by the enfranchisement of the blacks, the *Southern Planter and Farmer* lamented that universal manhood suffrage "is the confiscation of private property. If we cannot check the tendency of things, socialism, nihilism, is not far off. This malignant philosophy injected by force into our social and political system is doing its deadly work. We must bestir ourselves, and at once, or be forever undone." [32]

Determined to maintain elitist rule, the Funders worked tirelessly to limit the political power of the lower classes. They restricted the franchise by making the prepayment of the poll tax a requirement for voting, and they took the vote away from those who had been convicted of petit larceny. Disgusted by "the wrangling, the corruptions, [and] the lying" of popular elections, the debt-payers also sought to reduce the number of elected officials, particularly on the local level.[33] "We would," the *Dispatch* remarked candidly, "far prefer a diminution of the number of elective offices to an increase of them." [34] The faction's leaders endeavored to control the electorate, moreover, through a rigid system of one-party Conservative rule, and they generally followed the antebellum practice of attempting to prevent divisive issues from coming before the public. Perhaps most significantly, a majority of the Funders aban-

30. *Harrisonburg* (Va.) *Old Commonwealth,* April 1, 1880.
31. *Staunton* (Va.) *Vindicator,* February 11, 1881.
32. [L. R. Dickinson], "Editorial General," *Southern Planter & Farmer* 41 (1880):148.
33. *Richmond Daily Dispatch,* February 18, 1878.
34. Ibid.

doned their traditional hostility to free public education because of a growing conviction that the schools could serve as an effective means of social control, as a method of integrating the mass of new voters into the state's conservative political order. Such men as William Ruffner believed that education would serve as a bastion of the status quo, instilling in the multitude a proper appreciation for the unchanging truths of morality, economics, and politics.[35] All these efforts, from repression to education, reflected the debt-payers' fervent desire to perpetuate elitist government in a democratic world.

These commitments to economic orthodoxy and social and political elitism came naturally enough to most white Virginians, particularly in the aristocratic areas east of the mountains. Educated in private schools and colleges, the Funder leadership had been brought up on these principles, and the white masses also had an intuitive appreciation of them. Orthodox Christianity's emphasis on the afterlife had conditioned the common people to accept their earthly rulers and their humble stations in life. The Judeo-Christian teachings concerning personal thrift, character, and honesty, moreover, oriented them toward the principles of the classical economists, as did the farmers' individual experiences in the practical realm of commercial agriculture. Similarly, generations of relatively honest and capable aristocratic government motivated the people to accept elite rule, and the grim instincts of racial survival convinced them of their innate superiority to the ex-slaves. Binding together a broad cross-section of Virginia's white population, Funder thought reflected the main currents of the state's intellectual life.

The debt-payers represented, then, a continuation of the ideas and personnel of the Old Dominion's traditional agricultural-mercantile order. Their social thought constituted a conservative bulwark against the disruptive forces of the 1870s and 1880s. Many of them abandoned their essentially cautious and defensive attitude, however, when they discussed Virginia's economic future. Receptive to the early versions of the burgeoning New South creed, the party's spokesmen maintained that the people should abandon the leisurely ways of the agrarian past in order to seek their fortunes in the brave new worlds of industry and finance. "The old Virginia system," according to the popular novelist John Esten Cooke, "resulted in immense comfort, but it did not result in profit, which

35. Virginia, Superintendent of Public Instruction, *School Report,* 1881, pp. 118–20.

is a good thing, however it may be denounced by some. Profit means prosperity, and prosperity means . . . happiness." [36] Insisting that "Croesus rules the roost," the *State* pursued a similar line of thought. "Money," the newspaper argued, "is the key to everything; . . . therefore, get money and all else that is of value in this world shall be added, leaving the next for subsequent consideration." [37] The Funder governors of the 1870s laced their official messages with flamboyant references to the state's boundless natural resources, and the party's self-proclaimed prophets lined Virginia's shores with imaginary cities and dotted the dreary hillsides with hundreds of prospective factories and mines.[38] Opening the gates to foreign immigrants and investors, the debt-payers appeared to be seeking a new, industrialized society which would have little in common with the old.

Taking this New South rhetoric at face value, several historians argue that Virginia's leaders virtually abandoned the traditions and values of the antebellum order after Appomattox. C. Vann Woodward declares that the Old Dominion's Conservatives and the other "Redeemers" of the post-Reconstruction South "were of middle-class, industrial, capitalistic outlook, with little but a nominal connection with the old planter regime." [39] Arguing that these men neglected the needs of the state's farmers, he also maintains that they shunned the agrarian radicals of the West in order to cement a firm political alliance with the conservative, business-oriented Democrats of the industrialized Northeast. [40] While Woodward generally emphasizes the exploitative and opportunistic aspects of "Redeemer" rule, two younger historians accentuate the positive in their studies of the Virginia Conservatives. Jack P. Maddex, Jr., and Robert R. Jones insist that the state's leaders during the 1870s were relatively progressive and realistic. Declaring that the Conservatives sought "a regeneration of Virginia's economy along Northeastern capitalist lines," Maddex contends that they attempted "to fit Virginia into the pattern of Gilded Age America." [41]

36. Quoted by Robert Darden Little, "The Ideology of the New South: A Study in the Development of Ideas, 1865–1910" (Ph.D. diss., University of Chicago, 1950), p. 23.

37. *Richmond State,* May 10, 1879.

38. For the governors' statements see Virginia, Senate, *Journal,* 1871–72, p. 24; *Senate Journal,* 1879–80, pp. 25–26; and *Senate Journal,* 1881–82, p. 20.

39. C. Vann Woodward, *Origins of the New South, 1877–1913* (Baton Rouge: Louisiana State University Press, 1951), p. 20.

40. Ibid., pp. 49–50.

Jones reaches a substantially similar conclusion in his biography of Governor Kemper. "With Northern and foreign financial aid," he notes, "the Conservatives planned to develop Virginia's resources and to make Virginia an integral and important part of the national economic system." [42] Although such assertions admirably modify the traditional stereotype of the reactionary "Bourbon," they also tend to obscure several essential characteristics of the Old Dominion's "Redeemer" hegemony, particularly when applied to the dominant Funder wing of the Conservative organization. The elite had become increasingly urban-oriented during the postwar years, of course, but its essential ideals and values remained much the same. A planter could move to the city and begin a new career with relative ease, but it was much more difficult for him to shake off the thought patterns of a lifetime. The debt-payers realized that the war had irrevocably shattered the traditional system of plantation agriculture, and their New South editorials reflected only a commonsense preference for prosperity over poverty—not a fundamental change in personal values or standards. A closer analysis of the Funders' statements reveals, moreover, that they hedged their commitments to the new economic order with so many reservations and qualifications as to make them practically meaningless. They welcomed economic growth, but only so long as it did not disrupt their elitist political, social, and economic order in Virginia.

Emphasizing the affinity of the "Redeemers" for the industrial Northeast, such historians as Woodward tend to underestimate the degree of sectional hatred in the first decades after the war. Memories of abolitionism, invasion, and "black-and-tan" rule poisoned the Southern mind, and the "bloody shirt" rantings of the Republicans in the North only intensified the feud. Noting that "northern and southern men and women hate one another instinctively," the *State* doubted if there would ever be "friendly sympathy" between the sections.[43] Prominent Funder intellectuals such as Robert L. Dabney, John Esten Cooke, and George William Bagby exhorted Virginians to resist insidious efforts to Northernize them

---

41. Jack Pendleton Maddex, Jr., "The Virginia Conservatives: A Study in 'Bourbon' Redemption, 1869–1879" (Ph.D. diss., University of North Carolina, 1966), pp. 800, 815.

42. Robert R. Jones, "Conservative Virginian: The Post-war Career of Governor James Lawson Kemper" (Ph.D. diss., University of Virginia, 1964), p. 112.

43. *Richmond State,* March 5, 1880.

through the introduction of alien ideas and institutions.[44] The debt-payers, far from taking the industrialized Northeast as their model, were disgusted and alarmed by the region's teeming slums, dishonest business practices, exploitative monopolies, labor strife, and lack of respect for constitutional government. Abandoning its devotion to "Croesus," the *State* denounced the people of the North as a "rude," "uncultured," and ill-bred mob who lacked respect for the "traditional past" and who wasted their lives in a degrading struggle for "filthy lucre." [45] The *Dispatch* seconded these harsh sentiments and added that the region was the home of an "illiberal and dogmatical and presumptuous political puritanism." [46]

Plagued by doubts and suspicions, the Funders were never really comfortable in their alliance with the urban Democratic bosses of the North, and during the depression-ridden 1870s they showed signs of a marked desire to seek other friends. The Northern Democracy, torn by factional strife and badly divided on the currency and tariff issues, was of little help in the struggle for political supremacy. Some conservative Virginians were so disillusioned by the incompetence and selfishness of these allies that they even considered joining the hated Republicans. For most, however, the possibility of firm ties with the rebellious farmers of the West appeared much more palatable. "Observant and unprejudiced statesmen," the *Dispatch* declared hopefully, "must have arrived at the conclusion that the South and West not only have the power to direct the policy of this nation, but that they will unite for the purpose of doing so." [47] The debt-payers' fear of the industrial and financial power of the Northeast, moreover, led them to supplement their hostility to protective tariffs with a number of surprising stands on the other major issues of the day. Convinced that their agricultural-mercantile economy was threatened by the overbearing influence of the Northeastern "money power," the party's editors occasionally abandoned their laissez-faire scruples and expressed sympathy for federal railroad regulation, government ownership of the telegraph lines, criminal prosecution of monopolists, and an end to the exploitation of wage laborers.[48] Defying the national

44. George William Bagby, "The Southern Fool," in *Selections from the Miscellaneous Writings of Dr. George William Bagby,* 2 vols. (Richmond: Whittet & Shepperson, 1885), 2:170–71; Dabney, "The New South," *Discussions,* 4:16–19; John Esten Cooke to F.W.M. Holliday, June 12, 1881, Holliday Papers.

45. *Richmond State,* October 6, 1879.

46. *Richmond Daily Dispatch,* November 26, 1877.

47. Ibid.

and international trends of the day, the Funders also opposed the demands of Northern financial interests who favored the demonetization of silver and the creation of a monometallic gold standard for the currency. Realizing the potentially disastrous impact of this deflationary policy on their economy, conservative Virginians demanded the retention of silver as an integral part of the money supply and joined with Western agrarians to force the enactment of the pro-silver Bland-Allison Act.[49] The Funders were not enthusiastically eager to subordinate the needs of Virginia to those of Northeastern capitalists.

This commitment to the traditional order also colored and modified the debt-payers' New South pronouncements. Fearful of the social consequences of overcrowded cities and great industrial plants, they generally endorsed the concept of a balanced economy based on agriculture, commerce, and small-scale manufacturing.[50] The development of industry required the creation of a large pool of cheap labor, but the Funders were alarmed by the social dislocation which this would involve. The *Richmond State* repeatedly urged the agricultural masses, the most logical source of the labor pool, to remain on their farms instead of swelling the rush to the congested urban centers.[51] This conservatism also influenced the faction's approach to the problem of immigration. They did not seek to entice the ignorant peasant or industrial worker to come to the Old Dominion; they attempted, instead, to lure the wealthy and cultured person who would be able to understand and appreciate the state's traditions and who could afford to purchase and cultivate its unused farmland. Shunning the poor of Europe, the *State* endorsed

48. *Richmond State,* February 7, 1879; January 18, February 26, March 29, 1881; *Staunton* (Va.) *Vindicator,* February 18, March 4, 1881; *Richmond Daily Dispatch,* December 31, 1877; *Richmond Commonwealth,* April 15, 1880.

49. *Warsaw* (Va.) *Northern Neck News,* May 30, July 4, 1879; *Richmond Daily Dispatch,* February 9, 1878, December 30, 1879; Joseph Carlyle Ellett, "The Free Silver Movement, 1878–1900, with Special Reference to Virginia" (M.A. thesis, University of Virginia, 1933), pp. 65–68.

50. This assessment is based on the Funders' tendency to stress the essential harmony and interdependence of agriculture, commerce, and manufacturing. Their emphasis was on a program of economic diversification that would enable Virginians to use and process the products of their fields and mines. See Virginia, Commissioner of Agriculture, *Handbook of Virginia,* 1879, pp. 74–75, 79–81; *Richmond State,* September 1, 1879, April 26, 1880; J.L.M. Curry, *Thoughts for Farmers upon Present Distress* (Richmond: n.p., 1878), pp. 5–7, Virginiana Collection; and the report of a speech by F.W.M. Holliday in the *Richmond Daily Dispatch,* November 16, 1877.

51. *Richmond State,* April 26, July 12, 1879; see also the *State's* comparison of urban and rural life in its issue for February 2, 1880.

only "immigration of the best quality, of wealth, of enterprise, of industry . . . of education, and of good blood." [52] A latent nativism occasionally rose to the surface, moreover, and several debt-payer editors argued that it would be better to encourage young Virginians to remain in the state instead of urging potentially rebellious foreigners to take their places.[53] Similar suspicions even extended to outside capitalists who had money to invest in the state. Convinced that Virginians should reap the profits from their natural resources, thoughtful conservatives pondered the impact of an influx of foreign investors and money. "The poverty of the South," the *Norfolk Landmark* noted gloomily, "unhappily exposes us to the schemes of alien speculators, who parcel out our territory and consume our resources in the interests of outside communities." [54] Alexander H. H. Stuart, a leader in the movement to "redeem" the state from Radical rule, provided an even more dismal evaluation. "Already," he noted, "many of the most valuable estates, and the richest mines of coal and iron in Virginia and West Virginia, have passed into the hands of strangers for less than a tithe of their value; and, if the people of Virginia continue to remain quiescent and inactive, the day is not far distant when they will be supplanted by a more vigorous and energetic population, and their magnificent heritage will pass into the hands of strangers." [55]

These anxieties reflected more fundamental misgivings about the New South. Even while extolling the virtues of economic growth the debt-payers frequently revealed their nagging doubts and fears about the impact of materialism on their traditional society. "Our ears are constantly vexed," Governor Holliday intoned, "with cries of progress! progress! But alas! if we only knew it, oftentimes those very things that are regarded as evidences of progress, to a thoughtful man, are the millstones that are dragging us to barbarism." [56] Disturbed by the unrest and the tensions of the modern age, John Esten Cooke noted that life was "more satisfactory" in the old days "when men managed to live without telegraphs, railways,

52. Ibid., January 17, 1881. For additional references of this type see the *Norfolk Landmark,* September 10, 17, 1879; the *Warsaw* (Va.) *Northern Neck News,* July 11, 1879; and Rolfe S. Saunders, "Immigration to Virginia," *Southern Planter & Farmer* 41 (1880):443–44.
53. *Richmond State,* January 17, 1881; *Warsaw* (Va.) *Northern Neck News,* July 11, 1879.
54. *Norfolk Landmark,* September 24, 1879.
55. Alexander H. H. Stuart, "A Word of Advice to the Young Men of Virginia," *Southern Planter & Farmer* 42 (1881):20.
56. Holliday, *Higher Education,* p. 36.

and electric lights." [57] The *Lynchburg Virginian* pursued a similar line of thought and posed two searching questions. "With all this ceaseless activity," the newspaper asked, "are men any better than they used to be? Has the growth of moral principle kept pace with intellectual and material development?" [58] Such qualms led the party's spokesmen to insist again and again that good character was the real key to individual and social progress, and they firmly admonished that the single-minded pursuit of wealth for its own sake was a bitter delusion. More than mere rhetorical flourishes, these arguments reflected the persistence of the antebellum heritage with its emphasis on honor and personal integrity. Appalled by what Cooke described as the "dreary waste" of the postwar years,[59] the Funders looked to the past for their standards and values. Their literary endeavors—their essays, poems, novels, and histories—lauded the social peace and economic harmony of the slave era, and the refined "old Virginia gentleman" remained unchallenged as the dominant cultural symbol and ideal long after his plantation regime had crumbled. The four years of war had added new heroes to the Old Dominion's pantheon, moreover, and the elite was already sprinkling the cities and crossroads towns with monuments to Lee, Jackson, and the Confederate dead. Disdaining the crassness and vulgarity of the new era, the debt-payers generally approached the future with stoic resignation rather than hope. " 'The spacious times of great Elizabeth' come not again;" Doctor Bagby lamented, "there is no second age of Pericles." [60]

One of Bagby's stories, "What I Did with My Fifty Millions," provides additional insight into the elite's ambivalence toward economic progress. The hero of the tale, a loafer named Mozis Addums, mysteriously acquires $50 million from "Hindostan" and devotes his life to rebuilding the prosperity of Virginia and the South. "I will," he exults, "flood the South with money. Set every industry humming, restock every plantation, buy up every negro legislature, buy Congress, buy Grant bodily; my people shall not, no, by the gods! they *shall not* suffer any longer." [61] He exhausts his fortune in efforts to develop the region, but in the end he is old, lonely, forgotten, and embittered. Surrounded by "settlers

57. John Esten Cooke, *Virginia: A History of the People* (Boston: Houghton Mifflin Co., 1884), pp. 370–71.
58. *Lynchburg Tri-Weekly Virginian,* December 28, 1877.
59. Cooke, *Virginia,* p. 505.
60. Bagby, "The Old Virginia Gentleman," *Miscellaneous Writings,* 1:46.
61. Bagby, "What I Did with My Fifty Millions," *Miscellaneous Writings,* 2:246.

from strange places" and "money-seekers," his only close companion is a fiendish mechanical man who beats him and makes his life miserable. Near death, the aged philanthropist has a vision of a regiment of Confederate ghosts—men from the old times—who come to visit and feast with him. Addums is overjoyed to see them again, but the evil "automaton" bursts into the banquet room and breaks up the party. The hero and his friends struggle with the monster, which eventually destroys itself by falling down a well. The festivities begin anew, symbolizing the final victory of the romantic past over the grim realities of the postwar era.[62] The Funders, like the fictional Addums, paid lip service to the New South, but their hearts remained with the Old.

In many ways the tradition-oriented debt-payers resembled the contemporary "Mugwump" reformers of the North. Convinced of the eternal validity of natural laws and economic orthodoxy, both groups offered simplistic and moralistic panaceas for the complex problems of Gilded Age America. Faced by the rise of trusts and monopolies, they agreed that free trade and sound financial policies would restore the essential harmony between labor and capital. Both groups refused to recognize the dynamic character of the nation's democratic experience and worked diligently to secure the rule of the "best men" in politics. Representing the remnants of the agricultural-mercantile oligarchies which had dominated the country before the war, both seemed congenitally unable to understand the forces at work in the new industrial order.[63] The Funders wished to realize the New South's dream of industrial wealth, but only if it could be accomplished without disturbing their elitist class structure and patrician mores. Trapped by their traditionalist values, they were truly men against their time.

62. Ibid., pp. 241–318.

63. For information on the Mugwumps see John G. Sproat, *"The Best Men": Liberal Reformers in the Gilded Age* (New York: Oxford University Press, 1968).

4

A Confusion of Voices: Sections, Races, and Readjusters

The Funders elaborated their arguments throughout the 1870s, creating an ideology with strong popular appeal. During most of the decade, in fact, their regime appeared practically invulnerable. They had an iron grip on the overwhelming majority of the newspapers, the bulk of the wealth, and the Old Dominion's political machinery from statehouse to courthouse. Their opponents, on the other hand, encountered a depressing round of gubernatorial vetoes, adverse judicial decisions, and public ridicule. Assailed as "agrarians," "communists," "bolters," and "scum," the "original" Readjusters of the early 1870s were a disorganized and ineffectual group of malcontents, powerless and isolated on the fringes of the dominant agricultural-mercantile elite. The prolonged depression of the decade, however, coupled with a superabundance of debt-payer blunders, resulted in massive accretions to the insurgents' ranks. They expanded their appeal beyond the debt issue and rallied thousands of Virginians who were alienated from the Old Dominion's tradition-oriented political and economic hierarchy.

Unlike the Funders, who enjoyed a relatively coherent and unified political base among the urban upper classes and the conservative farmers of the Piedmont, the Readjusters amassed their support from a much more heterogeneous cross section of the people. Analysis of election returns from 1879 to 1883 reveals that the insurgents won consistent and repeated victories in counties scattered over each of the state's major geographical regions. They assimilated a large bloc of votes from the Negroes as well as the whites. Extending their influence beyond the countryside, moreover, they won elections in such urban centers as Norfolk, Danville, Petersburg, and Winchester. To a much greater extent than their debt-payer opponents, the insurgents reflected the variety of social and economic conditions which characterized postwar Virginia.

The Readjusters could count on a relatively loyal core of white voters, more than 30,000 in number, concentrated in the mountainous Southwest, the northern Valley, the eastern Piedmont, and the southern Tidewater.[1] Most of these men were farmers, devastated by the deflationary trends of the 1870s, but their political motives were frequently as varied as their sectional backgrounds. The aggressively democratic Southwest, for example, led all the white regions in its support for the new party. Hungry for outside capital investments, devoted to the public schools, and unhampered by the "Negro problem" which plagued eastern Virginia, the ambitious farmers and businessmen of this underdeveloped frontier frequently endorsed the Greenbacker movement as well as Readjustment. Similar aspirations propelled thousands of Valley whites into the Readjuster column. Enjoying the fruits of a flourishing agricultural economy and anxious to develop their untapped mineral resources, the energetic yeomen of such counties as Rockingham, Shenandoah, and Page turned a deaf ear to Funder oratory about the state's "sacred honor" and glorious past. At the other end of the Commonwealth the bustling southern Tidewater was also caught up in this yeoman revolution and provided a third source of strength for the new movement. Leavened with immigrants from Europe and the North, its cosmopolitan population welcomed political and economic change. Sandwiched between these progressive areas, moreover, lay the last and most unstable source of white insurgent votes—the depression-ridden tobacco belt of the eastern Piedmont. This tier of impoverished counties spawned a quarrelsome mass of broken-down aristocrats, aggressive Grangers, and a sizable

1. See Map 6. This map shows the distribution of the 31,674 votes that were cast for the Readjuster presidential electors in 1880. In this election the Funders, Readjusters, and Republicans fielded competing slates of electors, and the Readjusters retained the support of only their most loyal adherents. For the returns from the 1880 contest see the *Warrock-Richardson Maryland, Virginia and North Carolina Almanack for the Year of Our Lord 1882* (Richmond: James E. Goode, 1882), pp. 30–31. The results of other elections from 1879 to 1883 are available in the following sources: *Richmond Daily Dispatch,* November 19, 22, 1879; January 16, 1884; *Warrock-Richardson Almanack, 1884,* pp. 30, 34; and Ainsworth R. Spofford, ed., *American Almanac and Treasury of Facts, Statistical, Financial, and Political, for the Year 1884* (New York: American News Co., 1884), p. 262.

minority of "poor white" Readjusters. Basically committed to the traditional values of Virginia society and determined to preserve white rule in their heavily Negro counties, these eastern whites were an unreliable, troublesome element in the insurgent coalition.

More important numerically than any of these groups, however, was the great mass of Negroes in eastern Virginia. Concentrated in the southern Piedmont and the Tidewater, these rebellious blacks provided an ever-increasing percentage of the Readjuster vote. Most were tenants in the depressed tobacco belt, but a few of the more capable and ambitious had advanced into the land-owning class. Shunning the blighted countryside, the most energetic Negroes had migrated to the cities; there they provided the bulk of Virginia's tobacco-manufacturing proletariat and formed the nucleus for a small but influential middle class of skilled artisans, merchants, professional men, and federal officeholders.[2] In spite of their progress in the years since Appomattox, however, Virginia's ex-slaves still had considerable cause for dissatisfaction. Their movement into the urban areas had angered many working-class whites, and sensitive Negroes were disturbed by emerging patterns of segregation in transportation facilities, hotels, and restaurants. Even more troubling was their marked decline in political influence; their brief experience of power during the period of military rule only made their crushing defeat by the racist Conservatives all the more bitter. Poll taxes, chain gangs, whipping posts, inferior schools, and gerrymandered county boundaries provided ever-present reminders of their humiliating political impotence. Biased judges and local officials systematically excluded blacks from jury duty, and the common practice of employing white teachers in the Negro schools was a rankling source of discontentment and anger.[3] Many of the freedmen focused their hatred on their incompetent white Republican leaders, accusing them of being more interested in the federal patronage than in Negro rights.[4] Concerned about the disastrous

2. For evidence of the blacks' economic progress see George William Bagby's letters to the *Richmond State*, June 7, 1879; May 14, August 10, 1880; January 10, 11, May 27, June 21, 22, 1881. See also Orra Langhorne, *Southern Sketches from Virginia, 1881-1901*, ed. Charles E. Wynes (Charlottesville: University of Virginia Press, 1964), pp. 17, 37-38.

3. The racial discrimination of the 1870s is described in Jack P. Maddex, Jr., *The Virginia Conservatives, 1867-1879* (Chapel Hill: University of North Carolina Press, 1970), pp. 184-203; and Charles E. Wynes, *Race Relations in Virginia, 1870-1902* (Charlottesville: University of Virginia Press, 1961), pp. 12-14, 126-27.

4. *Petersburg* (Va.) *Lancet*, July 15, August 26, December 9, 1882; "The Week," *Nation* 30 (1880):204.

impact of the debt crisis on their schools, indifferent or hostile to the pleas of the bondholders, and convinced that the Readjusters offered at least a hope of renewed political power, they moved by the tens of thousands into the insurgent ranks.[5]

Ambitious yeomen, impoverished tobacco farmers, and rebellious blacks formed the backbone of the Readjuster coalition, and the party leadership reflected this variety of races and classes. Biographical information on 125 prominent insurgents reveals that they had little in common with Virginia's traditional ruling class of "gentleman" lawyers. A few patricians supported the revolt, particularly in the tobacco belt, but their influence was never great and declined precipitously. Instead a large number of struggling farmers, businessmen, and small-town attorneys jostled for position in the party councils. Disdaining the "fossils" and "fogies" who had ruled for generations, the majority came from the new middle class which had grown up on the fringes of the postwar social order. Self-made men, Negroes as well as whites, urban as well as rural, surged into the forefront of the movement. Slightly younger than their Funder contemporaries, less burdened with family pride, Confederate honors, and college degrees, they resented the power of Virginia's close-knit oligarchy and the infuriating pretensions of the pompous "brigadiers." [6] The depression had played havoc with their personal fortunes, however, reducing many to the uncomfortable status of lawyers without cases, financiers without finances, and businessmen without business.[7] They were convinced that their misfortunes had been intensified by the Funders' inept policies, and they feared that a continuation of these policies would only result in higher taxes, the annihilation of the schools, and the

5. James Hugo Johnston, "The Participation of Negroes in the Government of Virginia from 1877 to 1888," *Journal of Negro History* 14 (1929):253–55, 257–59; Robert E. Martin, "Negro Disfranchisement in Virginia," *Howard University Studies in the Social Sciences* 1 (1938):94–95.

6. Of the 125 men whose backgrounds were analyzed for this study, 50 had studied or practiced law, 38 had been farmers, and another 49 had been engaged in commerce or manufacturing. The median age of these Readjuster leaders in 1880 was 41.5 years, and their average age was 42.73 years. Nineteen out of 125 were Negroes. Information on states of birth is available on 79 of the leaders, and of these 68 were native Virginians. At least 43 had served in the Confederate war effort, and 29 had attained positions of authority in its military or political hierarchies. A minimum of 37 had attended college or law school. See Appendixes C and D.

7. *Richmond State*, July 1, 1878. See also the following in the William Mahone Papers, William R. Perkins Library, Duke University, Durham, N.C.: D. M. Ream to William Mahone, January 23, 1879; John Paul to Mahone, April 17, 1879; and William C. Kennerly to Mahone, October 5, 1879.

continued exploitation of the state by avaricious bondholders. Spurning the traditional shibboleths of their society, most of them longed for an innovative and genuinely new departure in the Old Dominion.

What held these diverse and potentially hostile races and classes together? In the most obvious sense they constituted a nega- tive-reference group, cemented by a common alienation from the elite's reactionary policies. Blasted by their myopic opponents as "communists" and "anarchists," the Readjusters responded in kind by viewing the unsettled conditions of the day through the eyes of political paranoia. The party's spokesmen followed in the footsteps of the Greenbacker theorists and interpreted the nation's difficulties in terms of an irreconcilable conflict between the virtuous "produc- ers" and the parasitical "special interests." At the local level they denounced the grasping, manipulating lawyers of the "courthouse cliques"; turning their attention to affairs in Richmond, they lacerated the bungling officials for selling Virginia's birthright to the "bloated bondholders"; at the national level, moreover, they envisioned an insidious conspiracy of insatiable "money kings" and monopolists, bent on taking control of the government and exploiting the toiling millions. Voicing the discontent of the masses, the insurgents branded the period's miasma of high taxes, depressed farm prices, tight money, and exorbitant railroad rates as the inevitable consequences of "Funderism" and "Bourbonism." [8]

Accepting this inflammatory rhetoric at face value, historians have generally described the Readjuster Movement as an "agrarian" revolt against the overweening power of urban capitalism. C. Vann Woodward, for example, viewed the insurgents as latter-day Jeffer- sonians, spearheads of a Southwide rebellion against the oppressive "Redeemers." [9] Other writers, some of them hostile to the party, attributed its mass appeal to the clannish sectionalism of the western mountaineers, the ignorance of the freedmen, and the poverty of

8. For examples of these Readjuster accusations see the following: Isaac A. Worley, *To the Voters of Washington County* (Abingdon, Va.: Standard Job Print, 1877), broadside, copy in the Baugh Family Papers, Edwin A. Alderman Library, University of Virginia, Charlottesville, Va.; notes for a speech by Edmund W. Hubard, October 1877, Edmund W. Hubard Papers, Southern Historical Collection, University of North Carolina, Chapel Hill, N.C.; and J. G. Cannon, *To the People! of the Senatorial District Composed of the Counties of Essex, King & Queen, Middlesex, Gloucester and Mathews* (n.p., [1879]), broadside, Mahone Papers.

9. The Readjusters figure prominently in the fourth chapter, "Procrustean Bed- fellows," of Woodward's *Origins of the New South, 1877–1913* (Baton Rouge: Louisiana State University Press, 1951), pp. 75–106.

the tobacco belt whites.[10] All in all, this emphasis on agrarian origins has fostered an image of the Readjusters as rural "have-nots," isolated socially, economically, and intellectually from the mainstream of postwar life. On the contrary, however, the election returns tell a significantly different story. Focusing their attention on the party's rural vote, these historians have completely ignored its strength in the towns and cities. The new organization's middle-class leaders worked tirelessly to unite the urban blacks with the Irish, German, and Jewish ethnic minorities and won substantial victories in Norfolk, Petersburg, Danville, Harrisonburg, Winchester, and Williamsburg.[11] True, the insurgents polled the bulk of their votes in the countryside, but this was also the case with their Funder opponents.[12] No political party, agrarian or otherwise, could hope to succeed in the overwhelmingly rural Virginia of the 1870s and 1880s without substantial support from the farmers. The Readjuster leadership, moreover, could hardly be described as agrarian in any strict sense of the word. Of the 125 prominent insurgents examined for this study only thirty-seven had engaged in agricultural pursuits to any significant extent, and at least twenty-two members of this minority had also been involved in other work besides farming.[13] Most of the party's spokesmen came, instead, from the periphery of the mercantile and professional classes of the towns. The debt struggle did not, therefore, produce anything approaching a clear-cut split between farmers and urbanites.

With the exception of the eastern "poor whites," even the Readjuster farmers scarcely fit the stereotype of the reactionary agrarian. In general the new party drew its support from the most change-oriented and potentially progressive groups in rural Virginia. The

10. Maddex, *Virginia Conservatives*, pp. 256–57; Charles C. Pearson, *The Readjuster Movement in Virginia* (New Haven: Yale University Press, 1917), pp. 104, 130, 154–55; Richard L. Morton, *The Negro in Virginia Politics, 1865–1902* (Charlottesville: University of Virginia Press, 1919), p. 119.

11. The Readjusters also won victories in such towns as Suffolk, Salem, Burkeville, Farmville, Nottoway Court House, and Lunenburg Court House. See election returns in the *Richmond State*, November 4, 1879; the *Richmond Daily Whig,* November 10–15, 1881; the *Harrisonburg* (Va.) *Old Commonwealth*, November 10, 1881, November 9, 1882; and the *Salem* (Va.) *Weekly Register,* November 11, 1881.

12. The 1879 Funder vote in Virginia's thirteen independent cities, which contained the overwhelming majority of the state's urban population, was only 6,780 out of the party's total vote of more than 60,000. See election returns in the *Richmond Daily Dispatch,* November 19, 1879. Comparable figures for subsequent elections are as follows: (1880) 14,473 out of 96,912; (1881) 13,201 out of 100,758; (1882) 15,071 out of 94,184; and (1883) 18,940 out of 144,885.

13. See Appendix D.

blacks had few ties to the state's traditional order, of course, and the mass of white insurgents were also straining to break away from the old regime. Most of these whites came from the counties with the widest distribution of land ownership, the greatest enthusiasm for the public schools, the most rapid rate of population growth, and the largest voter percentages in popular elections.[14] Examples of these trends abounded all over the state, but one of the most striking was provided by Fairfax County, a center of Readjuster strength in staunchly Funder northern Virginia. Set off from its debt-payer neighbors by the predominance of yeoman freehold agriculture and the presence of 600 families of energetic Northern settlers, Fairfax elected a Readjuster to the House of Delegates in 1879 and 1881 and voted for the party's gubernatorial candidate in 1881. Immigrants and ambitious "carpetbaggers" throughout eastern Virginia followed suit and gravitated into the insurgent ranks. Combining rebellious blacks, yeomen, newcomers, and alienated representatives of the middle class, the party had the potential for a genuinely progressive and forward-looking assault on the entrenched forces of tradition.

Virginians of the 1870s and 1880s, Funders and Readjusters alike, generally interpreted the debt struggle as an attack on the old regime by those who wished to destroy it. Astonished by their opponents' disdainful attitude toward state pride, honor, and the eternal truths of political economy, the Funders repeatedly denounced them as "radicals," the "rag-tag and bob-tail," the "mob," or the "rabble"—as marginal men who were beyond the pale of respectability.[15] The Readjusters, on the other hand, gloried in

14. For a graphic demonstration of Readjuster strength in areas where yeoman agriculture predominated, compare Map 6 with Map 1. The counties that supplied the heaviest white Readjuster vote were generally those in which farm tenancy had made the smallest advances. The insurgents' appeal in the educationally oriented counties is also easily demonstrated. In the section of Virginia's 1879 *School Report* entitled "Written Reports of County and City Superintendents—Digested," pp. iv-xi, Superintendent William H. Ruffner noted 30 counties where there was great anxiety over school closings; 24 of these counties voted Readjuster in the crucial 1881 election. With reference to Readjuster strength in areas with rapidly increasing populations, it should be noted that 47 counties had population growth rates which exceeded the state average of 2.34 percent per year during the 1870s. In 1881 the Readjusters carried 31 of these counties. See Spofford, *American Almanac, 1884*, p. 294, for statistics on population growth. The statement that the insurgents were strongest in the counties with large voter turnouts is based on George M. McFarland's analysis of the 1879 election in "The Extension of Democracy in Virginia, 1850-1895" (Ph.D. diss., Princeton University, 1934), p. 125.

15. *Richmond Commonwealth,* February 5, 6, 27, 1880; *Richmond State,* January 27, July 23, 28, 1879.

Table I
READJUSTER VOTE IN URBAN AREAS
(INDEPENDENT CITIES)

City	1879	1880	1881[a]	1882	1883
Alexandria	251	82	1,006	776	990
Danville	7	8	789[b]	841[b]	26[c]
North Danville	9	5	108	115	0[c]
Fredericksburg	36	48	247	227	301
Lynchburg	142	24	. . [d]	1,260	. . [d]
Manchester	76	51	305	333	571
Norfolk	678[b]	564	1,896[b]	1,531	2,407[b]
Petersburg	1,728[b]	725	2,173[b]	2,035[b]	2,182[b]
Portsmouth	579[b]	93	882	864	1,227
Richmond	4	402	3,328	3,020	5,278
Staunton	50	53	325	415	441
Williamsburg	69[b]	68	109[b]	175[b]	165[b]
Winchester	403[b]	146	481[b]	496[b]	429
Totals	4,032	2,269	11,649	12,088	14,017

[a]First year of effective coalition between Readjusters and Republicans at the state level.

[b]Indicates a Readjuster majority. The 1879 vote in Portsmouth is the total cast for Readjuster and Republican opponents of the Funder nominee for the state senate. The Republican was elected and subsequently sided with the Readjusters.

[c]Abnormally small vote as a result of intimidation of blacks in the election-eve Danville riot.

[d]Data not available in the sources consulted. Lynchburg's vote totals were generally (and unaccountably) combined with those of Campbell County.

SOURCES: *Richmond Daily Dispatch*, November 19–29, 1879, January 16, 1884; *Warrock-Richardson Maryland, Virginia, and North Carolina Almanacks* (Richmond: James E. Goode), *1882*, pp. 30–31, *1884*, pp. 30, 34; Ainsworth R. Spofford, ed., *American Almanac and Treasury of Facts, Statistical, Financial, and Political, for the Year 1884* (New York: American News Co., 1884), p. 262.

their defiance of the old order and its leaders. Loading their speeches and editorials with denunciations of "fogies," "fossils," and unrealistic "abstractionists," the party's spokesmen insisted that the state should abandon outmoded theories, seek practical results, and get in step with the dominant forces of the new era. The insurgent *Richmond Whig,* for example, declared that it represented "the original and independent thinkers who constitute the masculine minded men of these steam-power times." [16] Reflecting the positive,

16. *Richmond Weekly Whig,* September 27, 1878.

entrepreneurial side of their Greenbacker heritage, moreover, the movement's spokesmen insisted that their policies would free the productive energies of the people, achieve the harmonious cooperation of labor and management, encourage immigration and capital investments, and turn the state into a workshop of enterprise and progress.[17] Unlike their debt-payer opponents, they expressed no fondness for the antebellum slave regime. They spoke for the farmers, the alienated, and the disenchanted, but their eyes were on the future, not the past.

Throughout most of the 1870s, however, these dreams were nebulous. The Readjusters' aspirations were real enough, but they lacked a specific reform program, effective leadership, and the unity essential for action. The opportunity was there, nevertheless, amid this confusion of voices, and time would supply all these needs in due season.

17. H. H. Riddleberger, "Bourbonism in Virginia," *North American Review* 134 (1882): 427; statement by William Mahone in the *Richmond Weekly Whig*, January 7, 1881.

5

The Crisis of Confidence: Readjuster Leaders, 1877–1880

During the 1870s three Readjuster factions struggled to fill the party's crippling leadership vacuum. The first comprised the "original Readjuster" theorists of eastern Virginia, men whose impassioned arguments had battered the disastrous Funding Act of 1871. Drawn from the depressed rural heartland of the Piedmont and Tidewater, this handful of embittered patriarchs conformed closely to the historical stereotype of the reactionary agrarian.[1] They included some of the most prominent defenders of the old order—antebellum Governor Henry A. Wise, opponent of the Conservative organization's "dirt eating male bawds";[2] Lewis E. Harvie of Amelia, Calhounite spokesman of the ruined planter class; Edmund W. Hubard, leader of the prewar Democracy and enemy of the lawyer "ring" in Buckingham; James Barbour, secessionist scion of a distinguished Culpeper family; and Frank G. Ruffin, a patrician Granger from Chesterfield who repeatedly blasted the "Yankees" for destroying the graceful plantation society of his youth. "Land delights not me," Ruffin declared in a statement typical of these essentially tragic figures, "nor farming either. I am too old for the changed times."[3] Albemarle's "Parson" John E. Massey, the most influential of these "original Readjusters," came from a different mold. A self-made lawyer and preacher, an adroit stump speaker and pamphleteer, this aggressively ambitious "man of the people" gained great popularity with the movement's rank-and-file. Taken as a group, however, these eastern leaders were older men, well into their sixties and implacably hostile to the capitalist overseers of the Northeast. Lashing out at the "Shylock" bondholders of Wall Street and London, they advanced debt proposals which ranged from total repudiation to the payment of less than half of the $30 million recognized by the Funding Act.[4] Essentially conservative, even reactionary, in their political views, they obeyed their emotions and took an ultraradical stand on the debt issue.

Across the Blue Ridge a second, and very different, group of leaders rose to prominence. The Valley and Southwest produced a large number of ambitious insurgents in their thirties and forties, hostile to the traditional ruling class and eagerly receptive to the Greenbacker gospel of rapid economic growth. A trio of robust lawyers—Abram Fulkerson of Washington County, John Paul of Rockingham, and Harrison H. Riddleberger of Shenandoah—quickly came to the forefront of the revolt in this area. Unhampered by fears of Negro rule, aggressively democratic in their social and political opinions, these vigorous ex-Confederates had relatively little in common with their crotchety allies in the depressed tobacco belt to the east.

These two Readjuster factions enjoyed an uneasy balance of influence during the early and middle 1870s. Unable to exert any real influence on debt policy, they collaborated with some success on such peripheral issues as fertilizer inspection, railroad regulation, and tax reform. In spite of this surface harmony they continued to view the state's problems from radically divergent perspectives, voicing a common rhetoric with strikingly different accents. As

1. Here the term *agrarian* is meant to imply a state of mind hostile to the new forces of industrialism and social change at work in Gilded Age America. As noted in the previous chapter, I reject the indiscriminate use of the term to describe everyone from a rural area; this broader usage is misleading when applied to economic and occupational groups in Virginia's relatively close-knit, homogeneous, agricultural-mercantile society. For the continuing dispute over this controversial but apparently indispensable word see Thomas P. Govan, "Agrarian and Agrarianism: A Study in the Use and Abuse of Words," *Journal of Southern History* 30 (1964):35-47.

2. Quote is from Wise to James L. Kemper, August 18, 1873, in James A. Bear, "Henry A. Wise and the Campaign of 1873: Some Letters from the Papers of James Lawson Kemper," *Virginia Magazine of History and Biography* 62 (1954):336.

3. Ruffin to John H. Chamberlayne, October 18, 1875, Chamberlayne Papers, Virginia Historical Society, Richmond, Va.

4. Quote from Henry A. Wise in William C. Pendleton, *Political History of Appalachian Virginia, 1776-1927* (Dayton, Va.: Shenandoah Press, 1927), pp. 295-96; John E. Massey, *Autobiography of John E. Massey,* ed. Elizabeth H. Hancock (New York: Neale Publishing Co., 1909), pp. 65, 94-95; Frank G. Ruffin, *An Appeal to the 31,527 Readjuster Democrats of Virginia* (Richmond: n.p., 1883), p. 2, pamphlet in the Baugh Family Papers, Edwin A. Alderman Library, University of Virginia, Charlottesville, Va.

the decade wore on, however, a third group of insurgent leaders emerged to revitalize the movement. Drawn primarily from the cities of the Tidewater and fall line, this new faction mustered some of the most forward-looking business and professional men in the state. Norfolk's influential mayor William Lamb took the lead in his city, aided by steamship magnate Virginius Groner. In Richmond brilliant lawyer John S. Wise and vitriolic *Whig* editor William C. Elam blasted the Funder "ring." Petersburg insurgents, led by Mayor William E. Cameron, transformed their town into a Readjuster stronghold. Similar men assumed command in the smaller urban centers of southeastern Virginia. The debt issue itself had relatively little to do with the conversion of these leaders; indeed, several had expressed debt-payer views earlier in the decade.[5] Instead they gravitated into political revolt because of their alienation from the traditionalist Conservative elite and, more importantly, because of their ties to one of the most controversial and enigmatic figures in Virginia history, William Mahone.

Although he had fought his way to the top of the state's economic and political life, General "Billy" Mahone was the antithesis of the Old Dominion's traditional leadership type. A tavern-keeper's son, he personified the spirit of the dynamic middle class. Dyspeptic, shrill-voiced, about five-feet-five-inches tall and weighing less than a hundred pounds, he drew attention with his broad-brimmed Panama hats and his flowing beard. An epicure, he delighted in fine clothes, carriages, cigars, liquor, and an occasional all-night poker session with his cronies. During the war he served with distinction, leading the Confederates to victory in the dramatic "Battle of the Crater" and attaining the rank of major general. After Appomattox his executive skill won him a $25,000 annual salary as president of the grandiosely named Atlantic, Mississippi, and Ohio Railroad. He lost control of this magnificent trunk line during the financial panic of the 1870s but retained his reputation as a rail tycoon. Described as a "bundle of nerves and a prodigy in energy," Mahone elicited a fierce loyalty from his friends and a hatred which bordered on fanaticism from his enemies.[6]

5. For evidence of the debt-payer sympathies of Cameron, Lamb, and Mahone lieutenant Nathaniel B. Meade, see the following: Ruffin, *Appeal to Readjuster Democrats*, p. 2; Jack P. Maddex, Jr., *The Virginia Conservatives, 1867–1879; A Study in Reconstruction Politics* (Chapel Hill: University of North Carolina Press, 1970), p. 252; and Nathaniel B. Meade to William Mahone, August 9, 1875, McGill-Mahone Papers, Edwin A. Alderman Library, University of Virginia, Charlottesville, Va.

The diminutive general first became associated with the debt revolt when he made an unsuccessful bid for the Conservative gubernatorial nomination in 1877. Seeking to inject new life into his faltering campaign, he endorsed readjustment in a series of public letters in July of that year.[7] Although political opportunism obviously influenced this move, Mahone's revolt against the prevailing economic and political orthodoxy had deeper roots. Closely associated with the moderate "True Republicans" during the early 1870s, he resented the growing influence of the Funder elite's reactionary "Bourbon" element. His desire to settle old scores was intensified by the galling suspicion that prominent debt-payers had helped to deprive him of his railroad.[8] Impressed by the Readjusters' arguments, moreover, he concluded that the Funding Act was sapping the state's resources, destroying its schools, and paving the way for repudiation. Observing the magnitude of the financial crisis, the general decided that readjustment was both inevitable and desirable.[9]

Whatever his motives, Mahone's conversion had an electrifying effect on the debt revolt. Rallying Fulkerson, Riddleberger, Hubard, and other prominent insurgents to his banner, the erstwhile "railroad king" narrowly missed victory at the Conservative state convention in August. His bold stand overshadowed the proceedings, and Funder dark horse F.W.M. Holliday won the gubernatorial nod only after implying that he would allow the new General Assembly to reduce the debt burden. The party platform also contained a nebulous endorsement of Readjuster principles. After long years of frustration, the insurgents seemed near victory.[10]

---

6. Quote is from Charles T. O'Ferrall, *Forty Years of Active Service* (New York: Neale Publishing Co., 1904), p. 211. See also Nelson M. Blake, *William Mahone of Virginia: Soldier and Political Insurgent* (Richmond: Garrett & Massie, 1935).

7. The letters were published in newspapers and campaign broadsides. For an example see Mahone's letter of July 4, 1877, to M. M. Martin, published as *The State Debt, the Leading Issue in the Campaign: General Mahone's Opinion upon the Same* (Petersburg: n.p., 1877), broadside, copy in the William Mahone Papers, William R. Perkins Library, Duke University, Durham, N.C.

8. C. Vann Woodward, *Origins of the New South, 1877–1913* (Baton Rouge: Louisiana State University Press, 1951), p. 97.

9. Mahone to Harrison H. Riddleberger, August 19, 31, 1877, H. H. Riddleberger Papers, Earl Gregg Swem Library, the College of William and Mary in Virginia, Williamsburg, Va.; Mahone to E. W. Hubard, September 15, 1877, Edmund W. Hubard Papers, Southern Historical Collection, University of North Carolina, Chapel Hill, N.C.

10. *Richmond Daily Dispatch*, August 11, 1877; Charles C. Pearson, *The Readjuster Movement in Virginia* (New Haven: Yale University Press. 1917), pp. 74–75.

In the weeks following the convention Mahone analyzed the impact of these events on the broader patterns of Virginia politics. He noted that neither of the state's major parties had been able to come to grips with the problems of the post-Reconstruction years. The Republican machine was moribund, and, in the general's opinion, "the want of some political cause of coherent common interest . . . will soon throw our Conservative organization into chaos." [11] The debt struggle seemed, however, to offer the chance for a fundamental restructuring of the Old Dominion's political order. Writing to Riddleberger in the west and Hubard in the east, Mahone called for the creation of a "solid governing party" on a platform of readjustment, low taxes, public education, and "the promotion of enterprise and progress." While accepting the expediency of supporting the convention's state ticket in the approaching election, he argued that the Readjusters should concentrate on electing their own men to the General Assembly. The insurgent legislative majority could then proceed with the all-important "reformation of parties." [12] Pushing for independent political organization, the general emerged as the foremost strategist of the debt revolt.

The 1877 campaign confirmed Mahone's prophecy about the imminent disintegration of the Conservative machine. Mass resentment over coupons, deficits, and diverted school funds came to a boil, particularly in the Valley and Southwest. The Republicans failed to nominate a state ticket, moreover, and dozens of independent candidates entered legislative races in the eastern counties, appealing for the votes of the disorganized Negroes and disaffected whites. Apprehensive Funders debated whether to launch a counterattack. James A. Walker, the convention's nominee for lieutenant governor, made a debt-payer speech in Wytheville, but the hostile public response forced him to back down. The election proved anticlimactic. The Conservative Readjusters and independents swept to victory, winning majorities in both houses of the General Assembly. [13]

Plagued by the absence of coherent political organization, the new legislature convened on December 5, 1877. The Conservative party quickly splintered into feuding debt-payer and Readjuster

11. Mahone to Harrison H. Riddleberger, August 31, 1877, Riddleberger Papers.
12. Mahone to H. H. Riddleberger, August 19, 31, 1877, Riddleberger Papers; Mahone to Edmund W. Hubard, September 24, 1877, Hubard Papers.
13. For a Readjuster reaction to the victory see R. F. Walker to Mahone, November 7, 1877, Mahone Papers.

caucuses, but it appeared extremely doubtful that either of these groups could exert effective leadership. The Funders were stymied by their unpopular stand on the debt issue. Mahone and Fulkerson, on the other hand, struggled unsuccessfully to weld the dissident majority into a unified bloc. Weakened by poor strategy and the defection of "soft" men, the insurgent lawmakers allowed their Funder opponents to control elections for state treasurer, secretary, and other administrative posts. "It is evident," one of Mahone's correspondents lamented, "that a majority of the Legislature are earnestly in favor of readjusting and settling forever the debt question. But it is equally as evident that a majority of that majority have no definite plan and no well arranged system. All is chaos." [14]

During these weeks of uncertainty the revolt's eastern agrarian wing reasserted its influence. In the Senate "Parson" Massey took the lead, introducing a bill to require the payment of all school taxes in cash instead of bond coupons. Adopting a similar approach, James S. Barbour gained the limelight in the House by championing a measure to protect the revenues of the schools and other governmental agencies. His controversial Barbour bill restricted not only the use of the coupons but also the total percentage of state funds which could be devoted to interest payments. Designed primarily to restrain the flood of worthless paper into the treasury, neither the Barbour bill nor the Massey school bill really came to grips with the basic problem of readjusting the debt. The General Assembly passed these measures, nevertheless, and sent them to Governor Holliday for his signature. In a surprising move he vetoed them instead. [15]

The new governor had straddled the debt issue during the preceding campaign, and his unexpected opposition shocked and demoralized the Readjusters. "A single blow from Holliday," one House insurgent groaned, "has put our ranks in confusion." [16] Efforts to override the vetoes failed, and factional lines, already weak, began to dissolve completely. Responding to popular demands for some form of debt settlement, moderate Funders and Readjusters collaborated to pass

14. L. B. Anderson to Mahone, December 31, 1877, Mahone Papers. See also the following in the Mahone Papers: Abram Fulkerson to Mahone, December 13, 28, 1877; February 7, 1878; R. F. Walker to Mahone, December 14, 1877; and John Paul and Abram Fulkerson to Mahone, February 26, 1878.

15. For Holliday's veto messages see Virginia, Senate, *Journal*, 1877–78, pp. 361–66. For information on the Massey and Barbour bills see Massey, *Autobiography*, pp. 135–36; and the *Richmond Daily Whig*, February 12, 1878.

16. I. C. Fowler to Mahone, February 28, 1878, Mahone Papers.

the abortive Bocock-Fowler Act—an innocuous and worthless compromise which asked the creditors to exchange their old bonds for new ones at a reduced interest rate. Predictably, the bondholders ignored this futile gesture, and the new proposal was stillborn. Fulkerson impatiently denounced the whole affair as a "fizzle." [17] Thwarted and impotent, the legislature adjourned in March 1878.

During these discouraging months Mahone once again took the lead in urging the establishment of an independent Readjuster party. Such a move, he wrote Riddleberger, was "essential to protect the people at coming elections against the power and influence of the old Funder organization." [18] Seeking to reinvigorate the faltering debt revolt, moreover, the general also called for a new state constitutional convention which could reduce the debt burden without being hamstrung by the governor or the courts. Issuing appeals, writing letters, and presiding over conferences, he worked to rally the insurgent legislators behind this plan during the spring of 1878. In spite of his efforts, however, he generated little support; the memory of the hated "black-and-tan" Underwood convention was still too fresh. The Readjuster leaders continued to mention this proposal for months, but their enthusiasm for it gradually waned. [19]

Mahone's appeals for effective organization also fell on barren ground. During the 1878 congressional races the Funders managed to outsmart and outmaneuver their stumbling Greenback-Readjuster opponents at every turn. The courthouse cliques dominated the local Conservative conventions and forced the insurgents to run as independents, shorn of regular party support. Sensing the popular mood, moreover, the debt-payer incumbents neutralized the currency issue by temporarily championing inflationist views. Skilled at political in-fighting, the Funder bosses also took full advantage of the chaotic factionalism which plagued the debt revolt. In the Valley they supported a moderate Readjuster in order to defeat an extreme one. In the Southwest several insurgent candidates competed for the same seat, enabling a Funder to squeeze through with a plurality of the votes. Personal squabbles and weak candidates

17. Fulkerson to Leonidas Baugh, December 12, 1878, Baugh Family Papers. See also Virginia, General Assembly, *Acts and Joint Resolutions,* 1877–78, pp. 230–31.

18. Mahone to Riddleberger, March 2, 1878, Riddleberger Papers.

19. Mahone to Riddleberger, March 2, October 7, 1878, Riddleberger Papers; Mahone to James H. Williams, March 30, 1878, James H. Williams Papers, Edwin A. Alderman Library, University of Virginia, Charlottesville, Va.; William Mahone et al., *To the People of Virginia* (Petersburg: n.p., 1878), pamphlet, Mahone Papers.

hurt the Readjuster cause in other areas, and the debt-payer machine swept to victory. "Well," one insurgent commented ruefully, "the fight is over & as I anticipated the 'regulars' have every where triumphed; without organization nothing else could have been expected." [20]

Taking heart from this smashing victory, the Funders regained the offensive on the debt issue. Soon after the congressional election a group of thirty-nine prominent men announced the formation of a society "to preserve the credit of the State." Calling for the establishment of similar organizations in every locality, they advocated the election of debt-payers to the General Assembly and endorsed a 40 percent increase in property taxes to meet the interest payments. [21] This group failed to attract any appreciable following, but the boldness of their appeal indicated an amazing resurgence of Funder spirits. Even more significantly, the bondholders gave evidence of a real desire to reach a mutually agreeable compromise on the debt. Frightened by Readjuster militancy, capitalists in New York and London informed the governor that they would be willing to negotiate a lower interest rate after the General Assembly reconvened for its 1878–1879 session. Financial magnate Hugh McCulloch headed the bondholder delegation in the ensuing talks with a special legislative joint committee. The resulting proposal, known as the McCulloch bill, provided for the funding of the debt principal plus half of the unpaid interest in new bonds which would bear only 3 percent interest for the first ten years, 4 percent for the next twenty years, and 5 percent for the final ten years before maturity. This represented a substantial reduction from the original Funding Act's 6 percent rate, and the enthusiastic debt-payer press estimated that the measure would ultimately save the state $26 million. Praising the settlement as the "Bill of Peace," the Funders called upon all Virginians to support it. [22]

Thoroughly demoralized, the insurgent legislators had no positive program to offer in response. At the start of the session a few had suggested passing the Barbour bill again, even though a veto was certain. Others had advocated a more cautious and conciliatory

20. N. B. Meade to Mahone, November 10, 1878, Mahone Papers. See also Pearson, *Readjuster Movement,* pp. 81–83.

21. *Richmond State,* November 29, 30, 1878. See also William L. Royall to James L. Kemper, September 5, 1878, James Lawson Kemper Papers, Edwin A. Alderman Library, University of Virginia, Charlottesville, Va.

22. *Richmond State,* August 25, 1879. For the terms of the new settlement see General Assembly, *Acts,* 1878–79, pp. 264–68.

attitude toward Governor Holliday. Faced with the attractive alternative of the McCulloch bill, therefore, the fragile Readjuster coalition began to disintegrate once again. In the House twenty-two of the insurgents deserted in order to support the Funder-sponsored compromise. Defections were particularly heavy among the eastern delegates, anxious to preserve the old Conservative organization as a bulwark against Negro rule. Bolstered by these new recruits, the resurgent debt-payers enacted the McCulloch settlement into law in March 1879.[23]

This debt law soon proved to be one of the most ironical pieces of legislation in Virginia history. Instead of squelching the agitators, as its proponents claimed, it infused new life and vigor into the faltering debt revolt. Momentarily stunned by the debt-payer assault, the Readjuster leaders quickly demonstrated their resiliency by formulating a plausible and extremely damaging critique of the new act. Denouncing the settlement as a fraudulent "Broker's bill," they insisted that it placed both the state and the bondholders at the mercy of foreign speculators by turning the entire funding process over to a pair of New York and London syndicates. The McCulloch Act, moreover, perpetuated some of the worst features of the 1871 debt law. It retained the hated tax-receivable coupons, exempted the new bonds from taxation, and contained no provision allowing the people to vote on its terms. Although the settlement did reduce the interest rates, the Readjuster spokesmen maintained that Virginia would still be unable to support the debt burden without a massive tax increase. Compiling impressive columns of figures to buttress their case, Mahone and Massey argued that the act condemned the government to chronic deficits for years to come. Other attacks focused on features which discriminated against the peeler bondholders and on a provision which authorized the auditor to borrow money at ruinous rates if necessary to meet the interest payments. Summarizing these complaints, Massey insisted that the new act was "more objectionable than the Funding Bill of 1871." [24]

Recognizing these defects in the McCulloch settlement, the leaders

23. Only five of the 22 defectors came from west of the Blue Ridge; the rest were drawn, by and large, from the tobacco belt and the northern Tidewater. This calculation is based on a comparison of the votes on the Barbour and McCulloch bills. See Virginia, House of Delegates, *Journal,* 1877–78, pp. 284–85; and *House Journal,* 1878–79, p. 546.

24. Massey, *Autobiography,* pp. 142–43. See also the *Bridgewater* (Va.) *Enterprise,* April 3, 1879; and Wythe G. Bane, *A Letter* (n.p., 1879), broadside, Mahone Papers.

of the debt revolt set to work rallying their scattered forces. Fulkerson echoed Mahone by warning that a "permanent plan of organization" would be necessary to prevent the insurgent bloc from going "to pieces." [25] Weakened by massive defections, the Readjusters finally heeded this advice and established an efficient party apparatus. In January 1879 the insurgent legislators issued a call for the selection of delegates to a statewide Readjuster convention scheduled for the following month. Massey temporarily opposed this break with the "white-man's party," but the "westerners," independents, Republicans, and a scattering of eastern Conservatives pushed it through the caucus. Forging ahead, local Readjusters held meetings and sent 175 delegates to the state gathering at Richmond's Mozart Hall. Amid a shower of flamboyant rhetoric, the convention blasted the "Broker's bill," demanded a more lenient settlement, and laid the foundation for an effective party structure with Mahone as chairman of the executive committee. [26]

Reflecting the shifting tides of politics, this meeting marked the beginning of a massive revival of the debt revolt. During the ensuing 1879 campaign, Funders, Readjusters, and Republicans competed in legislative races which bordered on political chaos in many areas. Although both of the debt factions claimed the mantle of the old Conservative party, both appealed for Negro and Radical votes to an extent unheard of since the "True Republican" days of 1869. [27] Backing their statistics with inflammatory rhetoric, the insurgents maintained that the new debt law would destroy the schools and force a tax increase. [28] The debt-payers responded by arguing that the McCulloch Act was Virginia's last chance to avoid political, social, and economic anarchy. [29] The Funders held the upper hand immediately after the enactment of the new settlement, but the Readjusters chipped away at their support through effective propa-

25. Fulkerson to Mahone, December 9, 1878, Mahone Papers.
26. *Richmond State*, February 25, 26, 1879.
27. Pearson, *Readjuster Movement*, pp. 124–28; Richard L. Morton, *The Negro in Virginia Politics* (Charlottesville: University of Virginia Press, 1919), p. 107.
28. *Luray* (Va.) *Page Courier*, August 14, 1879; T. T. Fauntleroy, Jr., *To the Voters of Frederick County, Va.* (n.p., 1879), broadside, copy in Scrapbook 4, F.W.M. Holliday Papers, William R. Perkins Library, Duke University, Durham, N.C.; C. G. Howison, *To the Voters of Prince William County* (n.p., 1879), broadside, Mahone Papers.
29. The *Richmond State*, September 25, 1879, made the following statement concerning the McCulloch Act: "Unsettle the settlement, attempt to readjust the readjustment already made, and you might as well put a keg of powder under the Capitol and blow it up—the effect in either case will be the same."

ganda and intensive grassroots organization. Sporting a silk hat, a black suit, and a gold-headed cane, "Parson" Massey regaled enthusiastic crowds all over the state with his witty anecdotes and fiery denunciations of the "Broker's bill." Mahone also came to the fore. Scheduling rallies, appointing canvassers, offering encouragement, and supplying funds, the little "Hero of the Crater" became the nerve center for the entire Readjuster campaign. Even the forces of nature aided the insurgents; tobacco hornworms and a prolonged drought plagued the eastern counties, intensifying economic hardships and stimulating political revolt.[30] The overconfident Funders predicted a "Waterloo" for their opponents, but the election returns told a different story. The debt-payers and Readjusters split the Conservative vote almost equally between them, while the outnumbered Republicans won enough seats to hold the balance of power in both houses of the General Assembly.[31] Although the election was too close to be described as a clear-cut insurgent victory, it soon became obvious that the Funders had suffered a grievous setback. Evidence—if any were needed—came from New York and London. Discouraged by the prospect of a hostile legislature, the financial syndicates allowed the McCulloch settlement to die by abandoning their efforts to fund the debt.[32]

The new General Assembly convened in December 1879, amid an atmosphere of doubt and suspicion. Although the pivotal Republicans generally favored readjustment, the Funders still hoped to convert enough of them to retain control. Spies infiltrated the Readjuster caucus; ominous rumors circulated about bribes and an influx of "broker" money; the debt-payers were on the watch for "weak" men. Succumbing to these pressures, most of the white Republicans gravitated toward the Funder camp, and the Negro legislators appeared to be wavering. Mahone and his lieutenants laid their plans carefully, however, and won the thirteen crucial blacks with timely concessions on the patronage and other issues, notably poll tax repeal.[33] With this accomplished the insurgents

30. Nannie May Tilley, *The Bright-Tobacco Industry, 1860–1929* (Chapel Hill: University of North Carolina Press, 1948), p. 364; R. F. Jennings to Mahone, July 21, 1879, Mahone Papers; Richard A. Wise to Mahone, July 22, 1879, Mahone Papers.

31. The *Richmond State,* November 10, 1879, noted that the new General Assembly would be divided as follows according to party affiliations: Senate—14 Funders, 6 Republicans (2 Negroes), and 20 Readjusters; House—42 Funders, 16 Republicans (11 Negroes), and 41 Readjusters.

32. William Luster Grenoble, "A History of the Virginia State Debt" (M.A. thesis, University of Virginia, 1937), p. 69.

set to work welding their legislative majority into a coherent voting bloc. They recognized the importance of the political patronage as a unifying force, and Senator Riddleberger maneuvered the caucus into establishing the "committee on spoils." Composed of legislators from each of the state's congressional districts, this powerful group awarded the political plums with an eye to building the party's strength in every county and region. Tight discipline prevailed, and the insurgent solons elected the caucus nominees for state treasurer, secretary, and other administrative posts. The blacks received several minor offices, and a white Republican won the nod for second auditor. The corporation and county judgeships also came up for election during this session, allowing the insurgents to elevate dozens of their men to these politically potent offices. Improving on time-honored Conservative techniques, the Readjusters made full use of the spoils to unify their diverse following.[34]

In spite of this surface harmony, however, the insurgent caucus was frequently torn by dissension. It was impossible to satisfy all the hundreds of deserving office-seekers, and the Republicans protested that they had received inadequate recognition on patronage matters. Other squabbles focused on the Negro legislators' efforts to curb lynching and to reduce the legal penalty for racial intermarriage. The white Readjusters refused to handle this political dynamite, and the jubilant debt-payers attempted to widen the schism. Exploiting these tensions, a Funder legislator introduced a resolution requiring racial segregation in the House galleries, and the Funder press publicized the unsuccessful efforts of a black senator to buy a meal in one of Richmond's "whites-only" restaurants. "It looks today," one debt-payer sarcastically noted, "as if the thieves were falling out. *Intermarriage* is a most helpful move toward the devoutly to be desired consummation."[35] Through-

33. The Mahone Papers contain numerous letters reflecting the Readjusters' careful planning and painstaking approach to the black legislators; for examples see Robert A. Richardson to Mahone, November 7, 1879; D. J. Godwin to Mahone, November 12, 1879; and Rutledge P. Hughes to Mahone, November 13, 1879. For evidence of the Negroes' response see the report of a speech by black Senator Cephas L. Davis in the *Richmond Daily Dispatch,* December 11, 1879.

34. *Richmond State,* December 3, 1879; *Richmond Daily Dispatch,* December 4-6, 1879. The 1879-80 journals of the Senate and House of Delegates also provide evidence of the Readjuster machine's control over state patronage.

35. J. L. Williams to F.W.M. Holliday, February 4, 1880, Holliday Papers. For additional evidence of racial friction in the legislature see the *Richmond State,* December 6, 9, 1879; January 12, 21, March 8, 1880; and *House Journal,* 1879-80, pp. 161, 165-66, 466.

out the session, however, Mahone proved equal to such crises. Dispensing cigars, whiskey, and advice from his hotel suite, he soothed hurt feelings and restored harmonious relations between the groups. "General Mahone," the Funder Richmond *Dispatch* reported sourly, "rules everything. Whenever there is a hitch he is appealed to, and up to date he has been able to reconcile differences." [36]

Although this friction between Readjusters and Republicans was a continuing irritant, the omnipresent debt question posed a much more serious threat to party unity. Years of debate had produced no consensus on the issue, and opinions ranged from Mahone's desire for moderate cuts in the interest rate to agrarian demands for total repudiation. Attempting to hold their organization together, the insurgent senators and delegates began the legislative session by agreeing to submit all debt bills to the caucus for its approval. [37] More than two months of indecision followed before the group began to debate potential settlements. Mahone quickly abandoned his original position in order to work for a compromise, and the party approved a proposal submitted by Senator Riddleberger. Seeking a middle ground between the moderates and the repudiators, this Riddleberger bill disavowed approximately two-fifths of the debt, provided for the payment of 3 percent interest on the remaining $19.6 million, and placed drastic restrictions on the use of the tax-receivable coupons. [38] As expected, Governor Holliday vetoed the measure, but this time there was no disintegration of party lines like that which followed the Barbour bill veto. The insurgent ranks held firm, and the government was deadlocked. One incident during the debt debate provided graphic evidence of this new Readjuster solidarity. Backed and perhaps bribed by the debt-payers, a maverick Negro delegate from Mecklenburg named Ross Hamilton introduced a House bill offering the bondholders an opportunity to fund the entire outstanding debt in tax-exempt 3 percent coupon bonds. The insurgents saw through this effort to divide them and voted it down almost unanimously. [39] Even though Holliday's veto had temporarily thwarted them, the Readjusters were becoming a party in fact as well as name.

36. *Richmond Daily Dispatch,* December 8, 1879.
37. *Richmond State,* December 3, 1879.
38. Ibid., February 5, 7, 10, 14, 1880. See also Mahone to Abram Fulkerson, March 25, 1880, Mahone Papers (Letterbooks).
39. *Richmond State,* February 26, March 2, 1880; *House Journal,* 1879–80, p. 403.

The adjournment of the legislature in March 1880 marked the end of the formative period of the debt revolt. During the 1870s the Readjusters had expanded their appeal and emerged as a powerful force in Virginia politics. In the last half of the decade, moreover, a marked transformation had taken place in the party's leadership. By 1880 the influence of the eastern agrarians had plummeted. Henry Wise and Edmund Hubard were dead; Lewis E. Harvie had been defeated for reelection to the House of Delegates; Frank Ruffin occupied a minor clerkship in the Capitol; James S. Barbour was moving steadily into the Funder camp. Even "Parson" Massey's influence had been seriously impaired. He had suffered a shocking defeat in his race for the Virginia Senate in 1879, and the Readjuster-dominated General Assembly subsequently elected him state auditor. He quarreled with the caucus over the patronage in his office, however, and was reported to be jealous of Mahone.[40] During these same years, by way of contrast, the western Readjusters gained considerable power. John Paul played a prominent role in the General Assembly, and Abram Fulkerson frequently presided over the party's legislative caucus. Surpassing the others, "Harry" Riddleberger gained statewide prominence through his debt proposal. The rise of the eastern Mahoneites had been even more striking. The little general's influence permeated the debt revolt, and the Readjuster legislators recognized his services by electing him to the United States Senate.[41] Encouraged by these developments, Mahone protégés John S. Wise, Virginius Groner, and William E. Cameron were beginning to cherish gubernatorial ambitions.

How may these shifting leadership patterns be explained? Part of the answer lies in the greater youth, vigor, and organizing ability of the westerners and the Mahoneites. More importantly, these groups took charge of the debt revolt because of their willingness to break away from the Funder-dominated Conservative organization. The movement's agrarian spokesmen, on the other hand, were weakened by the reluctance of their traditionalist constituents to abandon the "white-man's party." Isolated by age and temperament from the blacks, the poor, and the new middle class, these "original Readjuster" theorists helplessly watched the steady erosion of their political base. The declining influence of this essen-

40. Massey, *Autobiography*, p. 178; Richard B. Doss, " 'Parson' John E. Massey, Relentless Readjuster," *Papers of the Albemarle County Historical Society* 11 (1950–1951):13–15.
41. *Senate Journal*, 1879–80, pp. 58–59.

tially reactionary group had a profound influence on the movement; it opened the way for a closer alliance between the Republicans and the more progressive Readjusters, between rebellious blacks and liberal whites. Effectively united, these groups would possess the political strength for a massive assault on the traditionalist order.

6

The Struggle for Coalition:
Readjusters and Republicans,
1880–1881

The battle over state finances shattered Virginia's Republican organization. During the 1870s the party's white leadership generally endorsed debt payment, but the Negro masses rebelled against a policy which raised their taxes and destroyed their schools. This split widened into a chasm when the General Assembly convened in December 1879. The black legislators joined the Readjuster caucus, but most of the whites jealously maintained their independence. Calling themselves "Straight-out" Republicans, these old-line party bosses worked behind the scenes to reestablish their authority. Hostile to "repudiation," they attempted to pass the innocuous "Ross Hamilton" proposal as a substitute for the more aggressive Riddleberger debt bill. They even bargained with the Funders in an abortive bid to block Mahone's election to the Senate. Searching for outside aid, they urged the national Republican administration to force the Negroes back into line.[1] These political gadflies quickly earned a reputation for deceit and intrigue, and their actions threatened to swing the balance of power against the debt revolt. The Readjusters responded vigorously. As winter turned to spring in 1880 Mahone and his lieutenants moved to smash the Straight-outs and capture complete control of the Republican party. The ensuing struggle rocked Virginia politics for almost two years and caused tremors all over the "solid South."

The weakness of the Republican organization made it highly vulnerable to Mahone's schemes. The party had held its own during the early 1870s, even managing to carry the state for President

Grant in 1872, but its strength plummeted soon afterward. Battered by gerrymanders, social ostracism, and election fraud, the Republicans retreated into a dwindling handful of predominantly Negro counties. Radical strength in the General Assembly slumped from fifty-six members in 1870 to only fourteen in 1878. The party failed to nominate a gubernatorial ticket in 1877, and its demoralized State Central Committee practically ceased to exist for the next three years.[2] Deprived of adequate organization and leadership, thousands of Republican blacks either lost interest in politics or drifted into the Readjuster camp. Shunted aside in state affairs, the Radical party degenerated into a machine for distributing the federal patronage in Virginia. A small ring of influential whites, mostly northern-born "grip-sackers," scooped up the choicest patronage plums—to the disgust and dismay of ambitious blacks. Negro resentment smoldered against the privileged occupants of the federal customhouses, revenue agencies, navy yards, and post offices, and by the end of the decade personal feuds and racial animosities had reduced the party to a shambles.[3]

The debt controversy fragmented the Republican leadership, hastening this process of decay. Prominent Negroes generally welcomed the Readjuster revolt as a golden opportunity to regain some leverage in state politics. Resentful of their white Radical overseers, the blacks responded eagerly when Mahone promised them a larger share of the spoils. A few of the more cautious, such as the Mecklenburg delegate Ross Hamilton, kept the new movement at arm's length, but the majority embraced it with enthusiasm.[4] Alarmed by these defections, the white Republican elite also began to splinter. One faction abandoned its debt-payer views and pressed for an alliance with the Readjusters, arguing pragmatically that this approach offered the only real chance to crush the tradition-oriented "Bourbon" oligarchy. This "Coalitionist" group included such politically potent figures as former United States Senator John F. Lewis, Richmond Postmaster George K. Gilmer, Federal Judge Robert W. Hughes, Richmond editor John

1. For evidence of these intrigues see John S. Wise to William Mahone, November 9, 1879, William Mahone Papers, William R. Perkins Library, Duke University, Durham, N.C.; and William E. Cameron to Lewis E. Harvie, November 21, 1879, Lewis E. Harvie Papers, Virginia Historical Society, Richmond, Va.

2. *Richmond Southern Intelligencer,* January 19, 1880.

3. "The Week," *Nation* 30 (1880):204; Charles E. Wynes, *Race Relations in Virginia, 1870–1902* (Charlottesville: University of Virginia Press, 1961), pp. 8, 14.

4. "The Week," p. 204.

R. Popham, Internal Revenue collector James D. Brady, and John Tyler, Jr., son of the antebellum president. Most of these men were native Virginians, and several had collaborated with Mahone in the railroad wars and the moderate "True Republican" movement of the Reconstruction years.[5] The anti-Readjuster Straight-outs occupied the opposite extreme. This clique included some native Virginians, notably railroad magnate Williams C. Wickham, but most of its members were settlers from the North—grip-sackers such as United States Congressmen John F. Dezendorf and Joseph Jorgensen. This group won its strongest support from federal office-holders who feared that an alliance with the debt revolt would alienate conservative national Republicans and cost them their jobs. The Straight-outs hated Mahone, moreover, and resented his influence with the blacks.[6] Battle lines between these factions were frequently indistinct, and many individuals gravitated from one to the other and back again according to the dictates of political expediency. Thus divided against itself, the Radical leadership offered a tempting target for partisan intrigue.

Groping through this political quagmire, both sides concocted relatively simple battle plans. The Straight-outs worked to maintain an independent Republican organization. Relying on old party loyalties, they hoped to siphon off enough black support to tip the scales against the debt revolt. The Readjusters and their Coalitionist allies counterattacked with a vigorous drive to hold the allegiance of the Negro masses. Moving beyond the threadbare debt issue, they promised the freedmen a larger share of the government jobs, better educational opportunities, honest elections, and an end to the political "color line." Proceeding along a second path, moreover, the insurgents struck at the heart of the old Radical machine. Mahone plotted to take over Virginia's federal patronage posts—the centers of Straight-out influence in the black counties. Opportunistic and calculating, the little general was willing to deal with either national party to achieve this goal. The stakes in the struggle were high; the unity of the debt revolt hinged on the outcome.

5. Charles C. Pearson, *The Readjuster Movement in Virginia* (New Haven: Yale University Press, 1917), pp. 22, 33, 36; C. Vann Woodward, *Origins of the New South, 1877-1913* (Baton Rouge: Louisiana State University Press, 1951), pp. 99-100.

6. John F. Lewis to George K. Gilmer, May 1, 1880, George K. Gilmer Papers, Virginia Historical Society, Richmond, Va.; John J. Wise to John S. Wise, November 1, 1880, Wise Family Papers, held by John S. Wise III, Charlottesville, Va.; letter from "Old Guard" to the *Richmond Southern Intelligencer,* February 9, 1880.

The 1880 presidential race marked a new phase in this conflict. Reviving old party hatreds, it threatened to shatter the fragile alliance between Democratic Readjusters and Republican blacks. Insurgent leader Abram Fulkerson grimly predicted that the Funders and Straight-outs would use the election to "draw our forces off, . . . drive the Radical [legislature] members from us, and create confusion generally." [7] Early in the year Mahone attempted to head off this disaster. Testing the political winds with a controversial trial balloon, he urged the Readjusters and Republicans to unite behind a fusion slate of independent, unpledged electors. Both groups could support this neutral ticket without offending their old party loyalties, and together they could smash the Funder Democrats. In a close national race, moreover, the insurgent *Richmond Whig* confided that the unpledged electors "would be in a commanding position well worth striving for." [8] Maneuvering between the great national parties, they might even be able to win control of the federal patronage in Virginia. Logical and bold in conception, the plan seemed ideally suited to the state's treacherous political terrain.

In spite of its merits, however, the unpledged electoral ticket suffered from one crippling defect: it lacked popular appeal. Republican reactions ranged from outright hostility to relative indifference. The Straight-outs predictably blasted the move as an ill-disguised power grab. Maintaining their independent stance, they argued that Virginia's Radicals should nominate their own electors and carry the state against a divided Conservative Democracy. Even the blacks wavered, perplexed and disturbed by Mahone's proposal. However much they endorsed debt scaling, they were extremely reluctant to abandon their national party. [9] The white Coalitionists dutifully lined up behind the fusion scheme, but they offered only lukewarm support. Popham's *Richmond Southern Intelligencer* clutched at straws to justify its stand, hinting that the unpledged electors would probably back the Republican nominees in order to fracture the "solid South." [10] The Readjusters encouraged rumors that they supported the Negroes' favorite, Ulysses S. Grant, for the presidency, but they made no firm commitment to the old "Stalwart's" third term hopes. [11] Walking a political tightrope,

7. Fulkerson to Mahone, November 10, 1879, Mahone Papers.
8. *Richmond Daily Whig,* January 31, 1880.
9. *Richmond Southern Intelligencer,* February 16, 23, 1880.
10. Ibid., February 7, 9, March 29, 1880.
11. *Richmond Daily Dispatch,* December 11, 1879; *Richmond State,* April 9, 1880; Mahone to D. M. Bernard, Jr., October 5, 1880, Mahone Papers (Letterbooks).

Mahone could scarcely afford to lean too far toward either side.

This struggle reached its climax at the Republican state convention in April. Arriving in the bustling Valley town of Staunton, the delegates soon became embroiled in a vicious political melee. Debate focused on whether the party should nominate electors pledged to the Republican ticket or endorse the fusion proposal. Pressured by Mahone, most of the Negro delegates reluctantly supported fusion, but Wickham's Straight-outs responded by packing the hall with federal officeholders from the Southwest and Valley. Dishonest vote counts, false fire alarms, and bitter haggling over trivial points of order almost tore the meeting apart. Rumors circulated about Funder bribes and "Bourbon" influence. Moving through the hotel lobbies, influential Readjusters tried to hold their "faithful allies" in line. A widespread and deep-seated distrust of Mahone eventually prevailed, however, and the Straight-outs carried their "regular" electoral slate by a narrow margin. The blacks refused to bolt the meeting, and the general's disgusted spokesmen took the night train out of Staunton. Attempting to reconcile the losers, the convention elected Coalitionist John F. Lewis to the party chairmanship. After their smashing victory the Straight-outs could afford to be generous.[12]

Although the Republicans had seriously wounded the unpledged electoral ticket, it remained for the Readjusters themselves to deliver the deathblow. Attacking from the opposite extreme, the debt revolt's tobacco-belt agrarians fought to maintain their ties with the national Democracy. James Barbour defected to the Funders because of Mahone's electoral scheme, and Lewis E. Harvie, his eyesight failing, resigned from the Readjuster Executive Committee to protest against abandoning the party of Calhoun and states' rights. In Richmond John E. Massey, Frank Ruffin, and other government officials endorsed Harvie's stand. The mass of Democratic insurgents in the western counties also began to grumble, and it appeared likely that thousands would bolt if Mahone forced the independent ticket on the party.[13] Taking advantage of this schism, the Funders

12. For the events of the Staunton convention see the *Richmond State,* April 22–24, 1880; and the *Richmond Southern Intelligencer,* April 26, 1880.

13. Many letters in the Mahone Papers offer proof of this rank-and-file unrest. For examples see D. R. Stokes to Mahone, April 14, 1880; and S. Brown Allen to Mahone, June 11, 1880. For evidence of Harvie's opposition to the independent electors see Harvie to Mahone, February 6, 10, 1880. Ruffin's attitude is indicated by Ruffin to Harvie, March 31, 1880, Lewis E. Harvie Papers, Archives Division, Virginia State Library, Richmond, Va.

opened their local meetings to all Democrats—regardless of their views on Virginia's financial problems. In May the resurgent debt-payers held a state meeting, nominated Democratic electors, and sent delegates to the national party's convention in Cincinnati.[14] Mahone had already lost the Republican vote, and now he stood to lose the white insurgents as well. Pressured from all sides, he reluctantly abandoned his independent elector plan. Readjuster delegates met in Richmond in July and fielded their own electoral slate pledged to the Hancock-English national Democratic ticket. Harvie urged cooperation with the Funders to avoid splitting the white vote, but band music drowned out his words. "I attempted," the old Amelia planter complained, "to get a hearing on the floor of the Convention but although I vociferated . . . at the top of my voice and on my feet, the president would not or did not recognize me." [15] Dominating affairs with an iron hand, Mahone ruthlessly preserved the independence of the Readjuster organization.

Although officially committed to the Democratic ticket, the general kept up his efforts to capture at least part of the Radical vote. Conditions in the Republican camp gave him cause for optimism. The Straight-out electors lacked the funds to conduct an effective campaign, and the G.O.P. National Committee seemed reluctant to spend money on the South. Mahone traveled northward, urging prominent Republicans to abandon Virginia to his anti-Bourbon crusade. The Coalitionist *Southern Intelligencer* gave him strong backing. Pointing to the Radicals' empty campaign chest, the newspaper urged them to hold another state convention and withdraw their Straight-out ticket.[16] Mahone was encouraged by these developments and even planned special ballots for use by the black voters. These ballots would "accommodate the prejudice" of the Negroes by leaving off the names of the national Democratic nominees and bearing only those of the Readjuster electors.[17] Such schemes were foredoomed, however, to failure. As the presidential race entered its final month the national Republicans launched a massive effort to carry the Old Dominion. Money and campaign literature flooded the state, and even the Coalitionists went to

14. *Richmond State,* May 19, 20, 1880.

15. Harvie to W. M. Tredway, July 12, 1880, Richard J. Reid Papers, Edwin A. Alderman Library, University of Virginia, Charlottesville, Va.; see also the *Richmond State,* July 7, 8, 1880.

16. *Richmond Southern Intelligencer,* August 9, 16, 30, September 13, 1880.

17. Mahone to James H. Williams, September 30, 1880, James H. Williams Papers, Edwin A. Alderman Library, University of Virginia, Charlottesville, Va.

work for the Garfield-Arthur ticket. Lubricated and fully manned, the Radical machine started down the Straight-out track once again. Another attempt at coalition had collapsed.[18]

The split in the Virginia Democracy convinced the Republicans that they had a chance to carry the state. The Funders and Readjusters kept their rival Hancock-English electoral tickets in the field, and they battered each other much more furiously than they did their Radical opponents. "The fight that I am more interested in," a leading debt-payer remarked, "than even the presidential, is our *state* fight. I consider that all that is worth living for is gone, if that party of Thugs—Mahone & Co.—get control of the State—and with it the federal patronage." [19] The insurgents responded in kind, and Virginia politics experienced a growing bitterness. Attention increasingly focused on the national Democrats' attitude toward this potentially disastrous schism. The Funders enjoyed close ties with the party hierarchy, and Mahone feared that it would intervene on their side. At first, however, the Democratic high command maintained a cautious neutrality, working behind the scenes to end the feud and restore a united front. Responding to this pressure, the Funders and Readjusters began a series of sporadic negotiations which extended over the first half of September. They batted proposals back and forth, suggesting either an equally divided fusion ticket or a party primary. to choose between the two electoral slates. Mahone opposed any real cooperation with the debt-payers, however, and the talks broke down.[20] Disturbed by the failure of these compromise efforts, the national politicos moved decisively to save the state for Hancock and English. Late in October the party's national chairman, William H. Barnum, endorsed the Funder electoral ticket and urged Virginia Democrats to support it.[21] Cut off from their erstwhile Republican allies and repudiated by their own national party, the Readjusters' campaign fell apart. Wholesale defections took place in many areas. Mahone optimistically predicted a 25,000 vote plurality for his ticket, but this forecast reflected more bravado than judgment.

18. For Mahone's response to this campaign see his letter to Lewis E. Harvie, November 5, 1880, Harvie Papers, Virginia State Library.

19. Beverley Tucker to R.M.T. Hunter, October 7, 1880, Hunter-Garnett Papers, Edwin A. Alderman Library, University of Virginia, Charlottesville, Va.

20. The talks broke down when Mahone insisted on allowing Republicans to vote in the primary to choose between the rival slates. See the *Richmond Southern Intelligencer*, September 23, 1880; and "The Week," *Nation* 31 (1880):212.

21. *Richmond State*, October 22, 23, 1880.

The election returns told the story: Funder Democrats, 96,449 votes; Republicans, 84,020; and Readjuster Democrats, 31,527. A shockingly poor third in a field of three, the insurgents carried only nine of the state's counties. "It seems," a Mahone confidante noted wryly, "that we have met a Bull run." [22] National politics had devastated the debt revolt.

Although depressed and shaken, the Readjusters soon discovered grounds for hope in the 1880 fiasco. They had preserved their party structure, even managing to elect John Paul and Abram Fulkerson to the national House of Representatives. More significantly, the campaign forced the insurgents to reexamine their old political biases, and many of them moved much closer to Republicanism. Cooperating with the Radicals, several of the Readjuster congressional candidates had endorsed protective tariffs so vigorously that they had won national Republican backing.[23] Defeat in the November election only accelerated this trend. Angered by Barnum's recognition of the Funder ticket, a large group of insurgents broke all ties with the Democratic party. "Northern democracy smote us," a Valley legislator declared, "& hereafter we intend to smite them." [24] The more adventurous even advocated an open alliance with President-elect Garfield and his Republican administration. Petersburg Mayor William E. Cameron argued that such a move offered the only real chance to control the Radical vote and beat the Funders. "It is," he noted grimly, "a case of neck or nothing." [25] Mahone watched these developments closely. "I wish you could be here," the little general wrote one of his cronies, "to read the tone of all the letters I am getting. They would surprise you. They are all from [Readjuster] Stalwarts with two or three exceptions, and they absolve allegiance to the Demo[cratic] party and ask for a new departure. Some are ready without method to go—others by gentle and progressive steps. All would be glad to have the Rep[ublican] party . . . come to us, and some would go there. . . . There is much in the temper of the sentiment to be Nat[ional] Rep[ublican] and Vir[gini]a Liberal." [26] This new eagerness for coalition became

22. Richard R. Farr to Mahone, November 5, 1880, Mahone Papers.
23. *Richmond Southern Intelligencer,* September 23, October 11, 1880; Mahone to Harrison H. Riddleberger, October 14, 1880, H. H. Riddleberger Papers, Earl Gregg Swem Library, the College of William and Mary in Virginia, Williamsburg, Va.
24. Dr. Joseph B. Strayer to Mahone, November 15, 1880, Mahone Papers. Many letters in the Mahone Papers for November of 1880 reflect a similar attitude.
25. Cameron to Riddleberger, December 27, 1880, Riddleberger Papers.

clearly evident during the early months of 1881. Preparing for the fall gubernatorial race, the insurgents courted the Republicans more aggressively than ever before. Readjusters in the racially tense Southside declared their willingness to give the blacks a fair share of the government jobs. Party spokesmen blasted the color line and defended Negro rights. Local Readjuster clubs opened their doors to blacks and passed resolutions aimed at winning their support. Old party lines began to crumble, old loyalties to dissolve.[27]

The 1880 presidential race had a similar impact on Virginia's Republicans, forcing them to take a new look at political realities. Faced by a divided opposition, they had still lost the state by more than 12,000 votes. The Coalitionists gained ground by blaming the Straight-outs for the disaster. "We lost the electoral vote of Virginia," John F. Lewis growled, "by the worst stupid management." [28] The disillusioned blacks also opened fire on the party's grip-sack leadership. More than a thousand Lynchburg Negroes demanded the removal of the federal spoilsmen in their town, and similar rebellions took place in Alexandria, Portsmouth, and Elizabeth City.[29] Black politicians in Richmond went a step further, issuing a call for a Negro state convention to endorse the Readjuster movement. The Straight-outs schemed to break up this meeting, but the Mahone clique worked even harder to secure the selection of "true and trusty" black delegates. Another political Donnybrook loomed when the convention met in Petersburg on March 14, 1881. In spite of "Funder money" and "Wickham influence," however, ,the Coalition forces carried the day. A few Straight-out blacks left the hall, but the mass of delegates stood firm. The convention attacked the political color line, censured the grip-sackers, and called for an alliance with the debt revolt. Eager for victory, Radicals as well as Readjusters jostled for place on the Coalition band wagon.[30]

This political ferment encouraged Mahone to take the most controversial step of his career. Striking at the Straight-outs' pa-

---

26. Mahone to Riddleberger, December 2, 1880, Riddleberger Papers.

27. For evidence of these attempts to lure the blacks see the following: *Richmond Weekly Whig,* March 4, April 1, June 3, 1881; *Richmond Daily Whig,* April 1, 23, 1881; and William E. Cameron to Riddleberger, March 22, 1881, Riddleberger Papers.

28. Lewis to George K. Gilmer, November 13, 1880, Gilmer Papers.

29. *Richmond Daily Whig,* April 26, 1881; *Richmond Weekly Whig,* January 7, 21, March 4, April 1, May 13, June 24, July 8, 1881; *Salem* (Va.) *Weekly Register,* February 25, March 11, 1881.

30. The events of the Petersburg convention are described in the *Richmond Daily Whig,* March 17, 1881; and William E. Cameron to H. H. Riddleberger, March 14, 1881, Riddleberger Papers.

tronage lifeline, he attempted to forge close ties with the new Garfield administration. He had been in touch with the Republican party's Grant wing since 1879, and his friendly contacts with these "Stalwarts" proved invaluable. Senator Roscoe Conkling of New York endorsed the debt revolt, and J. Donald Cameron of Pennsylvania urged the president to come to terms with Mahone. Washington editor George C. Gorham worked behind the scenes, assuring skeptics that the Readjusters were not agrarian radicals.[31] Sporadic negotiations wore on for months. The general took his Senate seat in March 1881, however, and put an end to the uncertainty. He sided with the Republicans, casting the decisive vote which gave them control of the chamber. Grateful party leaders rewarded him with four excellent committee assignments and nominated two of his friends for lucrative Senate jobs.[32] Shrugging off Democratic charges of "political miscegenation," the aggressive "hero of the Crater" lashed out at "Bourbonism" and won nationwide publicity. Mahone also hoped to capture Virginia's share of the federal spoils, but this goal eluded him. President Garfield felt uneasy about tainting his party with "repudiation," and he refused to smash the Straightouts with the patronage club. "Of course I have no trouble," he explained, "in removing Bourbon Democrats of whom there are plenty in Virginia, but I will not remove Republicans to appoint Mahone men. I shall do enough for Mahone to help him against the Bourbons but not abandon our organization." [33] Instead the White House maintained a precarious neutrality in the struggle, dividing its favors between the rival groups. Delegations of Straightouts and Coalitionists trekked to Washington, but the beleaguered president refused to commit himself to either side.

31. For commentary on the efforts of these Stalwart Republicans see Stanley P. Hirshson, *Farewell to the Bloody Shirt: Northern Republicans & the Southern Negro, 1877-1893* (Bloomington: Indiana University Press, 1962), pp. 95-96; Theodore Clarke Smith, *The Life and Letters of James Abram Garfield* (New Haven: Yale University Press, 1925), p. 1065; and David J. Rothman, *Politics and Power: The United States Senate, 1869-1901* (Cambridge: Harvard University Press, 1966), p. 32.

32. The Senate Republicans made Mahone chairman of the Agriculture Committee and appointed him to the committees on Naval Affairs, Post Offices and Post Roads, and Education and Labor. They also nominated George C. Gorham and Harrison H. Riddleberger for the posts, respectively, of Senate clerk and sergeant-at-arms, but a Democratic filibuster prevented their confirmation. See "The Week," *Nation* 32 (1881):178; and John Sherman, *John Sherman's Recollections of Forty Years in the House, Senate and Cabinet,* 2 vols. (New York: Werner Co., 1895), 2:814-15.

33. Garfield to John Hay, March 15, 1881, in Smith, *James Abram Garfield,* p. 1117.

The little general's alliance with the national Republicans proved extremely fragile, but it gave a massive boost to Virginia's Coalition drive. The blacks, in particular, responded favorably. "If such great men," a Richmond Negro argued, "as Conkling, Dawes, Hoar, Logan, the Camerons, Garfield, Arthur, and Gorham . . . can afford to aid this [Readjuster] party, I cannot see why we little fellows down here who are suffering cannot do the same thing." [34] The administration appointed dozens of Readjuster postmasters, and the white insurgents also formed ranks behind Mahone. Discarding old Democratic loyalties, party meetings all over the state endorsed the new departure.[35] The general's prestige soared.

This enthusiasm carried over into the 1881 Readjuster state convention. The delegates—a third of them Negroes—flocked to Richmond early in June. Hostile observers described the gathering as "ignorant," "disorganized," and "boisterous," but no one denied its pervasive optimism. The list of gubernatorial hopefuls virtually provided a *Who's Who* of the party leadership; William E. Cameron, Virginius Groner, John E. Massey, Harrison H. Riddleberger, and John S. Wise vied for the honor. Representing the revolt's agrarian bloc, Massey made a strong showing. All the Mahoneites shifted their support to Cameron, however, and the Petersburg liberal captured the nomination on the fourth ballot. The party broadened its appeal by naming Valley Coalitionist John F. Lewis for lieutenant governor and Frank S. Blair, a Southwestern Greenbacker, for attorney general. The Funders scoffed at this "sandwich ticket," but the insurgents had actually shown very good judgment. Uniting Republicans with western yeomen and eastern progressives, they threatened to build a new ruling majority in Virginia politics. Cameron sounded the battle cry for this bold foray. Accepting the gubernatorial nomination, he attacked the old barriers between Democrats and Radicals, Negroes and whites. "I am going forward," he proclaimed, "to preach Liberalism." [36]

This Coalition ground swell rocked the Straight-outs. Faced with impending disaster, they scanned the national headlines for scraps of hope. President Garfield had become embroiled in a vicious patronage fight with Mahone's "Stalwart" allies, and there were

34. Statement by R. A. Paul, quoted in the *Richmond Daily Whig,* April 26, 1881.

35. *Richmond Daily Whig,* April 1, 23, 1881.

36. *Richmond Weekly Whig,* June 24, 1881. For convention events see the *Richmond State,* June 3, 4, 1881; and "The Week" *Nation* 32 (1881):398.

rumors that he had turned against the Readjusters as well. His influential secretary of state, James G. Blaine, openly denounced the debt revolt. Convinced that the administration would support them, the grip-sackers attempted to regain the initiative. In June they ousted John F. Lewis from the party chairmanship and issued a call for a state convention.[37] Marshaling their strength, they schemed to impose a Straight-out ticket on the Republican masses.

These hopes were shattered by the crackle of gunfire in a Washington railway station. Stricken by an assassin's bullets on July 2, 1881, President Garfield began a prolonged, agonizing struggle with infection and death. Unable to perform his official duties, he abandoned the political vendettas which had previously scarred his term. The national Republicans began to curry favor with the "Stalwart" heir apparent, Vice President Chester A. Arthur. Moving with the prevailing winds, many of them also became much more favorable toward Mahone. Postmaster General Thomas L. James suspended leaves of absence for Straight-out officials in Virginia. The Commissioner of Internal Revenue, Green B. Raum, fired an employee for disrupting a Readjuster campaign meeting. Treasury Secretary William Windom and Interior Secretary Samuel Kirkwood also endorsed the Coalition movement, and the government's highest-ranking Negro officeholder, Frederick Douglass, did the same. Breaking away from the dying president's influence, rebellious administration leaders abandoned every pretense of neutrality in the debt struggle.[38]

This chain of circumstances decimated the Straight-outs, and their weakness became clearly evident at the Republican state convention in August. Swayed by developments in Washington, most of the federal spoilsmen deserted to the burgeoning Coalitionist camp. The defiant grip-sackers came to Lynchburg, however, with plans to purge enough of their opponents to retain control. Recognizing this threat, Lewis and his men rented another hall and held a separate convention of their own. The Radical party had broken in two. Pressing forward, the Coalitionist majority proclaimed its support for the Readjuster ticket. The dwindling Straight-out clique urged General Wickham to run for governor, but he refused to

37. *Staunton* (Va.) *Vindicator,* June 24, July 1, 1881. See also J. P. Kavenaugh to Mahone, July 3, 1881, Mahone Papers.

38. Letter from Douglass to J. Ambler Smith, published in the *Salem* (Va.) *Weekly Register,* July 22, 1881. See also the following in the Mahone Papers: J. P. Klingle to Mahone, July 13, 1881; H. W. Blair to Mahone, August 1, 1881; Green B. Raum to Mahone, August 2, 1881; and William Windom to Mahone, August 2, 1881.

make this futile gesture. The mass of Republican voters had left their old leadership far behind. Coalition had triumphed. "The Mahone party," a northern correspondent reported, "has . . . its coveted alliance." [39]

The insurgents had very little time to congratulate themselves on their victory. The Funders had nominated the popular John W. Daniel for governor, and they were preparing for a vigorous fight. Mahone responded to the challenge. Organizing the Readjuster campaign, he arranged schedules for speakers and ironed out local party squabbles. He encountered the greatest difficulty, however, in raising campaign funds. The general needed thousands of dollars to pay the poll taxes of indigent voters, and he looked to his national Republican allies for aid. During the summer of 1881 he dispatched John S. Wise, James D. Brady, and several others on fund-raising trips to the Northeast. These emissaries contacted the great and the near-great, but they failed to raise much money. President Garfield still clung to life, and the northern Republicans feared that contributions might antagonize him. Thoroughly disgusted by these refusals, Wise provided an interesting vignette of Gilded Age politics. He grumbled in a note to Mahone:

Well, after my last advice I went to Brighton beach to see poor old [Senator] Don Cameron who was knocked over with the gout. I found him at the Oriental Hotel in an awful agony & he amused himself [by] lying on the bed—squeezing my hand & yelling like a woman in childbirth. In the interval between the paroxysms he begged me to stay saying Garfield would die that night (Friday) & then etc. Then he would kick me in the belly & howl. Fearing results, as I was full of clams, & his darling beautiful little wife was present, I left after offering to nurse him. I knew Garfield was not going to die so soon so I came off. [40]

Senator Cameron finally agreed to "pass the hat" in New York City, but the results were disappointing. [41] The financial nabobs watched the medical bulletins from Washington and kept a tight hold on their purse strings.

Fate continued, however, to ride with the insurgents. Garfield died in mid-September, and the situation began to change almost immediately. President Arthur formed a close alliance with the

39. "The Week," *Nation* 33 (1881):125. See also the *Staunton* (Va.) *Vindicator*, August 12, 1881.
40. Wise to Mahone, August 28, 1881, Mahone Papers.
41. Thomas V. Cooper and Hector T. Fenton, *American Politics* (Philadelphia: Fireside Publishing Co., 1882), Book 1, p. 264.

debt revolt, believing that it offered an excellent chance to break the "solid South." The new chief executive removed the remaining Straight-out spoilsmen in Virginia and replaced them with Mahone-ites. Receiving the "go ahead" from Washington, federal officials all over the country contributed to the Readjuster campaign chest.[42] Protectionist businessmen in the Northeast also donated large sums.[43] Mahone paid the poll taxes, and the insurgents swept to victory. Aided by a disastrous drought which compounded rural distress, they elected their state ticket with a 12,000 vote majority and retained control of both houses of the legislature. Holding their own in the western areas, they carried almost all the black counties in the Southside and Tidewater. The Coalition formula had succeeded magnificently.[44]

This alliance between the Republicans and Readjusters achieved more than merely winning an election; it revitalized the debt revolt. Ambitious men such as Lewis and Brady moved into the inner circle of the leadership, and the blacks returned to the center stage in Virginia politics. At a more fundamental level Coalition also reshaped the insurgents' hopes and objectives. Sloughing off their agrarian trappings, they began to hammer out a comprehensive, progressive reform program which would appeal to all of the anti-Bourbon groups in the state. This trend was most clearly evident in the changing nature of the party's platforms. In 1879 the Read-justers had confined themselves to financial problems, stressing the need for debt adjustment, lower taxes, and support for the schools. In 1880 they tacked on demands for railroad regulation and poll tax repeal. By 1881 they were emphasizing "liberalism," sectional harmony, and federal aid to mining and manufacturing.[45] No longer tied to one issue, the insurgents had begun to draw up blueprints for a new Virginia. The triumph of Coalition gave them the chance to transform these dreams into reality.

42. For examples of these contributions see the following in the Gilmer Papers: John Connell to George K. Gilmer, October 28, 1881; and John B. Smith to George K. Gilmer, November 1, 1881. President Arthur's use of the patronage ax is noted in "The Week," *Nation* 33 (1881):223.

43. M. W. Cooper to Mahone, October 8, 14, 17, 19, 1881, Mahone Papers; James M. Swank to Mahone, October 14, 1881, Mahone Papers.

44. See the *Richmond Weekly Whig,* November 25, December 2, 1881, for analyses of the election returns.

45. For evidence of the evolution of the Readjuster program see the *Richmond State,* February 25, 26, 1879; June 2, 1881; *Richmond Daily Whig,* June 27, 1881; Pearson, *Readjuster Movement,* pp. 97–102, 139; and John E. Massey, *Autobiography of John E. Massey,* ed. Elizabeth H. Hancock (New York: Neale Publishing Co., 1909), pp. 185–89.

7

The Readjusters in Power:
Ideology and Action,
1879–1883

The Virginia debt struggle took place within the broader context of Gilded Age reform agitation. Stricken by the hard times of the 1870s, thousands of American farmers and industrial workers temporarily abandoned their old party loyalties. Rebellious Grangers exploited antimonopoly sentiment and captured the governments of several Middle Western states. "Sand lot" agitators on the Pacific slope lashed out against the privileged classes as well as against the despised Chinese immigrants. Northeastern laborites added to the turmoil by resorting to violent strikes and organizing for independent political action. Small farmers in the Appalachian highlands continually harassed the South's "Redeemer" elite. Uniting these strands of unrest, the national Greenbacker movement polled more than a million votes in the 1878 congressional elections. Apprehensive conservatives railed about "agrarianism" and "communism," and only the revival of prosperity at the end of the decade prevented a potentially disastrous confrontation.[1]

This great wave of unrest left its mark on the Readjuster movement. Although officially nonpartisan, the Virginia Grange propelled thousands of tobacco-belt farmers into the debt revolt. The insurgents enjoyed even closer ties with the Greenbackers, particularly in the Southwestern counties. In 1878 the Readjuster congressional candidates campaigned for currency inflation, and two years later the national Greenback party seriously considered giving Mahone its vice-presidential nomination.[2] Such developments reflected the fundamental similarities between the insurgents and these other reform movements. Readjusters, Grangers, and Greenbackers viewed the political issues of the day from a similar perspective. They employed a common rhetoric and shared a loose but fairly coherent body of assumptions and beliefs. Gaining control of the Old Dominion, moreover, this insurgent coalition won an opportunity to put this ideology to a practical test. The state became, for four tumultuous years, a laboratory for reform.

The Readjusters drew most of their intellectual ammunition from a cluster of nineteenth-century ideas known as "producerism." Contemplating their labor-starved economy, American thinkers had traditionally emphasized the value of productive enterprise. This tendency resulted in a sentimental glorification of farmers, manufacturers, and others involved in the creation of goods. In the early 1800s John Taylor of Caroline transformed this popular prejudice into a rousing political battle cry. The old Jeffersonian defined politics in terms of an irreconcilable conflict between the virtuous producers and the parasitical middlemen who dabbled in trade, transportation, and banking. Elaborating this theory of class struggle, he denounced all governmental favoritism toward these exploitative "special interests." [3] Such ideas enjoyed widespread appeal, and generations of Jacksonians, Radical Republicans, and Greenbackers used them to hammer away at economic privilege. The Readjusters also embraced this producerite rhetoric. Their propaganda abounded with praise for the laboring or producing classes—particularly the farmers. Taking the offensive, moreover, they attempted to link the Funders with the speculators and monopolists of the courthouse towns. A typical Readjuster harangue described the Virginia controversy as "a square life and death struggle between the *organized Money-ring power,* and the productive industry of

1. For insight into the economic and political upheavals of the 1870s see Irwin Unger, *The Greenback Era: A Social and Political History of American Finance, 1865–1879* (Princeton, N.J.: Princeton University Press, 1964); Robert V. Bruce, *1877: Year of Violence* (Indianapolis: Bobbs-Merrill Co., 1959); and Solon J. Buck, *The Granger Movement: A Study of Agricultural Organization and Its Political, Economic and Social Manifestations, 1870–1880* (Cambridge: Harvard University Press, 1913).

2. Henry Nichols to William Mahone, June 3, 1880, William Mahone Papers, William R. Perkins Library, Duke University, Durham, N.C. In 1880 the Greenbacker presidential candidate, James B. Weaver, endorsed the Readjuster movement; see the *Marion* (Va.) *Patriot and Herald,* July 15, 1880.

3. Taylor's views are analyzed in Eugene T. Mudge, *The Social Philosophy of John Taylor of Caroline: A Study in Jeffersonian Democracy* (New York: Columbia University Press, 1939).

the people—the brawny arms and manly brows which distill the sweat of obedience to God's decree for honest Labor!" [4]

Producerism involved more than a paranoic hostility to middlemen. It also had a positive, constructive side—a commitment to economic growth and expanding wealth for all. Drawing inspiration from America's vast resources, the producerites adopted an optimistic view of the future. John Taylor set the pattern by asserting that it would take many centuries for the nation's farmers to expand across its fertile soils.[5] Pressing beyond the old agrarian's laissez-faire stance, moreover, subsequent generations of producerites advocated governmental action to spur rapid economic development. During the Jacksonian era the aggressive "Locofocos" agitated for mass education, trade unionism, and the enactment of general incorporation laws. Appealing for the votes of "free labor," antebellum Republicans championed homesteads in the West and the creation of land-grant agricultural colleges. The hard times after the Civil War spawned even more demands. Greenbacker theorist Henry C. Carey called for protective tariffs and an abundant currency to increase the volume of trade within the country. Grangers and laborites filled the air with suggestions for a ten-hour workday, consumer cooperatives, and agricultural experiment stations. By the 1870s, therefore, producerism had evolved into a driving force for action. Its focus on economic growth appealed to the nation's basic optimism and entrepreneurial spirit. Democratic in tone, emphasizing a natural "harmony of interests" between farm and city, labor and management, producerism offered the attractive vision of an expanding, prosperous society of self-supporting workers—the middle-class paradise of the American dream.

The Readjusters shared this commitment to economic growth. Stressing the need for rapid industrialization, they spurned Virginia's hidebound agricultural-mercantile order. Their speeches flashed with scorn for "dead customs and effete traditions," for "fogies" and "fossils" who lived on memories and dreams. Instead these aggressive "new men" called for a dramatic break with the past. Congressman John Paul urged the people to abandon "dead issues and old methods of thought and action, . . . the supports on which

4. T. T. Fauntleroy, Jr., *To the Voters of Frederick County, Va.* (n.p., 1879), broadside, Scrapbook 4, F.W.M. Holliday Papers, William R. Perkins Library, Duke University, Durham, N.C.

5. John Taylor, *An Inquiry into the Principles and Policy of the Government of the United States* (Fredericksburg, Va.: Green and Cady, 1814), p. 556.

they have been wont to rely." [6] The Readjuster press also beat the drums for change. The *Lexington Enterprise* published a salute to "goaheadiveness," "life," and "business vim." Mahone's *Richmond Whig* argued that Virginia's interests lay with the "great and growing States of the North and Northwest" and not with the backward cotton South. Riddleberger's *Woodstock Virginian* maintained that the "line of wisdom" required the state to "combine manufactures with agriculture." Joining the chorus, the *Staunton Valley Virginian* took an even more advanced position. "We are," it exulted, ". . . a new people, living under new conditions, looking to new pursuits, new methods, and new results." [7] Similar views permeated the insurgents' private correspondence, rivaling the debt issue as a topic for discussion.[8]

This intellectual ferment produced a glowing dream of the future. The Readjusters envisioned a Virginia with opportunity for the able, democracy for the masses, and public education for all. Newcomers—immigrants and investors alike—would be welcomed without regard to their religious or political beliefs. Farmers and townsmen would share the profits of industrial growth. The races would also coexist in harmony, socially segregated but united by common political rights and economic needs. Above all, the future would be dynamic, changing, and progressive. Writing in a national magazine, Riddleberger outlined his dream of the Readjuster commonwealth: "Population and capital are attracted. Railroads are built. New industries spring up. Mines are opened. Manufactories are started. Vigor, thrift and industry are seen everywhere. Virginia is awake and alert." [9]

Such opinions reflected more than New South bombast. The insurgents moved beyond mere wishful thinking and attempted to come to grips with the problems of economic growth. Drawing on their producerite heritage, they demanded a wide-ranging pro-

6. Quoted in the *Richmond Daily Whig,* June 27, 1881.

7. Quoted in the *Marion* (Va.) *Patriot and Herald,* March 29, 1883. For the previous statements from the Readjuster press see the *Lexington* (Va.) *Rockbridge Enterprise,* February 19, 1880; the *Richmond Weekly Whig,* June 3, 1881; and the *Woodstock Virginian,* December 1, 1882.

8. For examples see the following in the Mahone Papers: Robert B. Winston to Mahone, October 11, 1883; R. R. Farr to Mahone, November 5, 1880; and Thomas H. Cross to Mahone, November 12, 1879.

9. H. H. Riddleberger, "Bourbonism in Virginia," *North American Review* 134 (1882):427. See also the interview with Isaac C. Fowler in the *Richmond Daily Whig,* May 5, 1882; and the letter from William Mahone to Governor John D. Long of Massachusetts in the *Richmond Daily Whig,* March 24, 1882.

gram of government action to build their utopia. Their party platforms called for tax reform, protective tariffs, and railroad regulation. The Grangers chimed in with proposals to help the rural masses, and the blacks exerted pressure for equal rights. Driven by this current, the debt revolt became a dynamo of reform. Traditional Jeffersonian maxims about laissez-faire crumbled under the impact. "The Liberal revolution," the *Whig* declared, "has relegated perfunctory government to the limbo of worn-out and discarded things . . . . [Readjuster rule] will illustrate . . . that a [democratic] government . . . is not a necessary evil to be endured with patient philosophy, but a positive good, actively beneficent and full of benefits for all law-abiding citizens—and a terror only to evil-doers." [10] Capturing the legislature in 1879 and the Governor's Mansion in 1881, the insurgents set to work transforming the state's feeble administrative machinery into a powerful lever for social and economic progress.

The Readjusters moved vigorously to bring order out of Virginia's financial chaos. Wheeling their heaviest producerite artillery into line, they argued that the state's excessive debt burden had to be reduced or it would completely stifle business enterprise. Otherwise capital would be siphoned off into high-interest bonds instead of agriculture and industry. Oppressive taxes would only accelerate the downward spiral by dampening the business climate and frightening immigrants away. "I have not seen," Mahone remarked, ". . . how we could expect desirable people to come to live among a people who are themselves in sore distress—whose serious thought is oppressed with burdens—who are miserable with debt." [11] Only the financial "rings"—the speculators and Wall Street "Shylocks"— could possibly benefit from this catastrophe. Taking vigorous action, the insurgents moved to redress the economic balance between "producers" and "non-producers." Their 1882 Riddleberger Act repudiated approximately a third of the state debt and slashed the interest rate on the remainder from 6 to 3 percent.[12] Not satisfied with merely reducing the pressure on the state treasury, the new party proceeded to reform the entire revenue structure. The General

10. *Richmond Daily Whig,* February 21, 1882.

11. Mahone to Addison Borst, June 16, 1879, Mahone Papers (Letterbooks). See also H. H. Riddleberger, *The Riddleberger Bill Vindicated: "Indemnity for the Past and Security for the Future"* (Richmond: *Whig* supplement, 1881), broadside, Virginiana Collection, Edwin A. Alderman Library, University of Virginia, Charlottesville, Va.

12. Virginia, General Assembly, *Acts and Joint Resolutions,* 1881–82, pp. 90–98.

Assembly helped the farmers with a 20 percent property tax cut, and local Readjuster assessors placed substantially lower valuations on agricultural land. Wine manufacturers, saloon keepers, merchants, and other small businessmen also benefited from tax revisions. Shifting the burden, moreover, the debt revolt forced the nonproducers to pay a much larger share of government expenses. The insurgents closed a loophole for speculators by making it extremely difficult to use bond coupons for the payment of taxes. Displaying a similar bias, the new regime stopped the disastrous practice of allowing the railroads to assess their own property for tax purposes. The state imposed substantially higher valuations of its own, and tax receipts from these corporations almost tripled between 1879 and 1883.[13] Reflecting these developments, a new spirit of efficiency pervaded the financial offices of the Capitol "basement." Auditor John E. Massey tightened bookkeeping procedures, cracked down on incompetent revenue officials, and collected hundreds of thousands of dollars in delinquent taxes. The results were dramatic. By 1883 the insurgents had transformed the chronic budgetary deficits of the 1870s into a hefty $1.5 million surplus.[14]

The Readjusters used this financial windfall to revitalize Virginia's impoverished social services, particularly the public schools. Enthusiastic party spokesmen emphasized the role of the state's "mental resources" in economic growth, and the *Whig* argued that mass schooling would encourage "a general ambition for local prosperity." [15] Pouring money into the struggling system, therefore, the insurgents boosted the number of schools, pupils, and teachers by almost 250 percent. Dissatisfied with this rate of progress, the legislature petitioned Washington for federal aid in the struggle with illiteracy.[16] Funds for higher education also skyrocketed. Ener-

13. For evidence of Readjuster tax reforms see ibid., pp. 10–12, 37–39, 166, 497; Harold Wesley Ward, "The Administration of Liquor Control in Virginia" (Ph.D. diss., University of Virginia, 1946), p. 14; Robert Clinton Burton, "The History of Taxation in Virginia: 1870–1901" (Ph.D. diss., University of Virginia, 1962), pp. 95–100; and Joseph A. Greene, Jr., "A Critical Investigation of Virginia's System of Taxing Railroads" (Ph.D. diss., University of Virginia, 1951), pp. 20–21.

14. Virginia, Treasurer, *Annual Report,* 1882–83, p. 5. See also John E. Massey, *Autobiography of John E. Massey,* ed. Elizabeth H. Hancock (New York: Neale Publishing Co., 1909), pp. 178–83.

15. *Richmond Weekly Whig,* December 31, 1881; see also Riddleberger, *Riddleberger Bill Vindicated,* broadside.

16. Virginia, General Assembly, *Acts and Joint Resolutions,* 1879–80, pp. 73–74. For evidence of increased educational appropriations see General Assembly, *Acts,* 1881–82, pp. 262–64, 473–74. Statistics on educational progress are available in Virginia, Superintendent of Public Instruction, *School Report,* 1885, pp. 243–47.

getic Readjuster officials modernized the state colleges by expanding course offerings, lowering tuition fees, and repairing dilapidated buildings. Taking over the government hospitals, moreover, well-financed insurgent physicians experimented with new techniques in the treatment of handicapped children and the mentally ill. The abundance of tax revenues also allowed the movement to reward its Negro followers with a new college and an up-to-date mental institution—both located in Petersburg. Even the antiquated state penitentiary came in for a major overhaul. The insurgents added a modern wing for the female inmates and placed the prison's industrial workshops on a profit-making basis.[17] Looking to the future, Readjuster officials envisioned a system of local asylums for the incurably insane, vocational training schools for aspiring craftsmen, a teachers' college for white girls, and a reformatory for youthful law-breakers.[18] Innovative and efficient, the debt revolt promised expanded social services for all.

The Readjusters carried this drive even further by focusing attention on the plight of the lower classes. They authorized county officials to provide the poor with free vaccinations during epidemics and free food during crop failures. Disturbed by the condition of the urban proletariat, moreover, the insurgents agitated for limits on child labor and a ten-hour workday in the factories. One of the party's legislators demanded the abolition of the chain gang, while another called for the admission of "poor whites" to the University of Virginia. Reflecting concern for the destitute, these proposals marked the cutting edge of Readjuster reform.[19]

This zeal for change spilled over into other areas. Filling the air with producerite rhetoric, the insurgents demanded strict regulation of the middlemen. They began by imposing rigorous standards on "foreign" insurance companies doing business in Virginia. State

17. Legislation to expand the penitentiary and to build a state college and a mental hospital for the blacks may be found in General Assembly, *Acts,* 1881–82, pp. 246–47, 283–86, 373. For additional evidence of progress in Virginia's state institutions see Virginia, Virginia Military Institute, *Annual Report,* 1882–83, p. 8; Virginia, Agricultural and Mechanical College, *Annual Report,* 1882–83, pp. 3, 12–13; Virginia, Eastern Lunatic Asylum, *Annual Report,* 1881–82, pp. 9–12; and Virginia, State Penitentiary, *Annual Report,* 1882–83, pp. 3–5.

18. *State Penitentiary Report,* 1882–83, pp. 58–59; *Eastern Lunatic Asylum Report,* 1881–82, pp. 8–9; *Marion* (Va.) *Patriot and Herald,* March 22, 1883; Henry Hudnall et al., *Address to the People of Richmond* (n.p., 1883), broadside, Mahone Papers.

19. General Assembly, *Acts,* 1881–82, pp. 169, 230, 463; Virginia, House of Delegates, *House Bills,* 1881–82, House Bills 231 and 256; *Richmond Southern Intelligencer,* February 9, 16, 1880.

inspectors drove substandard fertilizers off the market, and party spokesmen called for controls over the tobacco warehouses. The railroads came under even closer scrutiny. Taking their cue from the Grangers, the insurgents concocted plans for a Virginia railroad commission with extensive rate-making and supervisory powers. This ambitious proposal failed to become law, but it reflected the general drift of Readjuster thought. Breaking with the past, the new party urged a major expansion of the state's role in the economy.[20]

In spite of their hostility to the middlemen, however, the insurgents were not antibusiness in any doctrinaire way. They welcomed outside investments and granted more than one hundred corporate charters during their brief hegemony.[21] Stimulating economic growth, they boosted a wide range of productive interests. The Readjusters proposed to aid the farmers by establishing agricultural experiment stations. They encouraged wine manufacturing through changes in the revenue laws, and they urged their national Republican allies to repeal the crippling federal excise on tobacco products. Publicizing the state's mineral resources, the legislature petitioned Washington to extend the work of the United States Geological Survey into Virginia. Dairymen benefited from new restrictions on the sale of oleomargarine, while mechanics received legal protection from defaulting customers.[22] Defending the Old Dominion's oyster industry, moreover, Governor Cameron personally led several raids against out-of-state vessels poaching in Virginia waters. The new regime also called for a regulatory board to improve navigation in the Norfolk-Portsmouth harbor complex.[23] Perhaps most significantly, the Readjusters spurned their region's traditional free trade dogma. Instead they championed a comprehensive program of tariff protection for Virginia products from iron ore to sumac. "There is no enterprise which can be started in the South," a party newspaper declared, "but what needs protection." [24] In a symbolical act the legislature voted to move a weather-beaten statue of Henry Clay

20. General Assembly, *Acts,* 1879–80, pp. 87–88; General Assembly, *Acts,* 1881–82, pp. 399–400; *House Bills,* 1881–82, House Bills 121, 189, and 197.

21. Derived from the indexes of General Assembly, *Acts,* 1879–80, and *Acts,* 1881–82.

22. For Readjuster efforts to aid farmers and mechanics see General Assembly, *Acts,* 1879–80, pp. 49, 181–82; General Assembly, *Acts,* 1881–82, pp. 109–10; *House Bills,* 1881–82, House Bill 189; and Ward, "Liquor Control," p. 14.

23. *House Bills,* 1881–82, House Bill 143. For Governor Cameron's efforts to curb oyster poachers see Virginia, Adjutant-General, *Annual Report,* 1882–83, pp. 36–41.

24. *Marion* (Va.) *Patriot and Herald,* July 27, 1882.

from the Capitol grounds to a conspicuous place in the building's rotunda.[25] Restored to favor, the old Whig probably felt very much at home.

These economic reforms constituted only part of the Readjuster program. Arguing that Bourbonism blocked the road to progress, the insurgents blasted the remaining strongholds of the old patrician order. One democratic reform after another tumbled through the legislative mill. The General Assembly struck down the poll tax as a prerequisite for voting, abolished the whipping post, and placed strict prohibitions on the practice of dueling.[26] The new party also agitated for repeal of the state's inequitable road law—a feudal remnant which forced the poor to bear the burden of highway maintenance.[27] Zeroing in on the local centers of patrician strength, moreover, the Readjusters attempted to smash the grasping courthouse cliques. One new law protected the public from exorbitant county fees; another, from unfair tax assessors; a third, from defaulting attorneys.[28] The insurgents also threatened to deprive the lawyers of a lucrative source of income by calling for the appointment of bonded state officials to handle all judicial land sales. The revolt followed a similar pattern by slashing the salaries of county judges and demanding a cut in the number of circuit judgeships. Striking at entrenched privilege, these reforms marked a significant revolution in local government.[29]

On issue after issue, from protective tariffs to poll tax repeal, the Readjusters showed a striking eagerness to break with the past. Critics denounced them as revolutionary agrarians, but this flamboyant rhetoric only obscured the nature of the movement. Analyzing their own views, the insurgents generally described themselves as "liberals" who sought a middle ground between "radicalism" and "Bourbonism." This assessment hit close to the mark. The Readjusters adopted essentially moderate policies, and the basic patterns of social and economic life remained much the

25. General Assembly, *Acts,* 1881–82, p. 363.

26. Ibid., pp. 213–14, 401, 404–5.

27. *Richmond Daily Whig,* December 13, 1881; *Marion* (Va.) *Patriot and Herald,* October 11, 18, 1883; *Woodstock Virginian,* October 19, 1883.

28. General Assembly, *Acts,* 1879–80, p. 210; General Assembly, *Acts,* 1881–82, pp. 226–27, 338.

29. For evidence of these attacks on Virginia's judicial establishment see *House Bills,* 1881–82, House Bill 259; General Assembly, *Acts,* 1881–82, p. 171; and "The Address of the Readjuster Members, Virginia Legislature" in the *Marion* (Va.) *Patriot and Herald,* June 15, 1882.

same. The movement's primary thrust was to expand opportunities within the existing system, to create a more open and democratic climate for individual effort. Producerite in orientation, the insurgents accepted the main outlines of capitalism and attempted to make it work for "the men who want money as well as the men who have money." [30] The *Whig* captured this entrepreneurial spirit by describing Readjustment as an "honest shuffle and a new deal." [31] Mobilizing Virginia's resources, the debt revolt propelled the state into the vibrant mainstream of producerite reform.

30. *Richmond Weekly Whig,* March 24, 1875.
31. Ibid., October 6, 1882.

8

Mahoneism:
The Collapse of
the Readjuster Coalition

Consolidating their control over the state, the Readjusters compiled an impressive list of achievements. Overdue reforms followed one another in rapid succession, and the legislative calendar teemed with equally ambitious proposals. Even as the insurgents savored their triumph, however, dissension cropped up in their ranks. Key men began to defect from the coalition. Early in 1882 "Parson" Massey broke away from the party, carrying with him enough members of the state senate to deadlock that body.[1] The Readjuster legislative caucus seethed with a discontent which threatened to erupt into physical violence; fist fights broke out between party officials on the streets of Richmond.[2] Southwestern Congressman Abram Fulkerson backed Massey's revolt, and the Piedmont's embittered Frank G. Ruffin did the same. The Readjuster press blazed with accusations of treason and bribery, but the list of defectors continued to grow. Gaining renewed hope, the Funders welcomed the rebels to their ranks. By 1883 the insurgent coalition appeared well down the road to collapse.[3]

Analyzing the causes of this disintegration, conservative Virginians almost unanimously pointed to Mahoneism as the disruptive agent. Consequently *Mahoneism* became a catch phrase for all of the excesses, real and imagined, of the debt revolt. The Funders took advantage of the situation, moreover, and molded the concept into a strikingly effective propaganda weapon. Reduced to its essentials, the popular image of Mahoneism revolved around four central issues: the idea of General Mahone as an autocratic "boss"; the belief that Readjuster "spoilsmanship" had corrupted Virginia's civil service; the assertion that the debt movement had endangered "white supremacy"; and, finally, the argument that Mahone had attempted to "Republicanize" the state in return for a share of the federal patronage. These accusations constituted a damning indictment of the Readjuster revolt, and they attached a stigma to it which persisted for generations. There can be no doubt of the devastating impact of these charges, but there is reason to question their truthfulness. Spawned in the heat of political warfare, these attacks could make few claims to objectivity. An examination of each is in order.

Hostility to Mahone's alleged bossism pervaded the whole controversy. The little general's enemies, personal as well as political, delighted in picturing him as a ruthless despot who demanded unquestioning obedience from his followers. In order to evaluate this charge, however, it is essential to understand the climate which produced it. The Gilded Age was the great era of the political boss, the heyday of such flamboyant spoilsmen as Roscoe Conkling and Simon Cameron. A decade of civil service reform agitation had made the public acutely conscious of the evils of machine politics, and the term *boss* came easily to the mouths and pens of political partisans. The Readjusters' alliance with the corrupt "Stalwart" Republicans only increased the possibility of guilt by association. Equally important in creating the atmosphere for these charges, moreover, Mahone seemed tailor-made for the unsavory role of "boss." He had earned a reputation in the 1870s as an expert political manipulator. Working behind the scenes, he had won legislative concessions for his railroad and had exerted a surprising amount of influence over state affairs. Backstairs rumors exaggerated his activities and made him appear an even more adept politico than he actually was. Even the loss of his railroad failed to dim his reputation for intrigue. Further intensifying suspicions, his looks and habits also fitted him for the boss's role. A natty

1. Massey's revolt is discussed in Chapter 9.

2. A particularly embarrassing street fight between the two state auditors, S. Brown Allen and Harry Dyson, is noted in C. C. Clarke to William Mahone, April 29, 1882, William Mahone Papers, William R. Perkins Library, Duke University, Durham, N.C.

3. Fulkerson defended his stance in a letter to the *Abingdon Weekly Virginian,* July 19, 1883. Ruffin blasted Mahone in a devastating pamphlet, *Mahoneism Unveiled! The Great Plot to Sell Out Virginians to the Republican Party Exposed* (n.p., 1882?), copy in the Virginia State Library, Richmond, Va.

dresser, his flashing eyes shaded by a great Panama hat, his slender features half-concealed by his thick beard, the little general presented a peculiar, almost sinister, appearance. His frail body and squeaky voice made him more adept as a political organizer than as a party spokesman, and he generally shunned the limelight.[4] Working outside of the public view and shrouded by his reputation, Mahone offered a vulnerable target. Thousands were willing, even eager, to believe the worst about him.

The general looked like a "boss" in an age of "bosses," but the question remains as to how well he actually filled the role. There is no doubt that he emerged as the dominant figure in the debt revolt. Beginning with his unsuccessful drive for the Governor's Mansion in 1877, he quickly filled the party's leadership vacuum. As late as 1879 the Funders had regarded him as only one of a group of opposition leaders, but by 1881 he had emerged as the movement's undisputed top man. Why was he able to accomplish this coup? Historians have generally stressed Mahone's control of the spoils as the source of his preeminence.[5] Although superficially convincing, these accounts ignored an essential fact about machine politics. Merely controlling a large number of federal and state offices did not ensure victory or even the efficient functioning of a patronage machine. Successful "spoilsmanship" involved not only the rewarding of key individuals but also the careful balancing of sections and factions, seeing that each important group in the party received its share of the jobs. It was in this area that the true nature of Mahone's leadership became apparent. Instead of an arbitrary boss, he served primarily as a broker among the groups which composed the variegated Readjuster coalition. Attempting to maintain harmony, he constantly walked a tightrope between the party's competing factions, particularly its Democratic and Republican wings. Historians have stressed harsh, dictatorial aspects of the general's personality, and in so doing they have ignored the pragmatic streak which enabled him to make the coalition

4. Charles T. O'Ferrall, *Forty Years of Active Service* (New York: Neale Publishing Co., 1904), p. 211; Nelson M. Blake, *William Mahone of Virginia: Soldier and Political Insurgent* (Richmond: Garrett & Massie, 1935), p. 271; Charles Chilton Pearson, *The Readjuster Movement in Virginia* (New Haven: Yale University Press, 1917), p. 114.

5. Blake, *William Mahone,* p. 193; Pearson, *Readjuster Movement,* p. 159; William C. Pendleton, *Political History of Appalachian Virginia, 1776–1927* (Dayton, Va.: Shenandoah Press, 1927), p. 349; Allen W. Moger, *Virginia: Bourbonism to Byrd, 1870–1925* (Charlottesville: University Press of Virginia, 1968), p. 50.

function in the first place.[6] His voluminous personal papers reveal a frank, highly practical man, determined to hold his party together.[7] Mahone, indeed, gloried in his political pragmatism. Moving among a swirl of quarrelsome ideologues, he limited his intellectual commitments to a sort of rough-and-ready, man-on-the-make producerism. Scornful of the pretensions of Virginia's traditional ruling class, he described himself as a Jacksonian "barn-burner." [8] Ideological labels, however, like party names, weighed but lightly on the little general. Avoiding dogmatic stands, he showed a willingness to compromise on issue after issue. He abandoned his conservative debt views in order to back the caucus's Riddleberger bill. By the same token, he offered his independent elector scheme in 1880 as a means of patching the coalition together, and he withdrew it when mass opposition developed. In 1881, moreover, he had favored Riddleberger for governor, but he had acquiesced in the Readjuster convention's choice.[9] An experienced political tactician, he knew how to bend when the tide was against him. This willingness to compromise was essential in Virginia's Byzantine political situation.

Ignoring these constructive facets of Mahone's leadership, historians have focused disproportionate attention on his bossism. They have fastened particularly on two aspects of the Readjuster regime—the "Mahone pledge" and "caucus rule"—as proof of the general's arbitrary behavior.[10] Observed within the political context of the day, however, even these actions appear much less reprehensible. During the 1881 race Mahone attempted to obtain pledges from the Readjuster legislative candidates that, if elected, they would vote for all men and measures approved by the party caucus in Richmond. When this move became public, dissidents howled that the general was attempting to collar the legislature and bend

6. This emphasis on dictatorial aspects of Mahone's personality is evident in Blake, *William Mahone,* pp. 193, 266; Moger, *Virginia,* pp. 49–50; and Pendleton, *Appalachian Virginia,* p. 349.

7. For evidence of Mahone's pragmatic approach to politics see the copies of the following letters in the Mahone Papers: Mahone to William M. Burwell, November 17, 1880; and Mahone to W. L. Fernald, October 7, 1881. See also Mahone to Abram Fulkerson, March 25, April 5, 1880, Mahone Papers (Letterbooks).

8. Mahone to William M. Burwell, November 17, 1880, copy in the Mahone Papers.

9. Ruffin, *Mahoneism Unveiled,* pp. 2–3; John E. Massey, *Autobiography of John E. Massey,* ed. Elizabeth H. Hancock (New York: Neale Publishing Co., 1909), pp. 193–95.

10. Pearson, *Readjuster Movement,* pp. 152–54; Moger, *Virginia,* p. 50; Richard L. Morton, *The Negro in Virginia Politics, 1865–1902* (Charlottesville: University of Virginia Press, 1919), pp. 111–16.

it to his will.[11] While this explanation has a certain plausibility, an analysis of the actual circumstances of the 1881 race leads to a substantially different conclusion. Party lines, especially in the eastern counties, bordered on chaos. In some areas several putatively "Readjuster" candidates were competing for the same seat. Caught up in the struggle between Coalitionist and Straight-out Republicans, moreover, a number of Negroes with ill-defined views were also running for office. Readjuster campaign funds, desperately needed for poll taxes, were limited, and the little general was reluctant to waste the party's resources on "doubtful" men. Viewed within this context, requiring the "pledge" emerges as an eminently reasonable action. Indeed, the whole system of caucus rule in the legislature reflected a similar attempt to bring order out of political chaos. The state Senate and House of Delegates met in an atmosphere of doubt and suspicion, of rumors about Funder bribes and influence. More than a scheme to exalt Mahone's power, the legislative caucus and its activities marked a commonsense approach to preserving a measure of party regularity in a shifting and uncertain situation. It should also be noted that the Funders had, at various times, advocated a similar system of rigid caucus control.[12] The caucus issue, like the pledge, has been distorted out of all proportion to its intrinsic importance.

Returning to the central question, however, why did the little general gain such prominence in his party? The answer lies not so much in bossism or spoils as in Mahone's superior ability as a political organizer, his knack for reconciling divergent interests. Some of the other leaders, notably Massey and Fulkerson, enjoyed greater mass support, but they were too closely identified with the revolt's Democratic wing to serve as go-betweens or conciliators. Mahone and his urban liberals, by contrast, moved with ease in either the Democratic or Republican camps. Only the general, with his wealth, his war record, and his control over the vital *Richmond Whig,* commanded enough respect on all sides to give the movement its driving thrust and direction. Even during Mahone's senatorial term in Washington his supporters continued to demand help and

11. Letter from Massey to the *Harrisonburg* (Va.) *Rockingham Register,* January 26, 1882; A. M. Lybrook, *Mahoneism Unveiled! The Plot against the People Exposed* (n.p., 1882?), p. 2, pamphlet, Virginia State Library, Richmond, Va.

12. *Richmond State,* November 7, 8, 1879; Robert E. Withers to James L. Kemper, December 7, 1872, James Lawson Kemper Papers, Edwin A. Alderman Library, University of Virginia, Charlottesville, Va.

advice. When dissension emerged in the state legislature, for example, his lieutenants begged him to return to Richmond, apparently convinced that his presence alone would be enough to restore harmony. Disputants in local party quarrels also appealed for his aid in reconciling their differences. "You have no conception," Mahone declared in a letter to one of his supporters, "of the judging and detail that devolves upon me—not only in respect to matters here [in Washington]—but in respect to the party organization in Virginia." He continued: "No one there will do the requisite work. It demands vigilance and persistency of attention down to the veriest detail." [13] Cajoling, prodding, occasionally threatening, he attempted to force the ill-assorted gears of his "machine" to mesh smoothly. Given the antagonistic elements in the Readjuster coalition, therefore, the wonder is not that it disintegrated but that the general held it together as long as he did.

Using the philosopher's stone of propaganda, the Funders transmuted Mahone's normal activities as a party leader into the evil machinations of a "boss." They achieved a similar success in smearing the entire debt revolt with the pitch of corruption. Slashing away without restraint, they branded the mass of Readjuster officials as incompetents, grafters, and vicious partisans. "Such men as they put in office all over the State," an embittered Funder growled, "have not been seen grouped together, since Sir John Falstaff was in command of Mouldy, Shadow, Wart, Feeble, and Bull-calf." [14] The *Richmond State* compared the new officeholders unfavorably with "Billy the Kid." [15] Accepting such accusations at face value, historians have also blasted the insurgents for "petty extravagance and humiliating partisanship." [16] A closer examination reveals, however, that most of these charges, if not wholly inaccurate, are at least misleading.

At one level, of course, the attacks touched a solid core of reality.

13. Mahone to Lewis E. Harvie, July 3, 1882, Lewis E. Harvie Papers, Virginia Historical Society, Richmond, Va. See also the following in the Mahone Papers: William H. Turner to Mahone, March 23, 1882; and Duff Green to Mahone, February 9, 1882.

14. William L. Royall, *The President's Relations with Senator Mahone and Repudiation: An Attempt to Subvert the Supreme Court of the United States* (New York: E. J. Hale & Son, 1882), p. 30.

15. *Richmond State*, August 2, 1881.

16. Pearson, *Readjuster Movement*, pp. 148–49. See also Marshall W. Fishwick, *Virginia: A New Look at the Old Dominion* (New York: Harper & Brothers, 1959), p. 147; and Richard L. Morton, *Virginia since 1861* (New York: American Historical Society, 1924), p. 197.

The Readjusters were unabashed, self-proclaimed champions of the spoils system. Stressing the democratic aspects of "rotation in office," they described their appointees as "rough diamonds" who only needed "a little rubbing to become polished stones." [17] These "rough diamonds" absorbed an increasing share of attention. The party caucus became little more than a clearinghouse for state jobs, while Mahone struggled under a deluge of applications for federal posts. Continually tightening their grasp, moreover, the insurgents demanded reforms which, while desirable in themselves, would also create more jobs for the "faithful." Their land sales bill would have authorized the governor to appoint more than one hundred agents to handle judicial sales in the counties. Similar motives figured in their tobacco inspection proposal, and their railroad regulatory bill would have placed additional thousands under political influence. Seeking still more offices, the Readjusters also schemed to replace dozens of incumbent Funder school trustees, notaries public, and circuit judges.[18] They even attempted to gerrymander the congressional districts. Undismayed by Funder protests, the *Whig* apologized because the redistricting measure would give the debt revolt only eight of the ten congressmen, instead of the whole delegation.[19] None of these controversial bills became law, largely because of the efforts of Massey and his allies in the state senate. Such blatant partisanship proved sufficient, nevertheless, to alienate respectable opinion from the Readjuster movement.

In spite of these excesses, however, caution must be used in analyzing this aspect of the debt revolt. Readjuster "spoilsmanship" should be evaluated within the political context of the Gilded Age. Government jobs and assessments on official salaries provided the ammunition for the great party battles of the day, and the Readjusters were simply following customary procedures. Given the realities of Virginia politics, moreover, such partisan behavior is even easier to understand. Campaigns were expensive, and the spoils system offered the insurgents their only chance to match the resources of the entrenched elite. Monopolizing most of the state's wealth, the Funders could rely on wealthy bondholder syndicates and railroads for contributions. The Readjusters, by way of contrast,

17. *Richmond Daily Whig,* December 9, 1881.
18. Virginia, House of Delegates, *House Bills,* 1881–82, House Bills 121, 189, 197, 259, and House Joint Resolutions 272 and 337.
19. *Richmond Weekly Whig,* April 14, 1882.

enjoyed only the uncertain and sporadic aid of the national Republicans, plus what they could garner from the spoils. Political necessity, as well as greed, propelled them into the struggle for places. It should also be noted that the Readjusters did not introduce the spoils system into Virginia. For all their sanctimonious tone, the Commonwealth's patricians had been distributing the offices according to political dictates for generations. These deals had generally been made behind closed doors, where such groups as the antebellum "Richmond Junto" had exerted a shadowy influence.[20] The courthouse cliques, moreover, had also battened off the informal patronage of county fees and legal actions. Although marred by nepotism and inefficiency, these practices had gone on for so long that many of the patricians looked on them as prerogatives rather than spoils. Their fierce attacks on the Readjusters stemmed, consequently, at least in part, from a self-deception which bordered on hypocrisy.

Given the pervasive and continuing nature of the spoils system, therefore, the question boils down to whether or not the Readjuster officials actually impaired Virginia's civil service. Here the findings are mixed, but they indicate that the caliber of government generally improved during the insurgent regime. An embarrassing scandal occurred when the state's financial officers switched the contract for printing the new "Riddleberger" bonds from one company to another for political reasons, but this episode appears to have been the exception rather than the rule.[21] Most of the Readjusters' actions withstood close scrutiny. After recapturing the legislature in 1883 the Funders examined almost every aspect of the insurgents' administrative conduct. These investigators uncovered some evidence of petty graft, generally arising from vague and haphazard legislation, as well as some proof of poor judgment and incompetence in the construction of public buildings. There was also evidence of political partisanship in the management of state institutions, but this was mitigated by the Funders' similar conduct in the 1870s. Beyond these minor points, however, the insurgents' record was good, as several of the investigative committees grudgingly admitted.[22] Belying their accusations of wholesale malfeasance, the inquisitors

20. Joseph H. Harrison, Jr., "Oligarchs and Democrats: The Richmond Junto," *Virginia Magazine of History and Biography* 78 (1970):186–88.

21. See Virginia, Senate, *Journal,* 1883–84, pp. 500–507, for a report on this scandal.

22. The *Senate Journal,* 1883–84, published the results of these investigations. For evidence of laudatory findings see the following sections of the volume: Document 16, pp. 1–2; Document 32, pp. 1–3; Document 36, p. 1. For more hostile observations see Document 19, pp. 1–2; and Document 33, p. 9.

allowed the overwhelming majority of Readjuster officials to serve out their terms unmolested. They attempted to gather impeachment evidence against Attorney General Blair, Education Superintendent Farr, and a few others, but these efforts came to nothing.

The Funders' treatment of the insurgent judges merits special attention. Since 1879 they had accused the Readjusters of packing the courts with drunks, gamblers, political partisans, and men who were totally ignorant of the law.[23] Recapturing the General Assembly, therefore, they threatened a reign of terror against the offending judges. For all their extravagant charges, they removed only six of the defenseless jurists, while four more resigned under pressure. The justice of several of these removals was also questionable. In two cases the legislative inquisitors admitted finding no cause for punitive action. In another instance the judge requested a public impeachment trial to defend himself, but his plea was ignored. In yet another case the impaneling of Negro jurors was at least a side issue. Still the judges lost their posts.[24] Surviving these arbitrary proceedings, however, the overwhelming majority of the party's jurists—scores of them—completed their terms in peace. The Readjuster state supreme court avoided partisan bias and held office well into the 1890s. While evaluating the insurgents' performance, moreover, we should also note that the judiciary had not flourished under the previous Funder regime. Throughout the 1870s public resentment had simmered against the graft and favoritism of the courthouse cliques. On balance it seems likely that the insurgents harmed the judicial system very little, if at all.

The Readjusters' administrative achievements far outweighed their shortcomings. They completely revitalized Virginia's government. They cracked down on defaulting revenue agents, forced the corporations to pay a larger share of the taxes, and slashed the crippling debt burden. Hundreds of thousands of dollars poured into the state treasury, enabling the insurgents to begin a dramatic expansion of the public schools and other social services. This flood of money might also have permitted widespread graft, but the Readjusters held official salaries at approximately their previous level. Mounting an economy drive, in fact, they accomplished

23. *Richmond State,* January 19, 1880; John B. Minor to F. W. M. Holliday, March 6, 1880, F. W. M. Holliday Papers, William R. Perkins Library, Duke University, Durham, N.C.

24. See references to these removals and resignations throughout the *Senate Journal,* 1883–84. See also the *Richmond Daily Dispatch,* January 9, February 10, March 7, 1884.

significant reductions in the cost of the General Assembly, printed records, and in the courts.[25] Instead of plundering the treasury, they left it with a surplus of well over a million dollars.[26] Retrenchment and reform, the traditional watchwords of conservative government, took on a new dimension under this ostensibly "radical" regime.

Perhaps this administrative efficiency can be best observed by focusing on events at the state's most prestigious educational institution, the University of Virginia. The school had long served as a training ground for the traditionalist elite, and the insurgents had denounced it as a reactionary "sleepy hollow." When the debt revolt swept to power, therefore, the Funders predicted a Mahoneite takeover which would decimate the school's teaching corps and destroy its reputation. The new Readjuster Board of Visitors quickly calmed these fears. They retained the entire faculty and added new members on the basis of ability rather than politics. Bringing a new air of efficiency to the campus, moreover, they renovated its buildings and improved its sewage system. They also made forward-looking changes in the degree requirements and expanded course offerings to make the school more attractive to potential students. There was nothing at all destructive or corrupt in their activities, and they left the university with a solid budgetary surplus.[27] This was not an isolated or "showcase" instance, moreover, because similar conditions prevailed at the other state colleges and mental institutions.[28] Viewed in this light, the Readjusters' administration of government actually deserved considerable praise. This aspect of the Mahoneism issue has been distorted out of all proportion to reality. The insurgent officials were political partisans; they replaced older, established men in many cases; but it does not follow that they served the Commonwealth badly.

The attacks on Readjuster bossism and corruption amounted

25. Relevant statistics on governmental expenditures are available in Virginia, Auditor of Public Accounts, *Annual Reports,* as follows: *Annual Report,* 1878–79, Document 2, pp. 27–28; and *Annual Report,* 1882–83, Document 2, pp. 3–5, and Document 17, pp. 3–5.

26. *Senate Journal,* 1883–84, Document 16, pp. 1–2.

27. James T. Moore, "The University and the Readjusters," *Virginia Magazine of History and Biography* 78 (1970):87–101.

28. Virginia, Central Lunatic Asylum, *Annual Report,* 1881–82, pp. 3–8; John Perry Cochran, "The Virginia Agricultural and Mechanical College: The Formative Half Century, 1872–1919, of Virginia Polytechnic Institute" (Ph.D. diss., University of Alabama, 1961), pp. 127–49; Francis H. Smith, *The Virginia Military Institute: Its Building and Rebuilding* (Lynchburg: J. P. Bell Co., 1912), p. 240.

to little more than hypocritical bombast. The Funders drew blood only when they shifted to the third facet of Mahoneism—to the Negro's role in the debt revolt. Exploiting racial fears, they argued that the general's alliance with the blacks endangered "white supremacy." A Richmond newspaper set the pattern by warning that the very future of "pure white Saxon government" was at stake.[29] Allowing for melodramatic exaggeration, moreover, such charges reflected an essential truth: the debt revolt did loosen traditional lines of class and caste. The freedmen regained their rights, at least temporarily, and the whole structure of racial subordination tottered under the impact.

The Negroes' political power mushroomed during the brief Readjuster hegemony. They constituted almost a third of the electorate, and they held the balance of power in the debt struggle. Recognizing this fact, Mahone carried out a racial reform program unsurpassed in Virginia history, even during Reconstruction. The insurgents rewarded their black followers with a new state college, a mental institution, and a vastly increased number of public schools. They abolished the whipping post, a humiliating reminder of the old slave regime, and enfranchised thousands of impoverished Negroes by repealing the poll tax. The legislature required equal pay for black teachers.[30] Striking another blow at racial discrimination, moreover, insurgent judges allowed Negroes to serve on juries for the first time in years.[31] The debt revolt also created hundreds of jobs for the racial minority. Black teachers took charge of the education of their race, frequently displacing whites; Negro doctors and professors held important posts at the new state institutions; blacks served as government clerks, prison guards, and postal workers. After a decade of political impotence, the freedmen shared the benefits of a civil rights revolution.[32]

29. *Richmond State,* September 27, 1881.

30. Virginia, General Assembly, *Acts and Joint Resolutions,* 1881–82, p. 37.

31. Letter from John F. Lewis to President-elect James A. Garfield in the *Richmond Weekly Whig,* February 11, 1881; Carter M. Louthan to Mahone, March 13, 1882, Mahone Papers; W. N. Stevens et al., *An Address to the Colored Voters of the State of Virginia: The Record of the Bourbon-Democratic and Liberal-Readjuster Parties Contrasted—What the Leading, Most Influential, Intelligent and Representative Colored Men of Virginia Have to Say to Their People* (n.p., 1883), broadside, Baugh Family Papers, Edwin A. Alderman Library, Charlottesville, Va.

32. For evidence of patronage opportunities for Negroes see the *Petersburg Lancet,* September 2, 9, 1882; October 27, 1883; Stevens, *Address to the Colored Voters,* broadside; and George F. Bragg, Jr., to Dr. C. G. Woodson, July 27, August 26, 1926, in the *Journal of Negro History* 11 (1926):673–74, 678–80.

The insurgents justified these reforms in highly practical terms. They emphasized the importance of social justice in economic growth and argued that their approach offered the only alternative to racial warfare. "Our treatment of the colored people elevates them as citizens," Mahone noted, "and promotes their productive capacity." [33] Attempting to reassure their white followers, moreover, the party spokesmen denied that their program endangered "white supremacy." Instead they made a crucial distinction between "political" and "social" equality. They argued that recognizing the blacks' political rights in no way required the breakdown of social barriers between the races. The insurgents underlined this stance with repeated denunciations of racially mixed marriages and schools. The thrust of their program, in its main outlines, was to upgrade the Negroes' status within the basically segregated framework of Virginia society. "Our party," the *Whig* explained, ". . . encourages each race to develop its own sociology separately and apart from unlawful contamination with each other, but under a government which recognizes and protects the civil rights of all equally." [34]

In spite of the Readjusters' caution, nevertheless, their activities severely weakened the "white supremacy" mystique. This change took place as much within the minds of the blacks as in the structure of laws and institutions. A new, more militant spirit emerged. The number of Negro legislators tripled, rising to fifteen in the 1882 session. No longer isolated and powerless, these men participated actively in the law-making process. They led the fight for a Negro state college, and they played a crucial role in abolishing the whipping post.[35] A similar combativeness also cropped up at the local level. Testing their strength, the blacks demanded more delegates at party conventions, a larger share of the legislative nominees, and an even greater number of schools. Negro voters took over Danville's municipal government, and in Petersburg they threatened to boycott discriminatory merchants. In some areas they even began to organize militia companies. Disturbed by these developments, thousands of whites abandoned the debt revolt, particularly in the eastern counties.[36]

33. Quoted in the *Richmond Weekly Whig,* March 24, 1882.

34. *Richmond Weekly Whig,* September 21, 1883.

35. Charles E. Wynes, *Race Relations in Virginia, 1870–1902* (Charlottesville: University of Virginia Press, 1961), p. 28; Luther P. Jackson, *Negro Office-Holders in Virginia, 1865–1895* (Norfolk: Guide Quality Press, 1945), pp. 79–81.

36. The new black militancy found particular expression in the Negro press. See the *Richmond Virginia Star,* November 18, December 9, 1882; and the *Petersburg*

This racial crossfire created an insoluble dilemma for the Readjuster leaders. Exasperated by Negro aggressiveness, party conservatives demanded the shelving of all racial reforms. Mahone and his liberals stressed the importance of the black vote, however, and began to move beyond their separate-but-equal stance. The little general had previously endorsed segregated political clubs, but in 1883 he demanded full integration of the machine, top to bottom. "I do not approve of meetings and proceedings," he declared, "on the basis of color. The color line is the one thing we are striving to extinguish." [37] Shunning racist arguments, moreover, he frequently sided with the blacks in party squabbles. The fragile barriers between social and political equality were coming down. Governor Cameron dramatized this shift by appointing Negroes to the school boards in Petersburg and Richmond. These men would share in the management of the white schools as well as the black, and the Funders groaned about "Africanization." Refusing to back down, the insurgents defended the move as an act of simple justice to the mass of urban Negroes.[38] Such attacks touched the Readjusters at a vulnerable point. Although they disdained the more flagrant forms of racial mixing—miscegenation and integrated schools—their program still posed a very real threat to "white supremacy." As a result they encountered a swelling tide of opposition. However progressive their program, however reasonable its objectives, it proved far too advanced for the racist Virginia of the 1880s. Funder propaganda alarmed the masses, and the state rapidly degenerated into a snake pit of hatred, white against black.

Mahone's course in national politics only aggravated this unrest. He sided with the Republicans after taking his seat in the United States Senate. President Arthur rewarded him with Virginia's share of the federal patronage, and the debt revolt gravitated into the G.O.P. orbit. By 1882 the Readjuster congressional candidates were campaigning for office as "administration" men, Republican in all but name. Hammering away at these intrigues, the Funders added another bar to the Mahoneism refrain: the general was out not only to "Africanize" the state but to "Republicanize" her as well. They probed old Reconstruction wounds, lacerating the insurgents

---

Lancet, August 5, September 9, 16, November 4, 1882; May 19, July 28, October 13, 1883.

37. Mahone to W. R. Watkins, August 21, 1883, Mahone Papers (Letterbooks). See also William Mahone, *Circular* (Richmond: *Whig* office, 1882), broadside, Baugh Papers.

38. *Richmond Weekly Whig,* May 18, 25, 1883.

as office-hungry "scalawags." "Are you willing," a Funder newspaper asked, ". . . to become a turncoat? Or will you not rather remain true to your friends, your party, and your country." [39] These pressures took their toll, and a large bloc of Democratic whites abandoned the debt revolt. Old political loyalties had driven another wedge into the crumbling coalition.

Detracting from these charges, of course, this facet of Mahoneism involved the usual backlog of hypocrisy. The Funders belied their "anti-Radical" stance by courting the Republican vote in campaign after campaign. They pandered to the blacks with biracial barbecues and promises of "equal rights." They shared platforms with Negro speakers and encouraged the "best men" of both races to unite against "repudiation." Bargaining behind the scenes, they even urged Republican legislators to join the debt-payer caucus. Only when these efforts failed did they resort to color-line tactics. Consequently their outbursts against the Readjusters sounded much like the proverbial sour grapes. [40]

Recognizing political realities, therefore, it seems unfair to condemn Mahone for collaborating with the Republicans. Instead a more pragmatic approach is in order—an evaluation of the general's conduct in terms of its results. What did he achieve through his controversial alliance? By almost any standard he made impressive gains, at least in some areas. He captured the federal patronage, enabling him to dominate the Virginia branch of the G.O.P. He also won a pivotal position in national affairs. His vote allowed the Republicans to organize the Senate, and they rewarded him handsomely. Few senators start their careers as committee chairmen, but the little general immediately took charge of the agriculture committee and held seats on several others. Exploiting his new prestige, moreover, he publicized the Readjuster gospel in congressional speeches and interviews with the Northern press. Anti-Bourbon elements all over the South copied his political tactics. [41] Benefiting from Mahone's boldness, Virginians enjoyed real influence in Washington for the first time in decades.

---

39. *Richmond Daily Dispatch,* November 3, 1881.
40. The following sources provide evidence of Funder overtures to the Negroes: *Richmond State,* November 7, 8, 1879; *Warsaw (Va.) Northern Neck News,* November 7, 1879; *Richmond Commonwealth,* July 2, 1880.
41. Vincent P. DeSantis, *Republicans Face the Southern Question—The New Departure Years, 1877-1897* (Baltimore: Johns Hopkins Press, 1959), pp. 155-56, 159-63; Willie D. Halsell, "James R. Chalmers and 'Mahoneism' in Mississippi," *Journal of Southern History* 10 (1944): 37-38.

On the debit side, however, many factors combined to make the general's alliance with the national G.O.P. less than perfect. For one thing, the Republican machine of the early 1880s was extremely weak. The party had splintered into three quarreling factions—President Arthur's "Stalwarts," James G. Blaine's "Half-Breeds," and the reformist "Mugwumps." Only the president's clique favored the debt revolt, while the others scorned its "spoilsmanship" and economic radicalism.[42] After 1881 even the Arthur group became less friendly. Attempting to calm his critics, the president increasingly shied away from the controversial Readjusters. He angered Mahone by enforcing new civil service regulations and cutting down on the "spoils."[43] A fiscal conservative, he also refused to pump federal money into Virginia. He vetoed a $400,000 appropriation for the state's waterways and even leaned toward a lower tariff, violating a major article of the Readjuster creed. Budget cuts finally compelled the insurgents to beg for funds just to keep the Norfolk navy yard in operation.[44] The congressional Republicans proved equally disappointing. They alienated the South with "bloody shirt" oratory, and many of them opposed Mahone's efforts to repeal the punitive excise on tobacco.[45] Such occurrences blighted the whole alliance. Plagued by bad faith, in fact, this Washington involvement probably did the debt revolt more harm than good. It certainly played into the Funders' hands, providing the fourth and final image in the Mahoneism mosaic.

Concluding this analysis, therefore, what evaluation should be placed on the whole raft of Funder charges—from "bossism" to "Republicanism"? In terms of factual content they had little merit. They were frequently riddled with half-truths and hypocrisy, and most of them amounted to little more than myth-making exercises. Molded by the propagandists, prosaic facts took on strange shapes

42. James Warren Neilson, *From Protest to Preservation: What Republicans Have Believed* (Boston: Christopher Publishing House, 1968), p. 99; Stanley P. Hirshson, *Farewell to the Bloody Shirt: Northern Republicans and the Southern Negro, 1877-1893* (Bloomington: Indiana University Press, 1962), pp. 108-14.

43. Edwin James Harvie to Lewis E. Harvie, December 24, 1882, Harvie Papers, Virginia Historical Society; Mahone to William E. Chandler, June 6, 1882, January 19, 1883, William E. Chandler Papers, Manuscripts Division, Library of Congress, Washington, D.C.; James D. Brady to Mahone, August 7, 1883, Mahone Papers.

44. See the following in the Chandler Papers: J. E. Walker to William E. Chandler, September 1, 1882; and George E. Bowden to William E. Chandler, October 18, 1883. For comments on the waterway veto see Lybrook, *Mahoneism Unveiled,* p. 7; and Ruffin, *Mahoneism Unveiled,* pp. 13-14.

45. Lybrook, *Mahoneism Unveiled,* pp. 11, 15-16; Ruffin, *Mahoneism Unveiled,* pp. 13-14.

and colorations. The routine political tactics of "Gilded Age" America mushroomed mysteriously into the evil machinations of a "boss." Honest, capable officials degenerated into incompetent corruptionists. Negroes exercising their constitutional rights became subhuman enemies of the peace. Even the bungling national Republicans somehow evolved into crafty schemers, determined to subvert Virginia's institutions. Concocting such distorted images, the Funders offered mere caricatures of the truth.

Pockmarked with errors, therefore, Mahoneism provided only a partial explanation for the Readjuster collapse. Instead the root cause lay much deeper—in the diverse and antagonistic character of the groups which supported the debt revolt. These cliques had been bound together only by a common commitment to debt reduction, reinforced by common sufferings during the hard times of the 1870s. After the Readjuster victory in 1881, moreover, even these ties withered away. The enactment of the Riddleberger debt settlement effectively neutralized that issue, and the revival of prosperity allowed Virginians to slump back into their normal, quiescent conservatism. As the ties of party unity, never strong, began to unravel, the insurgents fought among themselves: Democrats against Republicans, whites against blacks, "liberals" against "conservatives." The Funders recognized their opportunity. Exploiting every weakness, they moved in for the kill.

9

Rebuilding a Majority: The Democratic Evolution, 1881–1883

The destruction of the insurgent regime involved more than propaganda blasts at Mahoneism. It also required major changes in the Funders' political tactics. In the 1870s their single-minded commitment to the bondholders had alienated the mass of Virginians, enabling the Readjusters to capture the state government. As early as the 1879 legislative race, however, the patricians had begun to broaden their appeal. Recognizing the unpopularity of their financial program, they attempted to divert attention to the dangers of "Negro rule" and "radicalism." In the 1880 presidential race they successfully ignored state finances and urged all Democrats, regardless of debt views, to support their electoral slate. Their 1881 platform included the usual attack on "repudiation," but their campaign that year emphasized white supremacy. Exploiting old racial and political loyalties, in fact, the patricians steadily expanded their strength. They captured only 42 percent of the vote in 1879, but their share increased to 44 percent in 1880 and 47 percent in 1881.[1] In spite of several bitter setbacks, therefore, the Funders' long-term prospects were promising. The momentum appeared on their side, and the shift of a few thousand votes was all that was needed to restore them to power.

Political defeat hit the traditionalists, nevertheless, with devastating impact. Middle-class "riff-raff" took charge of the government; Negroes enjoyed a measure of power; native Virginians sided with the "Radicals" in Washington. Shocked and frightened, the patricians interpreted the whole affair as a recrudescence of Reconstruction. Such arch-reactionaries as theologian Robert L. Dabney and lawyer William L. Royall dramatized their disgust by leaving the state.[2] Others lapsed into philosophical speculation about the cycles of "barbarism" and "renaissance."[3] Struggling for their political lives, however, the more practical searched for ways to tip the power balance in their favor. Defeated gubernatorial candidate John W. Daniel offered the most interesting suggestion. He argued that the elite should make a bold appeal for the Negro vote. Only in this way—by making concessions on such matters as poll tax repeal—could they hope to take "Africa . . . politically by the hand" and regain control. "This is painful," he reasoned, "but it is necessary."[4] The mass of Funders balked at this proposal, however, and it attracted little support. They leaned, instead, toward an attempt to win back the white insurgents—even at the cost of repudiating the debt. "The debt is gone," an influential Funder remarked in 1880; "I see no help for it."[5] Absalom Koiner, a legislator from the Valley, echoed these sentiments. "Is it possible," he asked, "to effect a reconciliation between the Readjusters & our side by adopting a modified plan of debt settlement?"[6] Moving beyond their "mossback" attitudes of the 1870s, Virginia's traditional leaders became more receptive to change. The elite was obviously in ferment.

Opportunities to splinter the insurgent coalition also became evident. A large bloc of Readjusters were ripe for revolt. The white agrarians of the eastern counties seethed with unrest, angered by the movement's drift toward Negro rights and national Republicanism. Other grievances were more personal in nature. "Parson" Massey believed that Mahone had prevented him from winning the Readjuster gubernatorial nomination in 1881, and his hatred blossomed accordingly. The aristocratic Frank G. Ruffin also resented boss

1. The Funder vote totals in these elections were as follows: (1879) 61,851 out of 144,242; (1880) 96,912 out of 218,606; (1881) 100,758 out of 214,231.

2. Thomas Cary Johnson, *The Life and Letters of Robert Lewis Dabney* (Richmond: Whittet & Shepperson, 1903), p. 443; William L. Royall, *Some Reminiscences* (New York: Neale Publishing Co., 1909), p. 116.

3. J. L. Williams to R. M. T. Hunter, December 27, 1881, Hunter-Garnett Papers, Edwin A. Alderman Library, University of Virginia, Charlottesville, Va.; R. H. Stuart to F. W. M. Holliday, May 14, 1880, F. W. M. Holliday Papers, William R. Perkins Library, Duke University, Durham, N.C.

4. John W. Daniel to J. Randolph Tucker, November 15, 1881, Tucker Family Papers, Southern Historical Collection, University of North Carolina, Chapel Hill, N.C.

5. W. H. Payne to J. Randolph Tucker, January 16, 1880, Tucker Papers.

6. Absalom Koiner to John L. Hurt, January 21, 1881, John L. Hurt Papers, Edwin A. Alderman Library, University of Virginia, Charlottesville, Va.

tactics, and the caucus's refusal to endorse him for state commissioner of agriculture only increased his alienation. Congressman Fulkerson joined the ranks of the disaffected, moreover, largely because the Arthur administration ignored his patronage requests for southwestern Virginia. Such antagonisms transformed the movement into a tangle of conflicting ambitions and personalities.[7]

Only a spark was needed to touch off the revolt, and the explosion came during the winter of 1881–1882. The General Assembly in Richmond provided the setting for the debacle. Convening amid rumors of a smallpox epidemic, the legislators began to quarrel over the election of a United States Senator. Funder incumbent John W. Johnston's term was expiring, and the Readjuster majority gathered to choose his successor. Ignoring Massey's bid for the seat, most of the insurgents rallied behind H. H. Riddleberger instead. The disgruntled "Parson" subsequently led his followers out of the caucus, and the party retaliated by firing him from his post as state auditor. The defiant "Masseyites," including four state senators, proceeded to battle the Readjuster machine on issue after issue. The debt revolt had begun to disintegrate.[8]

Recognizing their chance, the Funders quickly took advantage of this schism. One of them enthusiastically hailed Massey as "the modern Samson" who would "pull down the Temple of Iniquity."[9] They helped the "Parson's" followers to deadlock the General Assembly, clogging the legislative wheels with filibusters, quorum calls, and motions to adjourn. Well-heeled railroad lobbyists complicated affairs with extravagant charter bills, moreover, and rumors made the rounds about a "slush fund" running into thousands of dollars. Valuable time was also drained off by a Funder-inspired debate on whether to allow the counties to prohibit liquor sales. The Senate eventually stifled this local option uproar, but only after it revealed additional fissures in the insurgent ranks. Such tactics reduced the lawmaking process to a shambles, and even the calling of an extra session failed to break the logjam. "The

7. For evidence of these grievances see John E. Massey, *Autobiography of John E. Massey,* ed. Elizabeth H. Hancock (New York: Neale Publishing Co., 1909), pp. 193–95; letter from Ruffin to the *Harrisonburg* (Va.) *Rockingham Register,* September 7, 1882; and Fulkerson to Mahone, July 30, 1881, and January 14, 1882, William Mahone Papers, William R. Perkins Library, Duke University, Durham, N.C.
8. See the *Richmond Daily Dispatch,* January 12–February 24, 1882, for a running account of this struggle.
9. Alexander H. H. Stuart to J. L. M. Curry, January 19, 1882. J. L. M. Curry Papers, Manuscripts Division, Library of Congress. Washington, D.C.

Funders are obstructing legislation," a Mahone lieutenant reported grimly, "in every conceivable way." [10] Key caucus bills, including those for congressional redistricting and railroad regulation, were lost in the shuffle. Patrician opportunism had won a shocking victory.

The legislature limped to adjournment in the spring of 1882, and attention shifted to the fall congressional races, particularly the one for congressman-at-large. The 1880 census had entitled Virginia to an additional House member, and the General Assembly's failure to enact a redistricting bill made it necessary to elect him from the entire state instead of from an individual district. The contest offered the chance, therefore, for another test of strength on a statewide basis. Rallying their forces, the Readjusters nominated one of Mahone's ablest lieutenants, the brilliant and fiery John S. Wise. The Funders responded by pursuing a particularly Machiavellian course. "If we keep cool now, & are discreet," a debt-payer congressman hinted, "I think we can deal a death blow to Mahoneism in Virginia." [11] Appealing to Readjuster dissidents, the patricians refrained from nominating one of their own men and supported Massey for the post. They attempted to weaken the debt revolt at its other flank, moreover, by encouraging the Straight-out Republicans to run a third, "straw man" candidate for the office. The Straight-outs cooperated by nominating a Negro preacher, John M. Dawson. This peculiar struggle, pitting a Mahoneite against a renegade Readjuster and a Negro, reflected the fluid state of Virginia politics. Tight races also shaped up in several of the congressional districts. As for issues, the insurgents defended their Republican alliance and stressed their commitment to tariff protection for Virginia industries. Divided among themselves on the tariff, the Funders shunned that question in favor of a continuous barrage against Mahoneism. [12]

Perhaps Virginians had become tired of the incessant political agitation. Whatever the cause, apathy prevailed during the 1882 campaign. The voter turnout was light, and the election returns

10. W. H. Turner to Mahone, March 23, 1882, Mahone Papers. See also Massey, *Autobiography,* pp. 218–20; and Beverley B. Munford, *Random Recollections* (n.p., 1905), pp. 150–52.

11. George D. Wise to John L. Hurt, April 14, 1882, Hurt Papers.

12. The Readjusters' campaign tactics in 1882 are exemplified by Isaac Chapman Fowler, "The Political Issues, The Question Dispassionately Argued: Speech Delivered September, 1882," in T. W. Preston and C. Bascom Slemp, eds., *Addresses of Famous Southwest Virginians* (Bristol, Va.: King Printing Co., 1939), pp. 314–25. For Funder attacks on the Mahone machine see the *Richmond State,* April 19, July 5, August 24, 1882.

proved indecisive. It initially appeared that the Readjusters had carried the day, overcoming an antiadministration tide which had swept Democrats into power throughout the rest of the country. Holding the Southwest and the Negro counties, Wise squeaked out a 6,000 vote triumph over Massey. Dawson and the Straight-outs attracted only a few thousand ballots and failed to influence the outcome, except perhaps by cutting into Wise's margin.[13] The Readjusters also claimed five of the nine regular districts. Their success, however, proved more apparent than real. The debt-payer candidates successfully contested the results in two of the races, pointing to election frauds, and the Democratic House majority seated them.[14] Consequently the Readjusters secured only four of the ten seats. The narrowness of Wise's statewide victory (he received slightly more than 50 percent of the vote) also provided graphic evidence of the Funder resurgence. The two factions now stood virtually neck-and-neck in the race for political survival.

The Readjusters put up a bold front after the election and trumpeted their victory claims. Behind this facade, however, Mahone complained bitterly about overconfidence and spurred his lieutenants to begin preparations for the crucial 1883 legislative campaign.[15] Frustrating his efforts, nevertheless, new troubles cropped up at every hand. Governor Cameron's appointment of blacks to the Richmond school board touched off an explosive wrangle. The Readjuster state supreme court added to the turmoil by refusing to back the party on several issues. The jurists cut down an attempt to replace the Funder administrators at the state medical college, and they pursued a similar course in nullifying a controversial tag tax on fertilizers.[16] Mahone's relations with the national Republicans also grew worse. Northeastern businessmen, depressed by Democratic victories in their own states, proved increasingly reluctant to contribute to the insurgent campaign chest. As a result

13. The election returns gave Wise 99,992 votes, Massey 94,184, and Dawson 4,342. See the *Warrock-Richardson Virginia, Maryland and North Carolina Almanack for the Year of Our Lord 1884* (Richmond: James E. Goode, 1884), p. 34.

14. For details on the *O'Ferrall* v. *Paul* and *Garrison* v. *Mayo* imbroglios see Chester H. Rowell, *A Historical and Legal Digest of All the Contested Election Cases in the House of Representatives of the United States from the First to the Fifty-Sixth Congress, 1789-1901* (Washington: Government Printing Office, 1901), pp. 398-99, 402-3.

15. See the following in the Mahone Papers (Letterbooks): Mahone to I. C. Fowler, November 14, 1882; Mahone to W. B. Paris, November 21, 1882.

16. *Lewis and als* v. *Whittle and als*, 2 Hansborough (Va.) 415-24 (1883); *Blanton, Commissioner* v. *Southern Fertilizing Company and als*, 2 Hansborough (Va.) 335-43 (1883).

the Readjusters began the 1883 race divided, demoralized, and short on funds. Proof of their decline came with the local elections in the spring; the Funders swept county and municipal contests all over the state, even in the heavily Negro Southside.[17] The balance of political power was shifting.

Only one major obstacle still blocked the Funders' path—the debt issue. This old nemesis continued to haunt the public mind, giving the insurgents their last real hope. The patricians, by contrast, had become thoroughly disgusted with the whole problem—with the ingratitude of the bondholders as well as the "repudiationist" bent of the masses. Their rhetorical flourishes about the "public faith" and Virginia's "sacred honor" made it difficult, nevertheless, to abandon their old position. "In any other state & with any other people," one of them grumbled, "the conservatives would not lash themselves to a fatal fire & die with it. But with us it is noblesse oblige." [18] Fortunately for their cause, however, an 1883 judicial decision allowed them to retreat from their debt stand without losing face. In the case of *Antoni* v. *Greenhow* the United States Supreme Court upheld the "coupon-killer" provisions of the Readjuster debt settlement.[19] This dilution of the creditors' rights allowed the Funders to accept the legality of the settlement as well, effectively neutralizing the debt issue. Patrician editors had been demanding a more practical approach for years, and this court action paved the way for just such a campaign.

Meeting in Lynchburg in July 1883, the Funder state convention proceeded to overhaul the party's whole image. The enthusiastic delegates accepted the finality of the Riddleberger debt settlement and welcomed former Readjusters to their ranks. Also conciliating the insurgents, they dropped the party's "Conservative" label and called themselves simply "Democrats." Mahoneism emerged once again as their central issue, and their platform indicted the little general at length. They placed surprisingly little emphasis on the color-line, apparently hoping to capture a significant fraction of the Negro vote. The newly christened Democrats blasted the governor's appointment of integrated school boards, but they pledged continued support for Negro education. Indeed, they indicated a

17. *Staunton* (Va.) *Vindicator,* June 8, 1883; *Woodstock Virginian,* June 1, 1883. See also the following in the Mahone Papers (Letterbooks): Mahone to R. H. Rawles, June 2, 1883; Mahone to C. B. Crumpler, June 3, 1883; and Mahone to James H. Guthrie, June 5, 1883.
18. W. H. Payne to J. Randolph Tucker, February 6, 1880, Tucker Papers.
19. *Antoni* v. *Greenhow,* 17 Otto (U.S.) 770–82 (1883).

willingness to experiment with a totally segregated administrative setup which would give the blacks almost complete control over their own schools. Crowning these efforts, moreover, the patricians established a more responsive party machine and centered control in the hands of an efficient railroad executive, Congressman John S. Barbour. This new Democratic boss reorganized the party down to the precinct level, with emphasis on vigorous young men for leadership positions. Amply financed with railroad money, the elite took the offensive once again.[20]

The Readjusters recognized the threat posed by the Lynchburg convention, particularly by its willingness to compromise on the debt issue. "Was there ever before," a Mahoneite judge fumed, "in all the annals of the human race, such an exhibition of self stultified and self confessed political scoundrelism?"[21] The insurgents attempted to counter the challenge by promising tax cuts, railroad regulation, and other producerite reforms. They also struggled to tighten their party organization—to little avail. Despondency pervaded the reports which flowed into Mahone's headquarters. In the eastern half of the state the friction between whites and blacks was acute, and the Funders were picking up "weak men" by the hundreds. In some Southside counties only a handful of whites remained in the party—generally men with little education or leadership ability. Funder bribes lured away the poor of both races, and the insurgents lacked the funds for an effective counterattack. In the predominantly white counties of the Valley and Southwest the Readjusters retained considerable strength, but even there the opposition made inroads with diatribes against boss rule and Republicanism. Surveying the situation, in fact, even such party stalwarts as Governor Cameron predicted defeat. Mahone continued to exude a forced optimism, but at times he appeared to be fighting almost alone.[22]

As the campaign entered the fall of 1883, therefore, a decisive Democratic victory appeared in the offing. Unfortunately and wholly

20. For a description of the Lynchburg meeting see the *Staunton* (Va.) *Vindicator,* August 3, 1883. See also Allen W. Moger, "The Origin of the Democratic Machine in Virginia," *Journal of Southern History* 8 (1942):187–88.

21. T. T. Fauntleroy to Mahone, July 28, 1883, Mahone Papers.

22. Dozens of letters in the Mahone Papers reflect the decay of the Readjuster machine. For examples see the following: William F. Jones to Mahone, July 24, September 5, 1883; Campbell Slemp to Mahone, September 3, 1883; and Henry F. Brooks to Mahone, October 29, 1883. See also William E. Cameron to Lewis E. Harvie, August 2, 1883, Lewis E. Harvie Papers, Virginia Historical Society, Richmond, Va.

unnecessarily, however, Virginia experienced a wave of politically engineered racial hysteria. Disappointed with the results of their appeals to the Negroes, the elite threw off the cloak of racial moderation and launched another full-fledged color-line attack. "The coming contest is to decide," one of their newspapers declared in a typical editorial, "whether we shall have in Virginia Radical rule, with the Negro holding the balance of power, or whether the white man shall rule. Side issues have no place in this fight." [23] John W. Daniel echoed this refrain. "I am a Democrat," the flexible patrician informed a cheering throng, "because I am a white man and a Virginian." [24] The usual charges of miscegenation, "mixed schools," and "social equality" also came into play. Attempting to buttress their case, moreover, the Democrats singled out Danville as a prime example of "black rule." In that Southside tobacco town the Negro Readjusters had captured the municipal government, and racial militancy was on the rise. Black policemen strolled through a city marketplace controlled by black merchants. Negroes no longer automatically yielded the sidewalk to whites, and there were reports of shoving and insolent language. [25] Late in the campaign a group of the town's Funder businessmen published the "Danville Circular," an appeal to the whites of the western counties for help against this "viper of *negroism.*" [26] Democratic newspapers throughout Virginia referred to the Danville situation with alarm, and the state gravitated into the hazardous realm of political violence.

Indeed, violence had always lurked beneath the surface of the debt revolt. It had found expression in the fierceness of campaign rhetoric, in the heckling of speakers, and, most dramatically, in duels and political brawls. By and large the heckling had been good-natured, however, and even the duels had generally been bloodless. Such roughhouse tactics paled by contrast with the Funders' efforts in 1883. Their speakers refused to share platforms with the Mahoneites and insisted, instead, on ostracizing them by "dividing the crowd." Democratic campaign workers visited the homes of "doubtful" whites, frightening the women and children with tales of "social equality." [27] Such activities aggravated an

23. *Fincastle* (Va.) *Herald,* August 30, 1883.

24. Quoted in Charles E. Wynes, *Race Relations in Virginia, 1870–1902* (Charlottesville: University of Virginia Press, 1961), p. 29.

25. Ibid., pp. 29–31; Charles C. Pearson, *The Readjuster Movement in Virginia* (New Haven: Yale University Press, 1917), pp. 163–64.

26. *Coalition Rule in Danville* (n.p., 1883), p. 4, pamphlet, Baugh Family Papers, Edwin A. Alderman Library, University of Virginia, Charlottesville, Va.

already tense racial situation, and the results became apparent in the streets of Danville a few days before the election. A shoving incident touched off a riot in which one white and four blacks were killed.[28] The Readjusters subsequently claimed that the Democrats had provoked the confrontation for political effect, but the evidence on this point is inconclusive. What is certain, however, is that the Democrats exploited the incident to the fullest. Within hours, their newspapers were turning out distorted accounts of the skirmish, and within two days horsemen were galloping into even the remotest hamlets with news of a "Mahoneite" racial war in the Southside.[29]

The ensuing turmoil resulted in a massive outpouring of Democratic voters throughout the state—an event made possible, ironically enough, by the Readjusters' repeal of the poll tax. The traditionalists swept to victory, capturing 44,000 more votes than they had in 1881. The insurgents also managed a 13,000 vote increase, primarily in the Negro counties, but they failed to offset the Democratic tidal wave. The patricians won over 53 percent of the vote, shifting the power balance definitively in their favor.[30] Their victory margin was still narrow, and the Readjuster-Republican coalition continued to threaten their hegemony for almost two decades. The elite maintained and expanded its edge, however, while the opposition progressively weakened. Gerrymanders, unfair election laws, and a white supremacy constitution eventually completed the work begun in 1883. Virginia became, by the turn of the century, a one-party state.

Evaluating the long-term impact of the debt struggle, historians have generally stressed the emergence of younger, more liberal leaders in the Democratic machine.[31] New faces did emerge in the hierarchy, of course. Of fifty-six Funders who served in the state legislature during the 1879–1880 session only nine remained in

27. For evidence of these tactics, see the following in the Mahone Papers: William E. Talley to Mahone, September 23, 1883; C. A. Heermans to Mahone, October 17, 1883; and M. F. Swann to Mahone, October 18, 1883.

28. U.S., Congress, Senate, Committee on Privileges and Election, *Report upon Danville, Va., Riot. November 3, 1883,* 48th Cong., 1st sess., 1884, Rept. 579, pp. xii–xiv, describes the origins of the riot.

29. J. M. McLaughlin to Mahone, November 4, 1883, and W. O. Wesson to Mahone, November 9, 1883–both in the Mahone Papers.

30. For election returns see the *Richmond Daily Dispatch,* January 16, 1884.

31. For examples of this approach see Pearson, *Readjuster Movement,* pp. 176–77; and William DuBose Sheldon, *Populism in the Old Dominion: Virginia Farm Politics, 1885–1900* (Princeton, N.J.: Princeton University Press, 1935), p. 53.

1883–1884.[32] Obviously there had been a marked turnover in personnel, although the continued importance of a good many of the old-line leaders indicated that the change was far from complete. As for the "liberalization" of these men, moreover, this argument requires severe qualifications. The Virginia Democrats' underlying commitments to elitist government, white supremacy, and economic orthodoxy endured well into the twentieth century. Instead the debt struggle retaught them the need to make concessions in order to head off potential revolts. Consequently they defused the Populists in the 1890s by championing "free silver"; they obliterated a vigorous independent movement in the early 1900s by adopting a moderately Progressive stand on the popular election of senators; later they followed the prevailing winds on such issues as Prohibition.[33] In the process they abandoned the "mossback" reactionism of the 1870s and became conservatives once again, bending with the tide to preserve the main patterns of their agricultural-mercantile order. The debt struggle taught them a hard lesson, but they learned it well.

32. Derived from lists in the *Warrock-Richardson Almanack, 1881*, pp. 29–30; and the *Warrock-Richardson Almanack, 1885*, pp. 28–29.
33. Allen W. Moger, *Virginia: Bourbonism to Byrd, 1870–1925* (Charlottesville: University Press of Virginia, 1968), pp. 106, 109, 157, 167, 206, 216–18, 304–8.

10

Epilogue: Reflections on Economic Growth

After the collapse of the debt revolt the insurgent leaders made peace with reality in various ways. Some of the more disillusioned lapsed into a crotchety and bitter reactionism. Shedding his Republican ties, for example, Governor Cameron sided with the conservative "gold" Democrats in 1896 and helped to draft Virginia's 1901 "white supremacy" constitution. Abram Fulkerson followed a similar pattern, abandoning his Greenbacker heritage and assuming a staunch "hard money" stand in the 1890s. John E. Massey made an even greater shift. Returning to the Democratic party, he was elected lieutenant governor in 1885 and state education superintendent in 1890. He used both offices as sounding boards for anti-Negro tirades. Others retreated from their liberalism in less dramatic ways. John F. Lewis retired to the quiet life of a country gentleman, while John S. Wise began a new career as a corporation lawyer in New York City. John Paul left politics in 1883 and served the rest of his life as a federal district judge. Plagued by alcoholism, Harrison H. Riddleberger died in 1890—less than a year after completing his term in the United States Senate. Only Mahone continued to battle for Republicanism in Virginia, and he suffered repeated defeats. A bitter and broken man, shunned by his Petersburg neighbors, he died in 1895.

The Readjusters' most important legislative venture—their debt settlement—also collapsed within a few years. The Democrats faithfully defended the Riddleberger Act after their 1883 triumph, but the bondholders continued to fight in the courts. With the exception of the *Antoni* v. *Greenhow* case, moreover, the federal judiciary uniformly supported their claims. In 1885 the Supreme

Court proved its bias by striking down the entire Readjuster settlement—Riddleberger Act, "coupon-killers," and all.[1] Responding
to this pressure, Virginia's patricians attempted once again to work
out a compromise. In 1892 they accepted responsibility for a larger
share of the antebellum debt and agreed to pay interest for a century
instead of the fifty years required by the Riddleberger plan.[2] This
satisfied the creditors, and the protracted litigation drew to a close.

These developments marked the end of one of the most eventful
periods in Virginia's history. Abandoning the solid South, for a
time at least, the state had experienced real two-party competition.
Old political ties had dissolved; Negroes had held the balance of
power; producerite reforms had battered the traditionalist hierarchy.
In a broader sense, furthermore, the Commonwealth had become
a testing ground for two divergent theories of economic growth.
Shattered by wartime defeat, Virginians all across the political
spectrum wished to regain their prosperity and prestige. They
quarreled, nevertheless, over how to achieve the tantalizing New
South vision. The debt struggle brought these disagreements to
the surface in a particularly graphic way.

Representing the conservative classes, rural as well as urban,
the Funders adopted a cautious approach to the problems of economic development. They conceived of growth as a gradual process,
a natural evolution from the old agricultural-mercantile order. The
traditional values would remain undisturbed; the patrician elite
would continue to dominate; the only real change would be a
rise in the volume of commerce and wealth. The new society would
differ from the old in degree rather than kind. The Readjusters,
on the other hand, assumed a more radical stance. Rallying the
disaffected elements—the yeomen, the blacks, the new middle
class—they insisted that economic expansion would require a sharp
break with the old regime. Consequently they abandoned their
old political ties and aligned themselves with the Republican capitalists of the North. Drawing on their producerite heritage, moreover,
they emphasized the importance of mass schooling, racial cooperation, and political democracy in the growth process. Laissez-faire
shibboleths fell by the wayside. "We need that freedom of thought,
political action and honest enterprise," Mahone declared, "which

1. *Poindexter* v. *Greenhow*, 29 L. ed. 193 (1885); see also *McGahey* v. *Virginia*,
34 L. ed. 306 (1890).
2. Virginia, General Assembly, *Acts and Joint Resolutions*, 1891–92, pp. 533–42.

will invite capital and inspire industry." [3] For the insurgents, therefore, reform took precedence over stability.

The split on this issue cut to the very heart of the debt struggle. Which of the factions offered the best formula for growth? Practical experience offered strong support for the Readjuster point of view. During the 1870s, the Funder heyday, Virginia was economically stagnant. A few urban areas prospered, but property values in most of the counties actually declined.[4] Under the insurgents, by way of contrast, the state enjoyed a commercial boom. Tobacco prices and production leaped upward in the years from 1880 to 1885, while the value of Virginia's exports rose by almost 22 percent. Iron manufacturing, another vital index, grew fivefold during the same period. Railroad mileage expanded rapidly, moreover, and the seaports bustled with trade. Richmond merchants reported the best sales in their history.[5] These developments should not be attributed entirely to the Readjuster program, of course. The national economy also skyrocketed in the early 1880s, and the state's progress largely mirrored this upward curve of the business cycle. Still, it does not seem unreasonable to assume that the insurgents' tax cuts and liberal expenditures accelerated the local expansion. The Readjusters certainly claimed full credit for the boom. "With her face to the sunset in 1879," Mahone proclaimed, "Virginia has now turned her face to the morning, and all her population is rejoicing at the new and happy direction her eyes and feet have taken." [6]

Modern theories on economic growth also tend to support the Readjuster program. Analyzing the problems of underdeveloped countries, social scientists generally agree that industrialization requires a radical break with outmoded values and beliefs. They emphasize far-reaching reforms, particularly to eradicate traditional lines of class and caste. "In short," John Kenneth Galbraith argues,

3. Mahone to A. L. Kelly, September 8, 1882, William Mahone Papers (Letterbooks), William R. Perkins Library, Duke University, Durham, N.C.

4. Virginia, Auditor of Public Accounts, *Annual Report,* 1879–80, Document 20, pp. 3–5.

5. For evidence of Virginia's economic growth see John D. Imboden, "Virginia," in U.S., Treasury Department, Bureau of Statistics, *Report on the Internal Commerce of the United States: The Commercial, Industrial, Transportation, and Other Interests of the Southern States,* 1886, Document 8926, pp. 71, 114, 120–21, 124, 128, 157.

6. William Mahone, *Address of the Readjuster State Executive Committee* (Petersburg: n.p., 1883), pp. 13–14, pamphlet, Virginiana Collection, Edwin A. Alderman Library, University of Virginia, Charlottesville, Va.

"on even the most preliminary view of the problem, effective government, education, and social justice emerge as crucially important." [7]
Other prominent scholars, such as Walter W. Rostow and Robert
Heilbroner, offer similar appraisals. They stress, above all, the need
to create an educated, healthy, and energetic population—capable
of exploiting local resources and investments from abroad.[8] Judged
by these standards, the insurgent program was clearly superior;
it conformed almost perfectly, in fact, to the prescriptions of the
growth theorists.

Observing the developing nations, moreover, twentieth-century
analysts have noted another phenomenon which has relevance for
post-Civil War Virginia. They maintain that the growth process
frequently involves a two-stage transition in political leadership.
During the initial phase (generally following military defeat by
a more advanced country) members of the old ruling class attempt
to modernize their own regime. These reforms are generally of
a limited and defensive character. After this cautious beginning,
however the entire traditional structure starts to crumble. Disaffec-
tion crops up at every hand, particularly among ambitious bureau-
crats and intellectuals. These rebels eventually topple the old order
and launch the second phase of the modernization process, making
the radical changes necessary for real growth. Such countries as
Russia, China, and Turkey provide classic examples of this pattern.[9]

For twenty years after the Civil War Virginia moved down a
very similar road. Shattered by military defeat, the patricians
half-heartedly took up the New South creed. They even accepted
such reforms as Negro suffrage and mass schooling. Their elitism
persisted, however, and during the 1870s their hidebound policies

7. John Kenneth Galbraith, *Economic Development in Perspective* (Cambridge:
Harvard University Press, 1962), pp. 9–10.

8. W. W. Rostow, *The Stages of Economic Growth: A Non-Communist Manifesto*
(Cambridge: Cambridge University Press, 1960), pp. 30–31; Robert L. Heilbroner,
The Making of Economic Society (Englewood Cliffs, N.J.: Prentice-Hall, 1962),
pp. 209, 216. See also Simon Kuznets, *Toward a Theory of Economic Growth:
With Reflections on the Economic Growth of Modern Nations* (New York: W.
W. Norton & Co., 1968), pp. 38, 99–100; Paul Alpert, *Economic Development: Objectives
and Methods* (London: Collier-Macmillan, 1964), pp. 104–5, 300; Nicholas Kaldor,
Strategic Factors in Economic Development (Ithaca, N.Y.: Cornell University, 1967),
pp. 56–59; and Lauchlin Currie, *Obstacles to Development* (East Lansing: Michigan
State University Press, 1967), p. 66.

9. C. E. Black, *The Dynamics of Modernization: A Study in Comparative History*
(New York: Harper & Row, 1967), pp. 64–65, 120–21; Rostow, *Stages of Growth*,
pp. 30, 58.

alienated thousands. Exploiting this unrest, the aggressive "new men" of the Readjuster coalition swept into power. Reforms proliferated, and the state soon regained its prosperity. During the 1880s, on the other hand, this modernization drive began to break down. The mass of white voters relapsed into their normal conservatism, obliterating the insurgent regime. This reactionary trend short-circuited the whole process of political and economic change. Consequently Virginia drifted back to the tragic "Redeemer" limbo, suspended between the lost antebellum world and the industrial promise of the future.

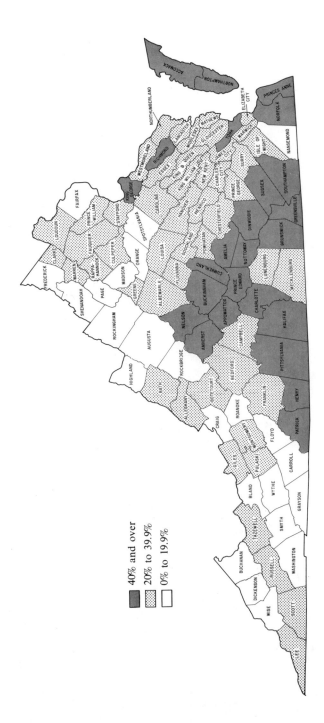

MAP 1. Sharecropping and Tenant Farming in Virginia, 1880

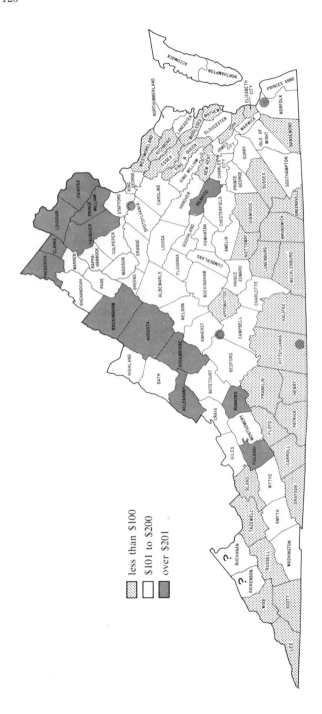

MAP 2.   Per Capita Property Valuations, 1880

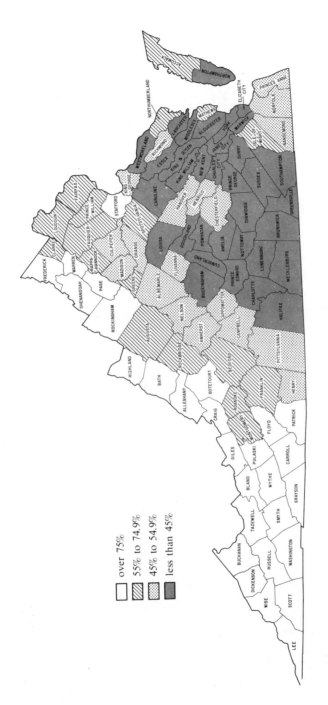

MAP 3. White Population of Virginia Counties, 1880

- over 75%
- 55% to 74.9%
- 45% to 54.9%
- less than 45%

128

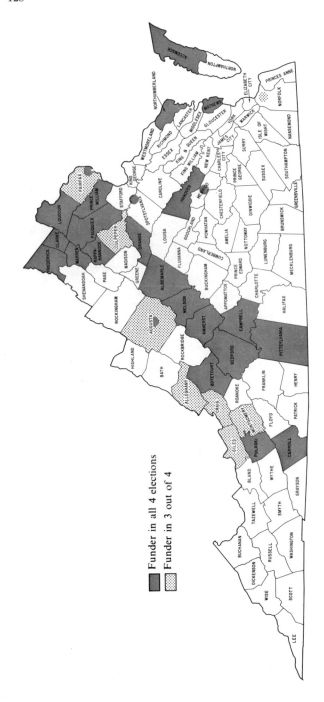

MAP 4. Funder Majorities in Virginia Counties, 1879–1883

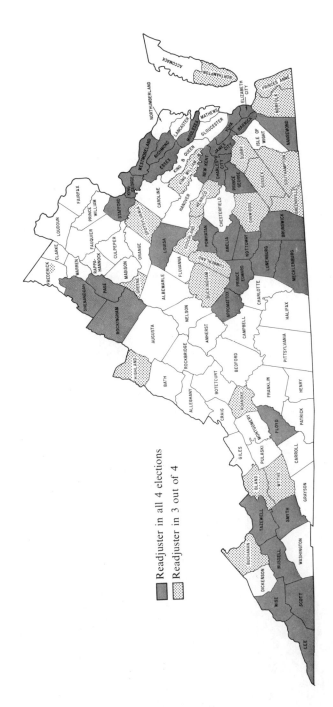

MAP 5. Readjuster Majorities in Virginia Counties, 1879–1883

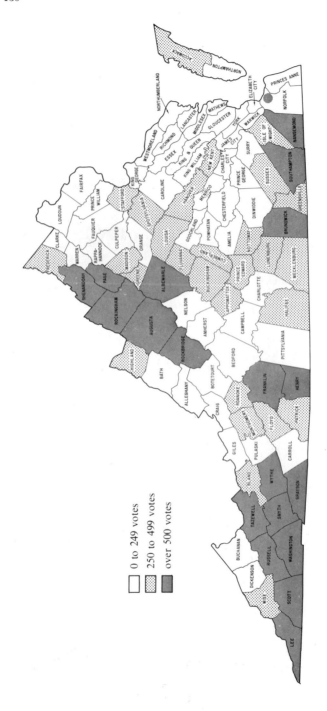

MAP 6. Distribution of White Readjuster Voters in 1880

☐ 0 to 249 votes

▨ 250 to 499 votes

■ over 500 votes

APPENDIX A

Biographical Information
on Prominent Funders,
1879–1883

ALLEN, HENRY CLAY: born 1838 in Botetourt County; educated at the University of Virginia; lawyer; Confederate veteran; Virginia House of Delegates, 1875–1879 (Speaker, 1877–1879); moderate Readjuster who joined the Funders in support of the McCulloch Act; unsuccessful Democratic candidate for the United States Congress in 1880.[1]

ANDERSON, FRANCIS T.: b. 1808 in Botetourt Co.; ed. at Washington College; lawyer, farmer, with iron interests; justice of the Virginia Supreme Court of Appeals, 1870–1882; replaced by a Readjuster judge in the latter year.[2]

ANDERSON, WILLIAM ALEXANDER: b. 1824; ed. at Washington College and U. Va. law school; Confederate veteran; Lexington lawyer; Va. Senate, 1869–1873; Va. House, 1883–1884.[3]

BAGBY, GEORGE WILLIAM: b. 1828 in Buckingham Co.; ed. at Delaware College and studied medicine at the University of Pennsylvania; doctor, journalist, humorist; appointed assistant secretary of the Commonwealth in 1870; custodian of the State Library, 1870–1878.[4]

BARBOUR, JAMES: b. 1823; resident of Culpeper; member of the 1850–1851 constitutional convention and a Secessionist in 1861; an "original" Readjuster (author of the "Barbour" Bill) who joined the debt-payers in 1880; Funder nominee for lieutenant governor in 1881.[5]

BARBOUR, JOHN S.: b. 1820 in Culpeper Co.; ed. at U. Va. law school; lawyer and railroad executive; Va. House, 1847–1851; U.S. House of

1. E. Griffith Dodson, *Speakers and Clerks of the Virginia House of Delegates, 1776–1955* (Richmond: n.p., 1956), p. 95.
2. Lyon Gardiner Tyler, *Encyclopedia of Virginia Biography,* 5 vols. (New York: Lewis Historical Publishing Co., 1915), 3:20.
3. Lois Grier Moore, "William Alexander Anderson: Attorney General of Virginia, 1902–1910" (M.A. thesis, University of Virginia, 1959), pp. 1–29.
4. Joseph Leonard King, Jr., *Dr. George William Bagby: A Study of Virginian Literature, 1850–1880* (New York: Columbia University Press, 1927).
5. *Staunton Vindicator,* August 12, 1881.

Representatives, 1880–1886; chairman of the Democratic organization during the 1883 campaign.[6]

BIGGER, JOHN BELL: b. 1829 in Prince Edward Co.; clerk in the U.S. Navy; Confederate veteran; clerk of Va. House, 1865–1879, 1883–1899.[7]

BOCOCK, THOMAS S.: b. 1815 in Appomattox Co.; ed. at Hampden-Sidney College; lawyer; U.S. House, 1847–1861; Confederate congressman; Va. House, 1869–1870; delegate to Democratic national conventions in 1868, 1876, and 1880; member of Funder U. Va. Board of Visitors deposed in 1882.[8]

BURKS, EDWARD C.: b. 1821 in Bedford Co.; ed. at Washington College and U. Va. law school; Justice on the Va. Supreme Court of Appeals, 1876–1882; replaced by a Readjuster in 1882.[9]

CABELL, GEORGE C.: b. 1836 in Danville; ed. at U. Va. law school; lawyer, editor; Confederate colonel; U.S. House, 1875–1886.[10]

CARDWELL, RICHARD HENRY: b. 1846 in North Carolina; farmer, Richmond lawyer; Confederate veteran; Va. House, 1881–1894.[11]

CHAMBERLAYNE, JOHN HAMPDEN: b. in Richmond; ed. at U. Va.; editor of the *Richmond State;* Confederate captain; Va. House, 1879–1881.[12]

CHRISTIAN, JOSEPH: b. 1828 in Middlesex Co.; ed. at Columbian College; lawyer; elected to Va. Senate, 1858; elected circuit judge in 1866; judge of Va. Supreme Court of Appeals, 1870–1882; replaced by a Readjuster.[13]

CONRAD, HOLMES: b. 1840 in Winchester; ed. at U. Va.; Winchester lawyer; Confederate major; U. Va. Board of Visitors; Va. House, 1881–1882.[14]

COOKE, JOHN ESTEN: b. 1830 in Winchester; lawyer, novelist, historian; Confederate major; educated in private schools.[15]

CURRY, JABEZ L. M.: b. 1825 in Georgia; ed. at University of Ga. and Harvard law school; member of Alabama House, 1847; U.S. House, 1858–1860; Confederate Congress; Confederate lieutenant colonel; college president, Baptist preacher, professor at Richmond College, 1868–1880.[16]

DABNEY, ROBERT LEWIS: b. 1820 in Louisa Co.; ed. at Hampden-Sidney

6. U.S., Congress, House, *Biographical Directory of the American Congress, 1775–1961,* 85th Cong., 2d sess., 1961, House Document 442, p. 514.

7. Dodson, *Speakers and Clerks,* p. 89.

8. Tyler, *Virginia Biography,* 3:38.

9. Ibid., p. 21.

10. *Directory of Congress,* p. 644.

11. Dodson, *Speakers and Clerks,* p. 105.

12. Paul Brandon Barringer, James Mercer Garnett, and Rosewell Page, *University of Virginia: Its History, Influence, Equipment and Characteristics, with Biographical Sketches and Portraits of Founders, Benefactors, Officers and Alumni,* 2 vols. (New York: Lewis Publishing Co., 1904), 1:400–401.

13. Tyler, *Virginia Biography,* 3:19.

14. Ibid., p. 244.

15. John O. Beaty, *John Esten Cooke, Virginian* (New York: Columbia University Press, 1922).

16. Jessie Pearl Rice, *J.L.M. Curry: Southerner, Statesman and Educator* (New York: King's Crown Press, 1949).

College, U. Va., and Union Theological Seminary; preacher and professor at the Union Theological Seminary of Virginia until 1883.[17]

DANIEL, JOHN WARWICK: b. 1842 in Lynchburg; ed. at Lynchburg College and U. Va. law school; Lynchburg lawyer; Va. House, 1869–1871; Va. Senate, 1875–1883; Democratic gubernatorial candidate in 1881.[18]

DAVIS, WILEY T.: a "master mechanic" in Richmond; Va. House, 1881–1882.[19]

DUKE, RICHARD THOMAS WALKER: b. 1822 in Albemarle Co.; ed. at V.M.I. and U. Va. law school; Confederate colonel; Albemarle common-wealth's attorney, 1858–1869; U.S. House, 1870–1874; Va. House, 1879–1880.[20]

DUNLOP, JAMES NATHANIEL: b. 1844 in Richmond; ed. at U. Va.; lawyer; Confederate veteran; Va. House, 1883–1887.[21]

FIELD, JAMES G.: b. 1826 in Culpeper Co.; schoolteacher, lawyer, farmer; Confederate major; Va. attorney gen., 1877–1881.[22]

FLOURNOY, H. W.: b. 1846 in Halifax Co.; ed. in private schools; lawyer, judge; Confederate veteran; elected secretary of the Commonwealth by the Democratic legislature in 1883.[23]

GARRISON, GEORGE T.: b. 1835 in Accomack Co.; ed. at Dickenson College and U. Va. law school; lawyer, farmer, and judge; Confederate veteran; Va. House, 1861–1863; Va. Senate, 1863–1865; U.S. House, 1881–1885.[24]

GOODE, JOHN, JR.: b. 1829 in Bedford Co.; ed. at Emory and Henry College; Norfolk lawyer; Confederate congressman; U.S. House, 1874–1880; U. Va. Board of Visitors.[25]

HANGER, JAMES MARSHALL: b. 1833 in Augusta Co.; ed. at U. Va. law school; Confederate colonel; Va. House, 1869–1883 (Speaker, 1871–1877).[26]

HARRIS, JOHN T.: b. 1823 in Albemarle Co.; Harrisonburg lawyer; member of the U.S. House, 1859–1861, 1871–1881.[27]

HOLLIDAY, FREDERICK W. M.: b. 1828 in Winchester; ed. at Yale and U. Va. law school; Winchester lawyer; Confederate colonel and congressman; governor, 1878–1882.[28]

17. Tyler, *Virginia Biography,* 3:143.
18. Richard B. Doss, "John Warwick Daniel: A Study in the Virginia Democracy" (Ph.D. diss., University of Virginia, 1955).
19. *Richmond State,* September 9, 1881.
20. *Directory of Congress,* p. 833.
21. Tyler, *Virginia Biography,* 3:249.
22. John Hammond Moore, "The Life of James Gaven Field, Virginia Populist, 1826–1902" (M.A. thesis, University of Virginia, 1953).
23. Tyler, *Virginia Biography,* 3:264.
24. *Directory of Congress,* p. 932.
25. Tyler, *Virginia Biography,* 3:40.
26. Dodson, *Speakers and Clerks,* p. 93.
27. Tyler, *Virginia Biography,* 3:119.

HOPE, JAMES BARRON: b. 1829; ed. at William and Mary College; served in U.S. Navy; lawyer, poet, editor of *Norfolk Landmark.*[29]

HUNTER, ROBERT M. T.: b. 1809 in Essex Co.; ed. at U. Va. and Winchester law school; lawyer, U.S. congressman and senator; Confederate senator and secretary of state; Va. state treasurer, 1877–1880.[30]

HURT, JOHN LINN: b. 1837 in Tennessee; ed. in private schools, studied law; court clerk, farmer; Confederate veteran; Va. Senate, 1876–1894.[31]

JOHNSTON, JOHN W.: b. 1818 near Abingdon; ed. at South Carolina College and U. Va. law school; Tazewell lawyer; Va. Senate, 1846–1848; circuit judge, 1866–1870; U.S. senator, 1870–1883.[32]

JONES, WILLIAM ATKINSON: b. 1849 in Richmond Co.; ed. at V.M.I. and U. Va. law school; lawyer in Richmond Co. and editor of the *Warsaw Northern Neck News;* commonwealth's atty., 1873–1883; alternate at the Democratic national convention in 1880.[33]

KEEZELL, GEORGE B.: b. 1854 in Rockingham Co.; farmer; Va. Senate, 1883–1887, 1895–1910.[34]

KEILEY, ANTHONY M.: b. 1835 in New Jersey; ed. at Randolph-Macon College; editor of Norfolk, Petersburg, and Richmond newspapers; lawyer; mayor of Richmond; Va. House, 1869; Richmond city atty., 1875–1885; chairman of Va. Democratic State Committee in 1881.[35]

KEMPER, JAMES LAWSON: b. 1823 in Madison Co.; ed. at Washington College; teacher, lawyer, involved in various promotional ventures; elected to Va. House in 1853 and served five terms; Confederate major general; governor, 1873–1877.[36]

KOINER, ABSALOM: b. 1824 in Augusta Co.; ed. at U. Va. law school; Staunton lawyer; Confederate colonel; Va. House, 1874–1875; Va. Senate, 1877–1888.[37]

LEE, FITZHUGH: b. 1835 in Fairfax Co.; ed. at West Point; farmer; Confederate major general; member of Funder Board of Visitors at Va. A. & M. College; considered for Funder gubernatorial nomination in 1881; governor, 1886–1890.[38]

---

28. Julian P. Porter, Jr., "Frederick William Mackey Holliday, Governor of Virginia, 1878–1881" (M.A. thesis, University of Virginia, 1969).

29. Janey Hope Marr, ed., *A Wreath of Virginia Bay Leaves: Poems of James Barron Hope* (Richmond: West, Johnson, & Co., 1895), pp. 5–7.

30. Barringer, Page, and Garnett, *University of Virginia,* 1:331–32.

31. Tyler, *Virginia Biography,* 3:237.

32. *Directory of Congress,* p. 1132.

33. Harold Gordon Wheatley, "The Political Career of William Atkinson Jones" (M.A. thesis, University of Virginia, 1953), pp. 2–10.

34. Tyler, *Virginia Biography,* 3:356.

35. James H. Bailey, "Anthony M. Keiley and 'the Keiley Incident,'" *Virginia Magazine of History and Biography* 67 (1959):65–81.

36. Robert R. Jones, "Conservative Virginian: The Post-war Career of Governor James Lawson Kemper" (Ph.D. diss., University of Virginia, 1964).

37. Tyler, *Virginia Biography,* 3:151.

38. Ibid., p. 7.

LOGAN, THOMAS M.: b. 1840 in South Carolina; ed. at South Carolina College; Richmond lawyer and railroad executive; Confederate brigadier general; chairman of Funder State Executive Committee in 1879.[39]

LOVENSTEIN, WILLIAM: b. 1840 in Henrico Co.; Confederate veteran; Va. House, 1869–1877, 1879–1880; Va. Senate, 1881–1896.[40]

LYONS, JAMES: Richmond lawyer; Va. House, 1879–1883.[41]

MARYE, MORTON: b. in Fredericksburg; lawyer; Confederate veteran; elected state auditor by Democrats in 1883.[42]

McKINNEY, PHILIP WATKINS: b. 1832 in Buckingham Co.; ed. at Hampden-Sidney College and Washington College (law); lawyer; Confederate captain; comm. atty. for Pr. Edward; Va. House, 1858–1865; Funder candidate for atty. gen., 1881.[43]

MOFFETT, WILLIAM WALTER: b. 1854; Rappahannock Co. lawyer and editor of the *Blue Ridge Echo,* 1878–1885; member, Democratic State Comm., 1883.[44]

MOON, JOHN B.: b. 1849 in Albemarle Co.; ed. at Washington College; Charlottesville lawyer; Va. House, 1881–1885.[45]

MUNFORD, BEVERLEY B.: b. 1856 in Richmond; ed. at William and Mary College and U. Va. law school; lawyer; Va. House, 1881–1887.[46]

O'FERRALL, CHARLES T.: b. 1840 in Frederick Co.; ed. at Washington College (law); lawyer, judge; Confederate colonel; won a contested election case and elected to U.S. House in 1882.[47]

PAGE, THOMAS NELSON: b. 1853 in Hanover Co.; ed. at Washington College and U. Va. law school; teacher, lawyer, writer; arch-Funder.[48]

POLLARD, HENRY R.: b. 1845 in King and Queen Co.; ed. at Columbian College (law); lawyer; Confederate veteran; Va. House, 1881–1888.[49]

ROYALL, WILLIAM L.: b. 1844 in Fauquier Co.; lawyer and editor of the *Richmond Commonwealth;* Confederate veteran.[50]

RUFFNER, WILLIAM HENRY: b. 1824 in Lexington; ed. at Washington

39. Ibid., p. 71.
40. George Wesley Rogers, *Officers of the Senate of Virginia, 1776–1956* (Richmond: n.p., 1959), p. 102.
41. *Richmond State,* September 9, 1881.
42. Tyler, *Virginia Biography,* 3:213.
43. Bernice Bryant Zuckerman, "Philip Watkins McKinney, Governor of Virginia, 1890–1894" (M.A. thesis, University of Virginia, 1967), pp. 1–12.
44. Tyler, *Virginia Biography,* 3:357.
45. Ibid., p. 325.
46. Beverley B. Munford, *Random Recollections* (n.p., 1905).
47. Charles T. O'Ferrall, *Forty Years of Active Service* (New York: Neale Publishing Co., 1904).
48. Harriet R. Holman, "The Literary Career of Thomas Nelson Page, 1884–1910" (Ph.D. diss., Duke University, 1947).
49. Henry Robinson Pollard, *Memoirs and Sketches of the Life of Henry Robinson Pollard: An Autobiography* (Richmond: Lewis Publishing Co., 1923).
50. William L. Royall, *Some Reminiscences* (New York: Neale Publishing Co., 1909).

College, U. Va., Union Theological Seminary, and Princeton Theological Seminary; U. Va. chaplain, farmer, preacher; appointed state superintendent of public instruction, 1870; replaced by a Readjuster, 1882.[51]

RYAN, JOHN FRANKLIN: b. 1848 in Dranesville, Va.; Loudoun Co. farmer and financier; Va. House, 1883–1906.[52]

SCOTT, ROBERT TAYLOR: b. 1834 in Fauquier Co.; ed. at U. Va.; lawyer; Confederate officer; Va. House, 1881–1883.[53]

SMITH, FRANCIS LEE: b. 1845 in Alexandria; ed. at V.M.I.; railroad lawyer, bank director; Confederate veteran; V.M.I. Board of Visitors; Va. Senate, 1879–1883.[54]

SPOTSWOOD, M. L.: Richmond lawyer; Va. House, 1881–1883.[55]

STUART, ALEXANDER H. H.: b. 1807 in Staunton; ed. at William and Mary and the U. Va. law school; lawyer in Staunton; Va. House, 1835–1839; U.S. House, 1841–1843; U.S. secy. of the interior under Fillmore; Va. Senate, 1857–1861, and again after the war, resigning in 1877; U. Va. Board of Visitors, 1876–1882; replaced by a Readjuster in 1882.[56]

STUART, CHARLES EDWARD: b. 1850 in King George Co.; lawyer; Va. House, 1881–1887.[57]

STUBBS, JAMES NEW: b. 1839 in Gloucester Co.; ed. at William and Mary College; lawyer; Confederate major; Va. House, 1869–1871, 1881–1882.[58]

TUCKER, JOHN RANDOLPH: b. 1823 in Winchester; ed. at U. Va.; Winchester lawyer; Va. atty. gen., 1857–1865; law professor at Washington and Lee; U.S. House, 1874–1887.[59]

TYLER, JAMES HOGE: b. 1846 in Caroline Co.; ed. in private schools, studied law; farmer in Pulaski Co.; Confederate veteran; Va. Senate, 1877–1879; defeated for reelection by a Readjuster.[60]

WALKER, JAMES A.: b. 1832 in Augusta Co.; ed. at V.M.I. and U. Va. law school; lawyer in Pulaski Co.; Confederate brigadier general; Va. House, 1871–1872; Va. lieutenant governor, 1877–1881.[61]

WHITTLE, STAFFORD GORHAM: b. 1849 in Mecklenburg Co.; ed. at Washington College and U. Va. law school; justice on Va. Supreme Court of Appeals, 1881–1882; defeated for reelection by a Readjuster.[62]

51. C. Chilton Pearson, "William Henry Ruffner: Reconstruction Statesman of Virginia," *South Atlantic Quarterly* 20 (1921):25–32, 137–51.

52. Dodson, *Speakers and Clerks,* p. 107.

53. Tyler, *Virginia Biography,* 3:186.

54. Ibid., pp. 268–69.

55. *Richmond State,* September 9, 1881.

56. Alexander F. Robertson, *Alexander Hugh Holmes Stuart, 1807–1891: A Biography* (Richmond: William Byrd Press, 1925).

57. Dodson, *Speakers and Clerks,* p. 103.

58. Tyler, *Virginia Biography,* 3:238.

59. *Directory of Congress,* p. 1731.

60. Rogers, *Officers of the Senate,* p. 61.

61. Ibid., p. 57.

62. Tyler, *Virginia Biography,* 3:26.

WICKHAM, HENRY T.: b. 1849 in Hanover Co.; ed. at Washington College and U. Va. law school; railroad lawyer; Va. House, 1879–1881; Va. Senate, 1882–1896.[63]

WICKHAM, WILLIAMS C.: b. 1820 in Richmond; ed. at U. Va. law school; farmer and railroad president; Confederate brigadier general; leader of "Straight-out" (Funder) Republicans.[64]

WISE, GEORGE D.: b. Accomack Co. in 1831; ed. at Indiana University and William and Mary College; Richmond lawyer; Confederate captain; U.S. House, 1881–1888.[65]

WITHERS, ROBERT ENOCH: b. 1821 in Campbell Co.; ed. at U. Va. (medicine); doctor, newspaper editor; Confederate colonel; Va. lieutenant governor, 1873; U.S. senator, 1875–1881.[66]

WOODS, MICAJAH: b. 1844 in Albemarle Co.; ed. at U. Va.: Charlottesville lawyer; Confederate lieutenant; U. Va. Board of Visitors, 1872–1876; chairman of Albemarle Co. Democratic party; Charlottesville commonwealth's atty., 1870–1903.[67]

63. Ibid., p. 326.
64. Ibid., p. 45.
65. *Directory of Congress,* p. 1838.
66. Robert E. Withers, *Autobiography of an Octogenarian* (Roanoke, Va.: Stone Printing & Manufacturing Co. Press, 1907).
67. Barringer, Page, and Garnett, *University of Virginia,* 1:457.

Occupational Background of Prominent Funders (Democrats)

Name	Lawyer	Editor	Teacher	Farmer	Preacher	Trade or Mfg.	Other
Allen	X						
Anderson, F. T.	X			X		X	
Anderson, W. A.	X						
Bagby		X					M.D., Author
Barbour, Jas.	—	—	—	—	—	—	—
Barbour, John S.	X					X	
Bigger							Clerk
Bocock	X						
Burks	X						
Cabell	X	X					
Cardwell	X			X			
Chamberlayne		X					
Christian	X						
Conrad	X						
Cooke	X						Author
Curry	X		X		X		
Dabney			X		X		
Daniel	X						
Davis						X	
Duke	X						
Dunlop	X						
Field	X		X	X			
Flournoy	X						
Garrison	X			X			
Goode	X						
Hanger	X						

Name	Lawyer	Editor	Teacher	Farmer	Preacher	Trade or Mfg.	Other
Harris	X						
Holliday	X						
Hope	X	X					Poet
Hunter	X						
Hurt	X			X			
Johnston	X						
Jones	X	X					
Keezell				X			
Keiley	X	X					
Kemper	X		X				
Koiner	X						
Lee				X			
Logan	X					X	
Lovenstein	–	–	–	–	–	–	–
Lyons	X						
Marye	X						
McKinney	X						
Moffett	X	X					
Moon	X						
Munford	X						
O'Ferrall	X						
Page	X		X				Author
Pollard	X						
Royall	X	X					
Ruffner				X	X		
Ryan				X		X	
Scott	X						
Smith	X					X	
Spotswood	X						
Stuart, A. H. H.	X						
Stuart, C. E.	X						
Stubbs	X						
Tucker	X		X				
Tyler	X			X			
Walker	X						
Whittle	X						
Wickham, H. T.	X					X	
Wickham, W. C.	X			X		X	
Wise	X						
Withers		X					Doctor
Woods	X						

APPENDIX C

Biographical Information on
Prominent Readjusters
(Coalitionists),
1879–1883

AKERS, WILLIAM T.: born 1838 in Patrick County; Confederate veteran; Virginia House of Delegates, 1877–1881.[1]

ALLEN, S. BROWN: b. 1845 in Bath Co.; educated in private schools; farmer in Augusta Co.; Confederate veteran; state auditor of public accounts, 1882–1883.[2]

BAILEY, DAVID FLOURNOY: b. 1845 in Charlotte Co.; ed. at Cumberland University (Lebanon, Tenn.); editor, printer, Bristol lawyer; delegate to the first Readjuster state convention at Mozart Hall in Richmond in 1879; Va. House, 1879–1881; Va. Senate, 1882–1885.[3]

BLAIR, FRANK S.: b. 1838 in Tennessee; son of a Tennessee congressman; ed. Washington College, Emory and Henry College, and the University of Tennessee; teacher, farmer, and Wytheville lawyer; Confederate lieutenant colonel; prominent Greenbacker; temporary chairman, Mozart Hall convention, 1879; Va. attorney general, 1882–1886; Readjuster Board of Visitors, U. Va.[4]

BLAND, EDWARD D.: Negro; born a slave in Prince George Co., 1851; his father was a shoemaker and minister; attended night school in Petersburg after the war; shoemaker, teacher, lighthouse keeper, whiskey gauger; Va. House, 1879–1884.[5]

BLANTON, JAMES M.: medical doctor, editor of the *Portsmouth Times*

1. S. Bassett French Biographical Sketches, Archives Division, Virginia State Library, Richmond, Va. French, an influential Readjuster, compiled a collection of several hundred biographical sketches of contemporary Virginians. These have been cataloged and microfilmed.

2. Ibid.; *Richmond Daily Whig,* October 29, 1881.

3. T. W. Preston and C. Bascom Slemp, eds., *Addresses of Famous Southwest Virginians* (Bristol, Va.: King Printing Co., 1939), p. 343.

4. Ibid., p. 374; *Marion* (Va.) *Patriot and Herald,* June 16, 1881.

5. Luther P. Jackson, *Negro Office-Holders in Virginia, 1865–1895* (Norfolk: Guide Quality Press, 1945), p. 3.

and the *Virginia Granger;* master of the Va. Grange; state commissioner of agriculture, 1882-1883.[6]

BOARD, GREEN B.: Salem banker; described by the *Woodstock Virginian* as the second "wealthiest man" in the General Assembly; Va. House, 1881-1882.[7]

BOLLING, STITH: b. 1835 in Lunenburg Co.; ed. private schools; farmer, Richmond merchant; Confederate assistant adjutant general; Va. General Assembly, 1870-1871; appointed state tobacco inspector by Governor Kemper and served until 1880; Mozart Hall delegate, 1879; prominent Readjuster speaker; appointed Petersburg postmaster in the early 1880s.[8]

BOWDEN, GEORGE EDWIN: b. 1852 in James City Co.; ed. in private schools; studied law; banker; federal collector of customs in Norfolk, 1879-1885; influential in the affairs of the Coalition party in Norfolk; U.S. House, 1886-1890.[9]

BOWEN, HENRY: b. 1841 in Tazewell Co.; ed. Emory and Henry College; farmer, livestock grower; Confederate captain; Va. House, 1869-1873; U.S. House, 1883-1885.[10]

BRADY, JAMES D.: b. 1843 in Portsmouth; moved to New York City at the age of 12; mercantile pursuits; lieutenant colonel in the Union army; returned to Portsmouth after the war; served as clerk of the Portsmouth corporation court until 1877; federal collector of Internal Revenue in Petersburg, 1877-1884; close ally of William Mahone and influential in achieving the Readjuster-Republican "Coalition" in 1881; elected to U.S. House in 1884.[11]

BROKENBOROGH, JOHN M.: b. 1823 (approx.) in Richmond Co.; resident of Essex Co.; Confederate brigadier general; register of the state land office and superintendent of public buildings, 1880-1883.[12]

CAMERON, WILLIAM E.: b. 1842 in Petersburg; lived in Missouri for several years during his youth; ed. in private schools and Washington University (St. Louis); editor in Norfolk and Richmond; Confederate captain in Mahone's brigade; mayor of Petersburg; governor, 1882-1886.[13]

6. *Richmond Weekly Whig,* January 26, 1883; J. M. Blanton to W. C. Elam, July 17, 1880, William Mahone Papers, William R. Perkins Library, Duke University, Durham, N.C.

7. *Woodstock Virginian,* January 20, 1882; Board to Mahone, September 14, 1881, Mahone Papers.

8. R. A. Brock, *Virginia and Virginians, 1606-1883,* 2 vols. (Richmond: H. H. Hardesty, 1888), 2:637-38.

9. U.S., Congress, House, *Biographical Directory of the American Congress, 1775-1961,* 85th Cong., 2d sess., 1961, House Document 442, p. 578.

10. Ibid.

11. Ibid., p. 587.

12. *Richmond Daily Dispatch,* December 10, 1879.

13. Lenoir Chambers and Joseph E. Shank, *Salt Water and Printer's Ink: Norfolk and Its Newspapers, 1865-1965* (Chapel Hill: University of North Carolina Press, 1967), pp. 21-22; Charles C. Pearson, *The Readjuster Movement in Virginia* (New Haven: Yale University Press, 1917), p. 111.

CAUSEY, CHARLES HENRY: b. 1837 in Delaware; ed. at Union College (Pennsylvania) and U. Va. law school; college teacher, lawyer; Confederate captain; clerk of the Va. Senate, 1880–1882; resident of Nansemond Co.[14]

CLAIBORNE, THOMAS B.: farmer and federal revenue official; Republican Readjuster; elected county judge of Franklin in 1880.[15]

CONRAD, THOMAS N.: b. in Fairfax Co.; ed. in the North; English professor at the Virginia A. & M. College (Blacksburg); influential in Readjuster affairs in the Southwest; president of Va. A. & M. College, 1882–1886.[16]

CROSS, THOMAS HARDY: b. 1841 in Nansemond Co.; ed. at U. Va.; medical doctor, farmer, teacher; Confederate surgeon; Nansemond Co. resident; Va. House, 1879–1882; clerk to the state railroad commissioner, 1880–1884.[17]

DAVID, CEPHAS L.: Negro; born a slave in Mecklenburg Co., 1843; ed. at Richmond Theological Institute; Baptist minister, teacher; Va. Senate, 1879–1880.[18]

DICKENSON, WILLIAM J.: b. Russell Co.; ed. at U. Va.; Russell Co. lawyer; Mozart Hall convention delegate, 1879; Va. House, 1878–1884.[19]

DODSON, AMOS A.: Negro; b. a slave in Mecklenburg Co.; son of a blacksmith; farmer, newspaper editor, deputy collector for the federal Internal Revenue; Va. House, 1882–1884.[20]

DODSON, JOHN S.: Richmond hotel proprietor; unsuccessful Readjuster candidate for the Va. House from the city of Richmond in 1881.[21]

DUNGEE, SHED: Negro; b. free in Cumberland Co., 1831; apprenticed as a shoemaker; shoemaker, farmer, preacher; Va. House, 1879–1882.[22]

DYSON, HORACE H.: b. 1842 (approx.); federal revenue official; Nottoway Co. sheriff; Republican Readjuster; state second auditor, 1880–1883.[23]

ELAM, WILLIAM C.: b. 1836 in North Carolina; ed. in common schools; lawyer, editor of the *Richmond Whig;* Confederate veteran; "old-line Whig" and opponent of secession in antebellum years; secretary of the Commonwealth, 1882–1883.[24]

ELLIOTT, WYATT M.: b. 1823 in Campbell Co.; ed. at V.M.I.; studied law; teacher, associate editor of the *Richmond Whig;* Confederate lieutenant colonel; Va. House, 1871–1873; Va. Senate, 1875–1882; president *pro tempore* of the Senate, 1879–1882; U. Va. Board of Visitors.[25]

14. George Wesley Rogers, *Officers of the Senate of Virginia, 1776–1956* (Richmond: n.p., 1959), p. 131.
15. *Richmond Daily Dispatch,* January 22, 1880.
16. *Richmond Daily Whig,* January 21, 1882.
17. S. Bassett French Biographical Sketches.
18. Jackson, *Negro Office-Holders,* p. 10.
19. S. Bassett French Biographical Sketches.
20. Jackson, *Negro Office-Holders,* p. 12.
21. *Richmond Daily Whig,* October 29, 1881.
22. Jackson, *Negro Office-Holders,* p. 13.
23. *Richmond Daily Dispatch,* December 9, 10, 1879.
24. *Richmond Weekly Whig,* January 13, 1882.

FARR, RICHARD R.: b. Fairfax Co., 1845; Confederate veteran; ed. at Roanoke College; studied law; teacher, county sheriff, and held various other local offices; Va. House, 1877–1883; unsuccessful candidate for the U.S. House, 1882; state superintendent of public instruction, 1882–1886.[26]

FAUNTLEROY, THOMAS T.: b. 1823 in Winchester; ed. at U. Va. law school; Confederate colonel; Va. Senate, 1877–1879; secretary of the Commonwealth, 1880–1881; elected to the state Supreme Court of Appeals in 1882.[27]

FISHER, JOHN W.: commission merchant; unsuccessful Readjuster candidate for the Va. House from the city of Richmond in 1881.[28]

FLANAGAN, WILLIAM M.: lawyer in Powhatan Co.; unsuccessful Readjuster candidate for the Va. Senate in 1883.[29]

FORD, HENRY M.: b. 1850 (approx.); self-educated; lawyer in Henry Co.; native of Campbell Co.; judge of Henry Co., 1880–1882; elected circuit court judge in 1882.[30]

FOWLER, ISAAC CHAPMAN: b. 1831 in Tazewell Co.; ed. at Emory and Henry College; mercantile pursuits, editor of the *Bristol News,* proprietor of the Great Natural Bridge and Tunnel Co.; Confederate Commissary Dept.; mayor of Bristol; Mozart Hall delegate, 1879; Va. House, 1875–1879, 1881–1883 (Speaker, 1881–1883).[31]

FRAZIER, JAMES A.: b. in Rockbridge Co.; ed. at Washington College; owner of a vacation resort in Rockbridge; Va. House, 1877–1882; Mozart Hall delegate, 1879; unsuccessful congressional candidate, 1880.[32]

FRENCH, S. BASSETT: b. 1820 in Norfolk; ed. private schools; lawyer, newspaperman on the staffs of the *Richmond Enquirer* and the *Richmond Whig;* held minor public offices under Governors Wise and Letcher; private secretary for William Mahone; elected corporation court judge of Manchester in 1881.[33]

FULKERSON, ABRAM: b. Washington Co. in 1834; ed. at V.M.I.; teacher, lawyer in Bristol, associated with William Mahone in the A. M. & O. Railroad; Confederate colonel; Va. House, 1871–1873; Va. Senate, 1877–1879; Mozart Hall delegate, 1879; U.S. House, 1881–1883; broke with Mahone in 1882; defeated for reelection to the House by Henry Bowen.[34]

GAINES, WILLIAM EMBRE: b. Charlotte Co. in 1844; ed. in common

25. Rogers, *Officers of the Senate,* pp. 96–97.
26. S. Bassett French Biographical Sketches.
27. *Richmond Daily Dispatch,* December 10, 1879; *Richmond Weekly Whig,* March 3, 1882.
28. *Richmond Daily Whig,* October 29, 1881.
29. Flanagan to Mahone, September 28, 1883, Mahone Papers.
30. *Richmond Daily Whig,* March 1, 1882.
31. E. Griffith Dodson, *Speakers and Clerks of the Virginia House of Delegates, 1776–1955* (Richmond: n.p., 1956), p. 101.
32. S. Bassett French Biographical Sketches, Frazier to Mahone, September 16, 1879, Mahone Papers.
33. S. Bassett French Biographical Sketches.
34. *Directory of Congress,* p. 919.

schools; Confederate adjutant; lawyer, tobacco dealer, and banker in Burkeville; elected to the Va. Senate in 1883.[35]

GIDDINGS, WILLIAM F.: native of Ohio, moved to Va. in 1865; lawyer, farmer; Republican Readjuster, elected to Va. House from Chesterfield, 1881–1883.[36]

GILLIAM, S. Y.: b. 1849 in Dinwiddie Co.; farmer, merchant; local Readjuster spokesman; elected Dinwiddie Co. sheriff, 1883–1887.[37]

GILMER, GEORGE K.: moved to Va. from West Virginia after the war; associated with Mahone in the "True Republican" and Readjuster movements; owned a vineyard in Henrico Co.; Va. House, 1869–1871; Readjuster Republican who helped to achieve "coalition" in the 1881 campaign; appointed postmaster of Richmond in 1880.[38]

GODWIN, DAVID J.: b. 1835 (approx.) in Suffolk; lawyer in Norfolk and Portsmouth; ed. at Union College (New York); editor; Confederate colonel and congressman; Democratic elector in 1876 presidential election; delegate-at-large to the 1876 Democratic national convention; elected corporation court judge of Norfolk in 1881.[39]

GOSE, GEORGE C.: farmer in Russell Co.; elected to the Va. House in 1883.[40]

GREEN, ARMISTEAD: Negro; b. a slave in Petersburg, 1841; grocer, undertaker; Va. House, 1881–1884.[41]

GREEN, DUFF: b. 1833; Stafford Co. farmer; Mozart Hall delegate, 1879; Va. House, 1879–1884.[42]

GRIGGS, NATHANIEL M.: Negro; b. a slave in Farmville, 1857; ed. in night school; tobacco factory hand, federal revenue official; Va. House, 1883–1884.[43]

GRIM, AMOS K.: Page Co. farmer; Va. House, 1881–1882; elected to Va. Senate in 1883.[44]

GRONER, VIRGINIUS D.: b. 1836 in Norfolk; ed. at Norfolk Military Academy; captain and assistant adjutant general in the Confederate army (Mahone's brigade); president and general manager of a Norfolk steamship line; helped to secure the election of Governor Walker, but subsequently declined offers of state jobs from him; president of Norfolk city council; dissident Readjuster member, State Conservative Committee, 1880; de-

35. Ibid., p. 924.
36. *Richmond Southern Intelligencer,* August 30, 1880.
37. S. Bassett French Biographical Sketches.
38. Robert Maurice Ours, "Virginia's First Redeemer Legislature, 1869–1871" (M.A. thesis, University of Virginia, 1966), pp. 25–26, 176.
39. S. Bassett French Biographical Sketches; *Richmond Daily Whig,* April 8, 1882.
40. *Bristol* (Va.) *News,* October 23, 1883.
41. Jackson, *Negro Office-Holders,* p. 18.
42. S. Bassett French Biographical Sketches.
43. Jackson, *Negro Office-Holders,* p. 19.
44. *Woodstock Virginian,* August 31, November 2, 1883.

feated for Readjuster gubernatorial nomination in 1881; ardent supporter of Mahone.[45]

HAMILTON, ROSS: Negro; b. a slave in Mecklenburg Co.; carpenter, storekeeper; Va. House, 1869–1882.[46]

HANSBOROUGH, GEORGE W.: Salem lawyer; ed. at the U. Va. law school; appointed Reporter of the Supreme Court of Appeals, 1883; Board of Visitors, U. Va.[47]

HARRIS, A. W.: Negro; b. free in Fairfax Co., 1854; ed. in Alexandria public schools and Howard University law school; Petersburg lawyer; Va. House, 1881–1882.[48]

HARVIE, LEWIS E.: b. 1809 in Richmond; ed. at U. Va.; lawyer, farmer; member of secession convention; antebellum railroad president; president of the Virginia Agricultural Society; publisher of the *Richmond Enquirer;* independent member of the Va. House from Amelia, 1877–1879; Readjuster spokesman.[49]

HENLY, R. L.: ed. at Bellamy College; Williamsburg lawyer; Confederate colonel; county judge, 1870–1882; elected circuit court judge in 1882.[50]

HINTON, DRURY A.: b. 1840 (approx.); ed. at U. Va. law school; Confederate veteran; elected to the state Supreme Court of Appeals in 1882.[51]

HOOPER, BENJAMIN STEPHEN: b. 1835 in Buckingham Co.; ed. in common schools; engaged in mercantile pursuits and tobacco manufacturing; Confederate veteran; U.S. House, 1883–1885.[52]

HUBARD, EDMUND W., JR.: Readjuster lawyer; Buckingham Co. commonwealth's attorney; member of the Readjuster Board of Visitors at Va. A. & M. College; defeated for Va. Senate, 1883.[53]

JONES, A. W.: native Virginian; lawyer; participant in the "Bloody Kansas" struggle; Confederate officer; served in the New Jersey legislature for three years after the war; unsuccessful Coalition candidate for the Va. Senate from Hanover and Caroline in 1883.[54]

JONES, JOSEPH R.: Negro; storekeeper and postmaster in Mecklenburg Co.; Va. Senate, 1881–1883.[55]

JONES, PARIS V.: Craig Co. attorney and insurance agent; elected

45. Brock, *Virginia and Virginians,* 2:555; Lyon Gardiner Tyler, *Encyclopedia of Virginia Biography,* 5 vols. (New York: Lewis Historical Publishing Co., 1915), 3:330.
46. Jackson, *Negro Office-Holders,* p. 19.
47. *Richmond Weekly Whig,* January 26, 1883.
48. Jackson, *Negro Office-Holders,* p. 20.
49. S. Bassett French Biographical Sketches.
50. Henly to Mahone, December 2, 1881, Mahone Papers.
51. *Richmond Weekly Whig,* March 3, 1882.
52. *Directory of Congress,* p. 1073.
53. Hubard to Mahone, January 9, 1882, October 20, 1883, Mahone Papers.
54. *Richmond Weekly Whig,* August 10, 1883.
55. Jackson, *Negro Office-Holders,* p. 23.

county judge of Alleghany and Craig during the 1879–1880 legislative session.[56]

KILGORE, GEORGE W.: b. 1843 (approx.); lawyer; elected to the Va. House in 1883 from Wise, Dickinson, and Buchanan.[57]

LACY, BENJAMIN W.: b. 1839 in New Kent; son of a distinguished "old-line Whig" legislator; ed. at U. Va.; lawyer and jurist in New Kent Co.; Confederate lieutenant; Va. House, 1874–1881 (Speaker, 1879–1881); unsuccessful congressional candidate, 1880; elected circuit judge, 1880–1882; elected to the state Supreme Court of Appeals in 1882.[58]

LAMB, WILLIAM: b. 1835; son of a Norfolk mayor; newspaperman, commission merchant, involved in railroad development; ed. at William and Mary College; Confederate colonel; mayor of Norfolk; close associate of Mahone and influential in Readjuster affairs; appointed to the Readjuster Board of Visitors at U. Va. in 1882.[59]

LEE, JOHN A. I.: lawyer; elected judge of Craig Co. during the 1881–1882 legislative session.[60]

LEWIS, D. S.: b. 1843 in Rockingham Co.; son of John F. Lewis (see below); ed. at U. Va. law school; lawyer; held various minor federal offices during the 1870s; Republican Coalitionist; appointed U.S. district attorney for the western district of Virginia in 1882.[61]

LEWIS, JOHN FRANCIS: b. 1818 in Rockingham Co.; ed. in common schools; farmer; antebellum Whig; member of 1861 secession convention but refused to sign the ordinance; elected lieutenant governor in 1869 as a "True Republican"; U.S. Senate, 1870–1875; appointed U.S. marshal for the western district of Virginia by President Hayes, 1878–1882; elected lieutenant governor on the Readjuster Republican "Coalition" ticket in 1881.[62]

LEWIS, LUNSFORD L.: b. 1846 in Rockingham Co.; ed. at U. Va. law school; lawyer; U.S. district attorney for eastern Virginia during the 1870s; elected to the state Supreme Court of Appeals in 1882.[63]

LEWIS, NEVERSON: Negro; born a slave in Powhatan Co.; farmer; Va. House, 1879–1883.[64]

LIBBEY, HARRY: b. 1843 in New Hampshire; ed. in common schools; mercantile pursuits; moved to Hampton, Va., in 1863; justice in Elizabeth City Co. in 1869; elected to U.S. House in 1882.[65]

LYBROOK, A. M.: Patrick Co. lawyer; elected to the Va. Senate in

56. Jones to Mahone, November 14, 1879, Mahone Papers.
57. *Bristol* (Va.) *News,* October 23, 1883.
58. Dodson, *Speakers and Clerks,* p. 97.
59. Tyler, *Virginia Biography,* 3:187–88.
60. Lee to Mahone, August 21, 1883, Mahone Papers.
61. *Richmond Daily Whig,* March 22, 1882.
62. Rogers, *Officers of the Senate,* p. 52.
63. *Richmond Weekly Whig,* March 3, 1882.
64. Jackson, *Negro Office-Holders,* p. 25.
65. *Directory of Congress,* p. 1217.

1881; member of the "Big Four" faction of Senate Readjusters who broke with the party during the 1881–1882 legislative session.[66]

McCAULL, PATRICK H.: b. 1851 in Scotland; Va. House from Pulaski Co., 1875–1879; secretary of the Mozart Hall convention, 1879; clerk of the Va. House, 1879–1883.[67]

McLIN, JOHN B.: b. 1833 (approx.); farmer, merchant; elected to the Va. House from Lee Co. in 1883.[68]

McTEER, JAMES P.: Wytheville lawyer; Mozart Hall delegate, 1879; elected county judge of Wythe and Pulaski during the 1879–1880 legislative session.[69]

MAHONE, WILLIAM: b. 1826 in Southampton Co.; son of a tavern keeper; ed. at V.M.I.; teacher, civil engineer, railroad president; Confederate major general; Va. Senate, 1863–1865; unsuccessful candidate for Conservative gubernatorial nomination in 1877; Mozart Hall delegate, 1879; U.S. Senate, 1881–1887.[70]

MARTIN, GEORGE A.: b. 1833 in Norfolk Co.; ed. at U. Va.; lawyer in New York City after the war; returned to Norfolk; Confederate lieutenant colonel; Va. Senate, 1881–1882; elected railroad commissioner during the 1881–1882 legislative session.[71]

MASSEY, JOHN E.: b. 1819 in Spotsylvania Co.; his father was a small farmer and mechanic; ed. at Richmond College; artisan, teacher, lawyer, preacher, farmer; Va. House from Albemarle, 1873–1877; Va. Senate, 1877–1879; Mozart Hall delegate, 1879; state auditor of public accounts, 1879–1882; broke with the Readjusters in 1882 and made an unsuccessful race for Congress.[72]

MAUCK, ROBERT G.: farmer and bank receiver; elected to the Va. House from Page Co. in 1883.[73]

MAY, DAVID F.: b. 1835 in Petersburg; ed. at William & Mary College and studied medicine at Jefferson Medical College; Petersburg doctor and public health official; Va. House, 1879–1882; superintendent of the Central Lunatic Asylum, 1882–1883.[74]

MAYO, ROBERT MURPHY: b. 1836 in Westmoreland Co.; ed. at William & Mary College and V.M.I.; studied law at Lexington law school; college

66. Lybrook to Mahone, June 24, 1881, Mahone Papers.
67. Dodson, *Speakers and Clerks,* p. 99.
68. *Bristol* (Va.) *News,* October 23, 1883.
69. McTeer to Mahone, November 14, 1879, Mahone Papers.
70. Nelson M. Blake, *William Mahone of Virginia: Soldier and Political Insurgent* (Richmond: Garrett & Massie, 1935).
71. Paul Brandon Barringer, James Mercer Garnett, and Rosewell Page, *University of Virginia: Its History, Influence, Equipment and Characteristics, with Biographical Sketches and Portraits of Founders, Benefactors, Officers and Alumni,* 2 vols. (New York: Lewis Publishing Co., 1904), 1:403.
72. John E. Massey, *Autobiography of John E. Massey,* ed. Elizabeth H. Hancock (New York: Neale Publishing Co., 1909).
73. *Woodstock Virginian,* August 31, 1883.
74. S. Bassett French Biographical Sketches.

math teacher, lawyer; Confederate colonel; Va. House, 1881–1882; elected to the U.S. Congress in 1882 and served until his election was successfully contested by George T. Garrison in 1884.[75]

MEADE, C. C.: b. 1828 (approx.); farmer; elected to the Va. House from Scott Co. in 1883.[76]

MEADE, NATHANIEL B.: b. 1828 in Clarke Co.; lawyer, farmer, editor of a Winchester newspaper and of the *Richmond Whig,* 1873–1877; chairman of the state executive committee of the Conservative party, 1873–1877; mayor of Culpeper; Readjuster presidential elector, 1880; elected corporation court judge of Alexandria in 1882.[77]

MINETREE, JOSEPH P.: purchasing agent for the Norfolk and Western Railroad; nominated William E. Cameron for governor at the 1881 Readjuster convention; president of the Readjuster Board of Visitors at V.M.I., 1882–1884.[78]

NEWMAN, W. W.: b. 1825 in (West) Virginia; farmer; unsuccessful independent congressional candidate in 1878; Mozart Hall delegate, 1879; elected judge of Hanover Co. during the 1879–1880 legislative session.[79]

NORTON, DANIEL M.: Negro; born a slave in Williamsburg, 1840; escaped to the North in 1850s and studied medicine in New York; doctor; Va. Senate, 1871–1873, 1877–1883; member, Board of Visitors, Virginia Normal and Collegiate Institute.[80]

NORTON, ROBERT: Negro; born a slave in Williamsburg; D. M. Norton's brother; escaped to the North in the 1850s; farmer; Va. House, 1869–1883.[81]

OWENS, LITTLETON: Negro; born free in Princess Anne Co., 1842; owned a small farm; Union veteran; Va. House, 1879–1883.[82]

PAIGE, RICHARD G. L.: Negro; born a slave in Norfolk; trained as a machinist in Boston, Mass.; ed. at Howard University; lawyer in Norfolk Co.; Va. House, 1871–1875, 1879–1882.[83]

PATTON, JAMES T.: lawyer, farmer, editor; elected county judge of Rockbridge during 1879–1880 legislative session.[84]

PAUL, JOHN: b. 1839 in Rockingham Co.; ed. at Roanoke College and the U. Va. law school; Harrisonburg lawyer; Confederate captain; Rockingham Co. commonwealth's attorney, 1870–1877; Va. Senate, 1877–1880; unsuccessful congressional candidate in 1878; Mozart Hall delegate, 1879; elected to U.S. House in 1880; appointed to a federal judgeship in 1883.[85]

75. *Directory of Congress,* p. 1280.
76. *Bristol* (Va.) *News,* October 23, 1883.
77. S. Bassett French Biographical Sketches.
78. *Richmond Daily Whig,* February 21, 1882; *Staunton* (Va.) *Vindicator,* June 10, 1881.
79. S. Bassett French Biographical Sketches.
80. Jackson, *Negro Office-Holders,* p. 30.
81. Ibid.
82. Ibid., p. 32.
83. Ibid.
84. Letter from "JAYSEM" to the *Richmond Commonwealth,* February 9, 1880.
85. *Directory of Congress,* p. 1435.

PHILLIPS, GEORGE R.: b. 1836 (approx.); businessman, postmaster, deputy sheriff, school board member; nominated for railroad commissioner by the party caucus in 1879 but declined when his character was impugned by the Funders.[86]

PHOEBUS, HARRISON: born in Maryland in 1840; only two years old when his father died; educated by his mother; Union army veteran; general agent for an express company and owner of the Hygeia Hotel at Old Point Comfort; considered for a Readjuster congressional nomination in 1882; close friend of Mahone.[87]

PORTLOCK, E. E.: b. 1840 in Norfolk; ed. in private schools; auditor of the A. M. & O. Railroad; Confederate colonel; Lynchburg resident; member, Readjuster Board of Visitors, V.M.I.[88]

POWELL, GUY: Negro; b. a slave in Brunswick Co., 1841; ed. at Wayland Seminary in Washington, D.C.; preacher; state senate, 1875–1878; Va. House, 1881–1882.[89]

PUMPHREY, W. F.: b. 1837 in Norfolk; Confederate veteran, wounded in combat; Mozart Hall delegate, 1879; elected Va. House sergeant-at-arms in 1881.[90]

RAWLES, RICHARD H.: Suffolk lawyer; Va. Senate, 1879–1883; elected county judge of Nansemond during the 1881–1882 legislative session.[91]

REDDY, J. V.: Richmond lawyer; unsuccessful Readjuster nominee for the Va. House in 1881.[92]

REYNOLDS, CORBIN M.: b. 1824 (approx.); college educated; farmer and businessman in Botetourt Co.; elected state treasurer in 1879 and served until 1881.[93]

RICHARDSON, ROBERT A.: b. 1829 in Charlotte Co.; Marion lawyer; Confederate veteran; unsuccessful independent candidate for lieutenant governor in 1877; elected to the state Supreme Court of Appeals in 1882.[94]

RIDDLEBERGER, HARRISON HOLT: b. 1844 in Shenandoah Co.; ed. in common schools; photographer, teacher, editor, lawyer in Woodstock; Confederate captain; Va. House, 1871–1875; member of the Conservative state committee until 1875; Democratic presidential elector, 1876; Shenandoah Co. commonwealth's attorney, 1876–1880; Va. Senate, 1879–1882; Mozart Hall delegate, 1879; Readjuster presidential elector, 1880; U.S. Senate, 1882–1888.[95]

86. *Richmond Daily Dispatch,* December 10, 1879.
87. G. W. Bagby to the *Richmond State,* April 13, 1881; *Richmond State,* August 30, 1882; Phoebus to Mahone, August 29, 1883, Mahone Papers.
88. S. Bassett French Biographical Sketches.
89. Jackson, *Negro Office-Holders,* p. 35.
90. *Richmond Daily Whig,* December 9, 1881.
91. Rawles to Mahone, October 13, 1879, Mahone Papers.
92. *Richmond Daily Whig,* October 29, 1881.
93. *Richmond Daily Dispatch,* December 10, 1879.
94. *Richmond Weekly Whig,* March 3, 1882.
95. Howson White Cole III, "Harrison Holt Riddleberger, Readjuster" (M.A. thesis, University of Virginia, 1952).

ROGERS, ASA, JR.: railroad official on Mahone's line, business manager of the *Richmond Whig;* Confederate veteran; Mozart Hall delegate, 1879; elected state railroad commissioner by the legislature during its 1879–1880 session; occupied the position until 1881.[96]

RUFFIN, FRANK G.: b. 1820; Chesterfield Co. farmer, edited *Richmond Enquirer* and the *Southern Planter;* Confederate lieutenant colonel; Grange spokesman; state treasury official and Readjuster spokesman; broke with the party in 1882.[97]

SCOTT, ARCHER: Negro; truck farmer; Va. House, 1875–1877, 1879–1884.[98]

SCOTT, WINFIELD: Floyd Co. merchant; elected general agent and storekeeper of the state penitentiary during the 1879–1880 legislative session.[99]

SIEBERT, KARL: architect of German descent; unsuccessful Readjuster nominee for the Va. House from Richmond in 1881.[100]

SIMS, WILLIAM E.: b. 1842 in Mississippi, moved to Va. in 1869; ed. at Yale; Chatham lawyer; Confederate colonel; unsuccessful Readjuster candidate for the U.S. House in 1882 and for the Va. Senate in 1883.[101]

SLEMP, CAMPBELL: b. 1839 in Lee Co.; ed. at Emory and Henry College; teacher, farmer, involved in mining and the lumber industry; Confederate colonel; Va. House, 1879–1883.[102]

SMITH, DABNEY: Negro; b. a slave in Charlotte Co.; house servant, merchant, farmer, mail carrier; Va. House, 1881–1882.[103]

SMITH, HENRY D.: Negro; b. a slave in Greensville Co., 1834; large landowner, farmer, distiller; Va. House, 1879–1880.[104]

STATHAM, CHARLES W.: Lynchburg tobacco dealer and bank vice president; Coalition leader in Lynchburg.[105]

STEVENS, WILLIAM N.: Negro; b. free in Petersburg, 1850; Suffolk lawyer; Va. Senate, 1871–1878, 1881–1882.[106]

STOVALL, JOHN T.: tobacco dealer; dissident Readjuster member, state Conservative committee, 1880; Va. Senate, Patrick and Henry, 1879–1881; unsuccessful Readjuster congressional candidate in 1880.[107]

96. *Richmond Daily Dispatch,* December 12, 1879.
97. Ruffin to Mahone, August 26, 1881, Mahone Papers; Nannie May Tilley, *The Bright-Tobacco Industry, 1860–1929* (Chapel Hill: University of North Carolina Press, 1948), pp. 398, 403.
98. Jackson, *Negro Office-Holders,* p. 36.
99. *Richmond Daily Dispatch,* December 10, 1879.
100. *Richmond Daily Whig,* October 29, 1881.
101. *Woodstock Virginian,* October 6, 1882; John T. S. Melzer, "The Danville Riot, November 3, 1883" (M.A. thesis, University of Virginia, 1963), pp. 40–41.
102. Tyler, *Virginia Biography,* 3:127.
103. Jackson, *Negro Office-Holders,* p. 38.
104. Ibid., p. 39.
105. Statham wrote a large number of letters to Mahone; for examples see Statham to Mahone, January 6, 7, 1882, Mahone Papers.
106. Jackson, *Negro Office-Holders,* p. 40.
107. *Richmond State,* September 22, 1879; *Richmond Daily Dispatch,* March 11, 1880.

STRAYER, JOSEPH B.: farmer in Shenandoah Co.; Va. House, 1879-1883.[108]

STROTHER, PHILIP WILLIAMS: b. 1839 in Rappahannock Co.; lawyer; Confederate lieutenant; Va. Senate, 1865-1867; county judge of Giles and Bland; Va. House, 1875-1877; influential in the Readjuster party in the southwest.[109]

TAYLOR, HEZEKIAH: farmer; elected county judge of Albemarle by the General Assembly in 1880.[110]

TAYLOR, JAMES C.: b. 1826 in Montgomery Co.; "self-made" man, merchant's clerk, lawyer, director of Mahone's railroad; Confederate major; Va. Senate, 1862-1865; elected state attorney general on the "True Republican" ticket in 1869; Va. House from Montgomery Co., 1881-1883.[111]

TURNER, WILLIAM H.: Norfolk real estate dealer and notary public; the *Woodstock Virginian* described him as "the wealthiest man in the Virginia legislature" and estimated his wealth at $500,000; Va. House, 1879-1883.[112]

VAIDEN, VOLASKI: teacher, farmer, New Kent Co. treasurer; chairman of the Mozart Hall convention, 1879.[113]

WADDILL, EDMUND, JR.: b. 1855 in Charles City Co.; ed. at U. Va. law school; Richmond lawyer, court clerk; elected Henrico Co. judge during the 1879-1880 legislative session; appointed U.S. district attorney for eastern Virginia in 1883; elected to U.S. House in 1890.[114]

WALKER, JOSEPH: native of Massachusetts; Union veteran who settled in Va. after serving in the state with General Ben Butler; Chesterfield Co. livestock breeder; Republican Readjuster in the Va. Senate, 1879-1883.[115]

WALKER, RICHARD F.: b. 1831 in Buckingham Co.; journalist, connected with the *Richmond Enquirer* and the *Richmond Whig;* served several terms as state superintendent of public printing during the 1870s before being defeated for reelection in 1877; elected printing superintendent again by the Readjuster legislators in 1879.[116]

WEBB, JOSEPH B.: doctor, farmer in Rockingham Co.; Va. Senate, 1881-1883; defeated for reelection in 1883.[117]

108. Strayer to Mahone, September 1, 1879, July 20, 1880, Mahone Papers.

109. William C. Pendleton, *Political History of Appalachian Virginia, 1776-1927* (Dayton, Va.: Shenandoah Press, 1927), p. 355.

110. *Richmond Daily Dispatch*, January 23, 1880.

111. S. Bassett French Biographical Sketches.

112. *Woodstock Virginian*, January 20, 1882; *Richmond Daily Whig*, December 10, 1881.

113. Vaiden to Mahone, June 22, 1881, Mahone Papers.

114. *Directory of Congress*, p. 1758.

115. *Richmond Daily Dispatch*, December 13, 1879.

116. S. Bassett French Biographical Sketches; *Richmond Daily Dispatch*, December 10, 1879.

117. *Harrisonburg* (Va.) *Old Commonwealth*, August 9, September 13, 20, November 8, 1883.

WILLIAMS, JAMES HARRISON: b. 1836 in Woodstock; ed. at U. Va. law school; lawyer in Woodstock and Winchester, associated with the B. & O. Railroad; moved to Iowa before the war and won election to the state legislature there in 1859; returned to Va. and attained the rank of judge advocate general in the Confederate army; brigadier general of the Virginia militia; Va. House, 1874–1875; unsuccessful candidate for the U.S. House on the Readjuster ticket in 1880; brother of penitentiary superintendent Samuel C. Williams.[118]

WILLIAMS, SAMUEL C., JR.: b. 1842 (approx.) in Woodstock; agent for the B. & O. Railroad in Rockingham Co.; superintendent of the state penitentiary, 1879–1883.[119]

WINDSOR, DAVID A.: partner in a Washington, D.C., lumberyard; chairman of the Readjuster party in Alexandria; appointed postmaster of Alexandria by President Arthur.[120]

WISE, JOHN S.: b. 1846 in Rio de Janeiro, Brazil; son of Governor Henry A. Wise; ed. at V.M.I. and the U. Va. law school; Richmond lawyer; Confederate lieutenant; unsuccessful congressional candidate in 1880; U.S. district attorney for eastern Virginia, 1882–1883; U.S. House, 1883–1885.[121]

WISE, RICHARD ALSOP: b. Philadelphia, Pa., in 1843; son of Governor Henry A. Wise and brother of John S. Wise; ed. at William & Mary College and the Medical College of Virginia; doctor, professor at William & Mary, 1869–1881; Confederate veteran; dissident Readjuster member, state Conservative committee, 1880; influential in party affairs in the Tidewater; superintendent of Eastern Lunatic Asylum, 1882–1884.[122]

WITTEN, JAMES RICHARD: b. 1830 in Tazewell Co.; Va. House, 1879–1882.[123]

WOOD, HENRY CLINTON: b. 1836 in Scott Co.; farmer, merchant, railroad president; Confederate major; Va. Senate, 1875–1882; president *pro tempore* of the Senate, 1882.[124]

WOOD, J. H.: b. 1843 (approx.); lawyer; Confederate veteran; unsuccessful Readjuster nominee for the Va. House from Washington Co. in 1883.[125]

118. Manuscript control folder, James H. Williams Papers, Edwin A. Alderman Library, University of Virginia, Charlottesville, Va.
119. *Richmond Daily Dispatch,* December 10, 1879.
120. Windsor to W. C. Elam, May 31, 1880, Mahone Papers.
121. *Directory of Congress,* p. 1838.
122. Ibid., p. 1839.
123. Pendleton, *Appalachian Virginia,* p. 337.
124. Rogers, *Officers of the Senate,* p. 98.
125. *Bristol* (Va.) *News,* October 23, 1883.

Occupational Background of Prominent Readjusters (*Coalitionists*)

Name	Lawyer	Editor	Teacher	Farmer	Preacher	Trade or Mfg.	Other
Akers	—	—	—	—	—	—	—
Allen			X				
Bailey	X	X				X	
Blair	X		X	X			
Bland			X			X	Govt. worker
Blanton		X					Doctor
Board						X	
Bolling				X		X	Govt. worker
Bowden	X					X	Govt. worker
Bowen			X				
Brady						X	Govt. worker
Brokenborough	—	—	—	—	—	—	—
Cameron		X					
Causey	X		X				
Claiborne			X				Govt. worker
Conrad			X				
Cross			X	X			Doctor
Davis			X		X		
Dickenson	X						
Dodson, A. A.		X		X			Govt. worker
Dodson, J. S.						X	
Dungee				X	X	X	
Dyson							Govt. worker
Elam	X	X					
Elliott	X	X	X				
Farr	X		X				

Name	Lawyer	Editor	Teacher	Farmer	Preacher	Trade or Mfg.	Other
Fauntleroy	X						
Fisher						X	
Flanagan	X						
Ford	X						
Fowler		X				X	
Frazier						X	
French	X	X					
Fulkerson	X		X			X	
Gaines	X					X	
Giddings	X			X			
Gilliam				X		X	
Gilmer				X			
Godwin	X	X					
Gose				X			
Green, A.						X	
Green, D.				X			
Griggs						X	Govt. worker
Grim				X			
Groner						X	
Hamilton						X	
Hansborough	X						
Harris	X						
Harvie	X	X		X		X	
Henly	X						
Hinton	X						
Hooper						X	
Hubard	X						
Jones, A. W.	X						
Jones, J. R.						X	
Jones, P. V.	X					X	
Kilgore	X						
Lacy	X						
Lamb		X				X	
Lee	X						
Lewis, D. S.	X						Govt. worker
Lewis, J. F.				X			Govt. worker
Lewis, L. L.	X						Govt. worker
Lewis, N.				X			
Libbey						X	
Lynbrook	X						
McCaull	—	—	—	—	—	—	—

Name	Lawyer	Editor	Teacher	Farmer	Preacher	Trade or Mfg.	Other
McLin				X		X	
McTeer	X						
Mahone			X			X	
Martin	X						
Massey	X		X	X	X	X	
Mauck				X		X	
May							Doctor
Mayo	X		X				
Meade, C. C.				X			
Meade, N. B.	X	X		X			
Minetree						X	
Newman				X			
Norton, D. M.							Doctor
Norton, R.				X			
Owens				X			
Paige	X					X	
Patton	X	X		X			
Paul	X						
Phillips						X	Govt. worker
Phoebus						X	
Portlock						X	
Powell					X		
Pumphrey	–	–	–	–	–	–	–
Rawles	X						
Reddy	X						
Reynolds				X		X	
Richardson	X						
Riddleberger	X	X	X			X	
Rogers		X				X	
Ruffin		X		X			
Scott, A.				X			
Scott, W.						X	
Siebert						X	
Sims	X						
Slemp			X	X		X	
Smith, D.				X		X	Govt. worker
Smith, H. D.				X		X	
Statham						X	
Stevens	X						
Stovall						X	
Strayer				X			

Name	Lawyer	Editor	Teacher	Farmer	Preacher	Trade or Mfg.	Other
Strother	X						
Taylor, H.				X			
Taylor, J. C.	X					X	
Turner						X	
Vaiden			X	X			
Waddill	X						
Walker, J.				X			
Walker, R. F.			X				
Webb				X			Doctor
Williams, J. H.	X					X	
Williams, S. C.						X	
Windsor						X	
Wise, J. S.	X						
Wise, R. A.			X				Doctor
Witten	–	–	–	–	–	–	–
Wood, H. C.				X		X	
Wood, J. H.	X						

Bibliographical Essay

C. Vann Woodward's *Origins of the New South, 1877-1913* (Baton Rouge: Louisiana State University Press, 1951) remains the starting point for any analysis of Southern history in the post-Reconstruction years. Woodward's bold generalizations, especially his emphasis on the Whiggish, industrially oriented nature of the South's "Redeemer" ruling class, have dominated the historiography of the period for more than two decades. In spite of its general popularity, nevertheless, this "Redeemer" thesis has come under increasing attack in recent years. As Clement Eaton demonstrates in *The Waning of the Old South Civilization, 1860-1880s* (Athens: University of Georgia Press, 1968), there was considerable continuity between the Old South and the New. All things did not change with Appomattox—much less with the Hayes-Tilden election. Similarly, William J. Cooper's study of *The Conservative Regime: South Carolina, 1877-1890* (Baltimore: Johns Hopkins Press, 1968) stresses traditionalist aspects of the Wade Hampton hegemony in that state. My own work with the ideas and attitudes of the Virginia Funders has led me to a similar conclusion. Jack P. Maddex, Jr., on the other hand, argues that Woodward is substantially correct with reference to the Old Dominion. His analysis of *The Virginia Conservatives, 1867-1879: A Study in Reconstruction Politics* (Chapel Hill: University of North Carolina Press, 1970) emphasizes the innovative, dynamic characteristics of the Conservative regime. Given these interpretive disagreements, therefore, it seems likely that additional state studies will neither wholly confirm nor completely undermine the Woodward thesis. Instead they will probably discover complex patterns of "Redeemer" conduct and belief which will vary markedly from faction to faction and from state to state. Avoiding this historiographical impasse, Paul M. Gaston suggests an alternative approach to the period in his analysis of *The New South Creed: A Study in Southern Mythmaking* (New York: Alfred A. Knopf, 1970). He maintains that the intellectual mood of the post-Civil War years should be discussed in terms of the myth-making process, of Southern efforts to escape the grim realities of the day through delusive dreams of wealth, progress, and social harmony.

The New South may well have been a myth, but Virginia did experience some very real social and economic changes in the postwar decades. George M. McFarland provides a particularly valuable survey of these developments in "The Extension of Democracy in Virginia, 1850–1895" (Ph.D. diss., Princeton University, 1934), and Allen W. Moger traverses much of the same ground in *Virginia: Bourbonism to Byrd, 1870–1925* (Charlottesville: University Press of Virginia, 1968). James Douglas Smith's "Virginia during Reconstruction, 1865–1870: A Political, Economic and Social Study" (Ph.D. diss., University of Virginia, 1960) is excellent for the years covered. The evolution of a crucial sector of the state's economy is described in B. W. Arnold, Jr., *History of the Tobacco Industry in Virginia from 1860 to 1894* (Baltimore: Johns Hopkins Press, 1897), and Nannie May Tilley, *The Bright-Tobacco Industry, 1860–1929* (Chapel Hill: University of North Carolina Press, 1948). Another vital form of business activity is treated in Allen W. Moger's "Railroad Practices and Policies in Virginia after the Civil War" *Virginia Magazine of History and Biography* 59 (1951): 423–57. Economic and social developments are also noted in a large number of local histories, but most of these works are so ladened with tangential anecdotes and genealogical data as to be of little use. Welcome exceptions to this rule are provided by William Edward Webb, "Charlottesville and Albemarle County, Virginia, 1865–1900" (Ph.D. diss., University of Virginia, 1955) and Thomas J. Wertenbaker, *Norfolk: Historic Southern Port* (Durham: Duke University Press, 1931).

Virginia's postwar political history has also received considerable attention. Hamilton J. Eckenrode provides a brief but valuable introduction to the period in *The Political History of Virginia during the Reconstruction* (Baltimore: Johns Hopkins Press, 1904). This work has been supplemented in recent years by Richard Grady Lowe's "Republicans, Rebellion, and Reconstruction: The Republican Party in Virginia, 1856–1870" (Ph.D. diss., University of Virginia, 1968). Jack P. Maddex, Jr.'s analysis of the state's Conservative regime (noted previously) makes an important contribution to our understanding of the 1870s, and Allen W. Moger's *Virginia: Bour-bonism to Byrd, 1870-1925* (also noted previously) surveys the poli-tics of the period in an incisive manner as well. The debt controversy itself is probed in Charles C. Pearson, *The Readjuster Movement in Virginia* (New Haven: Yale University Press, 1917). Pearson be-gan his graduate studies under the direction of William A. Dunning of Columbia University, and *The Readjuster Movement in Virginia* is marked by the typical virtues and defects of a "Dunning school" monograph. The book combines careful research—especially on economic issues—with a pervasive bias against Republicans and blacks. The involvement of the national Republicans with the Readjuster movement is discussed with surprising thoroughness in Stanley P. Hirshson, *Farewell to the Bloody Shirt: Northern Republicans & the Southern Negro, 1877-1893* (Bloomington: In-diana University Press, 1962), and Vincent P. DeSantis, *Republicans Face the Southern Question—The New Departure Years, 1877-1897* (Baltimore: Johns Hopkins Press, 1959).

Mahone's alliance with Virginia's Negroes has proved even more controversial than his ties with the Republican leaders in Washing-ton. Racial antagonisms exerted a strong influence on white histori-ans for several decades after the debt struggle, and the early accounts generally describe the blacks as venal and ignorant cogs in the Readjuster machine. William L. Royall provides a particularly virulent example of this viewpoint in his *History of the Virginia Debt Controversy: The Negro's Vicious Influence in Politics* (Rich-mond: George M. West, 1897), and Richard L. Morton offers a more subdued version of the same story in *The Negro in Virginia Politics, 1865-1902* (Charlottesville: University of Virginia Press, 1919). Resenting this derogatory stereotype, of course, black histori-ans set to work in the 1920s creating a more positive image of Negro activities. They denied the charges of corruption, and they argued instead that their race had shown good political judgment in the post-Civil War decades. A. Alrutheus Taylor began this reappraisal with his sympathetic study of "The Negro in the Recon-struction of Virginia," *Journal of Negro History* 11 (1926):243-415, 425-537, and James Hugo Johnston expanded the narrative in "The Participation of Negroes in the Government of Virginia from 1877 to 1888," *Journal of Negro History* 14 (1929): 251-71. Luther P. Jackson also bolstered the new interpretation with his analysis of *Negro Office-Holders in Virginia, 1865-1895* (Norfolk: Guide Quality Press, 1945), a work that stresses the accomplishments of black politicians during the Readjuster hegemony. Influenced by the modern-day civil rights movement, moreover, white historians have also begun to adopt a more favorable view of the Negro political activism of the 1870s and 1880s. Indeed, scholars have tended in recent years to exaggerate the interracial harmony of the Mahone era. This trend is clearly evident in Charles E. Wynes's *Race Relations in Virginia, 1870-1902* (Charlottesville: University of Virginia Press, 1961) and Carl N. Degler's "Black and White Together: Bi-Racial Politics in the South," *Virginia Quarterly Review* 47 (1971):421–44.

Studies of a biographical nature offer a potentially valuable way of cutting through the complexities of the period, and a number of worthwhile efforts along this line have been completed. Chief among these is Nelson M. Blake's pathbreaking *William Mahone of Virginia: Soldier and Political Insurgent* (Richmond: Garrett & Massie, 1935). Blake never really captures the flavor of Mahone's dynamic personality, but he does force a recognition of the general's positive impact on Virginia life. Also of significance in understanding the debt struggle are Audrey Marie Cahill, "Gilbert Carleton Walker: Virginia's Redeemer Governor" (M.A. thesis, University of Virginia, 1956); Howson White Cole III, "Harrison Holt Riddleberger, Readjuster" (M.A. thesis, University of Virginia, 1952); Curtis Carroll Davis, "Very Well-Rounded Republican: The Several Lives of John S. Wise," *Virginia Magazine of History and Biography* 71 (1963):461–87; Richard B. Doss, "John Warwick Daniel: A Study in the Virginia Democracy" (Ph.D. diss., University of Virginia, 1955); Richard B. Doss, " 'Parson' John E. Massey, Relentless Readjuster," *Papers of the Albemarle County Historical Society* 11 (1950–51):5–18; Robert R. Jones, "Conservative Virginian: The Post-war Career of Governor James Lawson Kemper" (Ph.D. diss., University of Virginia, 1964); Charles C. Pearson, "William Henry Ruffner: Reconstruction Statesman of Virginia," *South Atlantic Quarterly* 20 (1921):25–32, 137–51; and Julian P. Porter, Jr., "Frederick William Mackey Holliday, Governor of Virginia, 1878–1881" (M.A. thesis, University of Virginia, 1969).

Thoroughly biased in their presentations, the autobiographies and memoirs of participants in the debt struggle reflect the heated political climate of the day. John S. Wise spells out the "Mahoneite" version of affairs in *The Lion's Skin: A Historical Novel and a Novel History* (New York: Doubleday, Page & Co., 1905), and William L. Royall offers an ultra-Funder perspective in *Some Reminiscences*

(New York: Neale Publishing Co., 1909). John E. Massey's *Autobiography,* ed. Elizabeth H. Hancock (New York: Neale Publishing Co., 1909) is crucial for a proper understanding of its tempestuous author. Of lesser interest are John Goode, *Recollections of a Lifetime by John Goode of Virginia* (New York: Neale Publishing Co., 1906); Beverley B. Munford, *Random Recollections* (n.p., 1905); Charles T. O'Ferrall, *Forty Years of Active Service* (New York: Neale Publishing Co., 1904); Henry Robinson Pollard, *Memoirs and Sketches of the Life of Henry Robinson Pollard: An Autobiography* (Richmond: Lewis Printing Co., 1923); and Robert E. Withers, *Autobiography of an Octogenarian* (Roanoke, Va.: Stone Printing & Manufacturing Co. Press, 1907).

Manuscript collections also shed light on political activities and attitudes. The following collections proved particularly valuable for the purposes of this study: John W. Daniel Papers, F.W.M. Holliday Papers, and William Mahone Papers (all at Duke University); William H. Ruffner Papers (Historical Foundation of the Associate and Reformed Presbyterian Church, Montreat, N.C.); Chester A. Arthur Papers, William E. Chandler Papers, and J.L.M. Curry Papers (all at the Library of Congress); Edmund W. Hubard Papers and Tucker Family Papers (University of North Carolina); Baugh Family Papers, Gilliam Family Papers, John L. Hurt Papers, James Lawson Kemper Papers, and Richard J. Reid Papers (all at the University of Virginia); George W. Bagby Papers, John H. Chamberlayne Papers, George K. Gilmer Papers, and Lewis E. Harvie Papers (all at the Virginia Historical Society); S. Bassett French Biographical Sketches and Lewis E. Harvie Papers (Virginia State Library); Harrison H. Riddleberger Papers (College of William and Mary); and Wise Family Papers (in possession of John S. Wise III of Charlottesville, Va.). The Mahone Papers at Duke deserve special notice. Massive in volume, they provide an unparalleled view of the day-to-day operations of the Readjuster machine.

The newspapers of the period are another indispensable source of information concerning the debt struggle. Bitterly partisan in tone, their editorial pages mirror the evolution of political ideologies and attitudes. The University of Virginia has a large collection of newspapers from the 1870s and 1880s—as does the Virginia State Library. I have relied most heavily on the Richmond press, especially the *Richmond Commonwealth,* the *Richmond Whig* (daily and weekly editions), the *Richmond Daily Dispatch,* the *Richmond Southern Intelligencer,* and the *Richmond State.* Other Virginia newspapers of importance for the period are the *Abingdon Virginian,* the *Bristol News,* the *Harrisonburg Old Commonwealth,* the *Lynchburg Tri-Weekly Virginian,* the *Marion Patriot and Herald,* the *Norfolk Landmark,* the *Petersburg Lancet,* the *Salem Weekly Register,* the *Staunton Vindicator,* the *Warsaw Northern Neck News,* and the *Woodstock Virginian.* I have also made extensive use of two periodicals, the *Nation* and the *Southern Planter & Farmer.*

Virginia's public documents offer additional insight into the problems of the day. The *Journals* of the state Senate and House of Delegates provide roll call votes on crucial bills—along with the reports of various investigative committees. Debt settlements and other key pieces of legislation are incorporated in the *Acts and Joint Resolutions of the General Assembly,* and the *Annual Reports* of state institutions and officials contain much significant data as well. These documents are all available at the University of Virginia and the Virginia State Library. The State Library also has copies of Readjuster reform proposals in a bound volume of *House Bills* for the 1881–82 legislative session.

Index